To Pete

D1333983

ALL TOGETHER NOW?

ONE MAN'S WALK
IN SEARCH OF
A LOST ENGLAND

Mike Carter

First published by Guardian Faber in 2019
Guardian Faber is an imprint of Faber & Faber Ltd,
Bloomsbury House, 74–77 Great Russell Street,
London WC1B 3DA

This paperback edition first published in 2020

Guardian is a registered trade mark of
Guardian News & Media Ltd,
Kings Place, 90 York Way, London N1 9GU

Typeset by Faber & Faber Limited
Printed and bound by CPI Group (UK) Ltd, Croydon CR0 4YY

We are grateful to the following for permission to reproduce copyright material:
An extract from *Amusing Ourselves to Death* by Neil Postman published by
William Heinemann, copyright © 1985, 1986 by Neil Postman. Reproduced by
permission of The Random House Group Ltd and Viking Books, an imprint
of Penguin Publishing Group, a division of Penguin Random House LLC. All
rights reserved. Any third party use of this material, outside of this publication,
is prohibited. Interested parties must apply directly to Penguin Random House
LLC for permission; and the poem 'Cloud Weavers' by Tom Wyre, from *Clay,
Fire & Gold*, copyright © Tom Wyre. Reproduced with kind permission.

The right of Mike Carter to be identified as author of this work
has been asserted in accordance with Section 77 of the Copyright,
Designs and Patents Act 1988

A CIP record for this book
is available from the British Library

ISBN 978-1-78335-157-2

2 4 6 8 10 9 7 5 3 1

CONTENTS

PROLOGUE: THE SMOKER
(BIRMINGHAM)

It is a bitter winter's morning in 2010. Two men, both in their early seventies, are on a bus, somewhere in Birmingham. The windows are steamed up. Outside it is still dark, a brilliant frost shimmering under the tungsten glow of the street lights. One of the men walks along the top deck, the other along the bottom, each handing out forms to the passengers along with little pens, like the ones you get in Argos. They are questionnaires from the bus-operating company, asking: 'Dear Customer, how many times a week do you travel?'; 'at what time?'; 'are you happy with the service?'; 'what can we do to improve?' At the bottom of the form there is a box marked 'other comments'.

The two men often skim through the responses, though it isn't part of their remit to do so. Many of the customers seem happy with the bus service, but there are complaints about the prices. In the 'other comments' section, some people write that bringing back conductors would make them feel safer, especially at night. These must be older people, the two men reckon, as there haven't been conductors on Birmingham's buses since the 1970s. On one form, somebody had scored through the word 'customer' and written 'passenger', followed by three exclamation marks. Quite a few people write that they'd like to see the buses being run by the council again, that since deregulation in the mid-eighties, things had got steadily worse. There are always a few forms adorned with giant penises and hairy balls, or 'WBA rule', or 'Villa scum', depending on which route they were following. But they all get filed away in the bags that the two men carry.

At the terminus, the two old men alight and sit on a low wall, hunched up and freezing, waiting for the next bus. From a distance, the cold, pre-dawn air makes it look as if they are both chain-smoking, with huge plumes emitting from their mouths. One of the men does light a cigarette, his chest rasping and wheezing. He's been a heavy smoker from the age of twelve and he will be dead from lung cancer within a year. But at that moment he has no idea of the cellular changes going on within his body. He is immortal.

This is the first time the two men have worked together. They haven't even exchanged names. They start talking. The non-smoker speaks a little about his family, about his grandchildren. He had retired a decade ago, but he got bored at home, and his pension isn't enough to survive on, so he picks up shifts working on the buses, handing out forms.

The smoker says that he couldn't afford to retire either.

The non-smoker says the bus work is OK, but it is a bit, well, demeaning, compared with his old career.

What was that, asks the smoker.

Copper, the non-smoker says. Spent all of his life in the force. Worked his way up to be an undercover officer. That was exciting work. Dangerous too.

The smoker asks a lot of questions, offers not too much information about himself. The ex-copper is happy to talk endlessly: he can't believe his luck, that this stranger seems to find his life so interesting and important, as if he were a famous actor or politician. He hasn't felt this way in years.

Emboldened, the ex-copper starts telling a story about a surveillance job he'd been on in the early 1970s. He had been assigned to a team watching a 'notorious communist troublemaker, a nasty piece of work'. They had taken over a room on the first floor of a pub in Aston, from where they filmed and recorded the comings and goings at the troublemaker's house opposite, twenty-four hours a day. The man in question had led the building workers' strike in Birmingham in 1972, stirring up trouble. The strikers said that they were fighting against the building firms' introduction of casualised labour, or 'the lump', as it was called, and wanted to protect the terms and conditions of building workers. But, the ex-copper said, anybody could see that it was just the work of communist agitators, trying to bring down the state.

Does he remember the name of the pub, the smoker asks.

The Guild Arms on the Witton Road, the ex-copper replies. The bloke had two young kids; all sorts of people would come and go at all hours. God knows what was going on in that house. But the biggest thing, he said, was that his wife was stunning and yet he was a right ugly bugger. That had annoyed the lads.

Can you remember his name, the smoker asks.

I'll never forget it, the ex-copper says. His name was Pete Carter.

The smoker throws his butt onto the floor, crushes it under his foot, and turns to the other man, holding out his hand.

'Pete Carter,' he says. 'Nice to meet you.'

I

THE MUG
(WEST MIDLANDS TO LONDON)

Pete Carter was my father. I was one of his two kids. He died on 11 October 2011, aged seventy-three. Pete had left school in West Bromwich aged fifteen in 1953, illiterate, one of six children of alcoholic parents. He trained as a bricklayer and had been politically radicalised on the building sites in the late fifties. He joined the Young Communist League and his political career flourished: in the early seventies, he'd led the Birmingham building workers in their successful strike action against the use of casual labour; he played his part in the miners' strike of 1984–85, and went on to become the industrial organiser of the Communist Party of Great Britain.

Pete was not an 'important' man, like the usual subjects of national newspaper obituaries. He was neither a general nor a bishop. Yet he'd had enough old friends at the *Guardian* to agitate for a proper send-off in print. Pete, his friends had argued, was one of the last of a breed of self-educated, working-class, chest-thumping orators; part of a generation who'd fought for the huge changes in social mobility that peaked in the UK in the mid-1970s. Men and women like Pete had campaigned for the Sex Discrimination Act and the decriminalisation of homosexuality. They had fought against US nuclear bombs being sited in the UK, and were in the vanguard of the nascent green movement. Pete was an engaged citizen, belonging to a generation of

5

working-class people who felt that their moment had come and that it would last forever.

In 1981, Pete had been asked by the TUC to be one of the three main organisers of the People's March for Jobs. Organising it was to be his greatest achievement. With shades of the 1936 Jarrow Crusade, the People's March for Jobs saw around three hundred unemployed men and women walk from Liverpool to London in protest against Margaret Thatcher's Conservative government. Elected in May 1979, Thatcher introduced monetarist policies that had, within two years, ripped the heart out of Britain's traditional manufacturing base and sent unemployment rocketing towards three million.

I was born in 1964, so was only fifteen when Thatcher came to power, not yet old enough to vote. I was seventeen in 1981 when those marchers set off from Liverpool. Although I had been unemployed myself, and although Pete had asked me to march, I had not been among them. For Pete was effectively dead to me at that time.

Accompanying that *Guardian* obituary was a photograph of my father in a donkey jacket, addressing a group of building workers, their feather haircuts making the photo look like a still from *Top of the Pops* circa 1972. In their hands were placards shouting: 'We will fight to kill the lump'. In the text, Pete was described as an idealist, with a 'turbulent' love life.

That 'turbulence' had ended Pete's marriage to my mum, Norma, four years before the People's March. I stayed with her, and went off the rails. Mum had got cancer not long after Pete left, and by 1987 she was dead. Somewhere along the line, my elder sister, Sue, and I told ourselves a story that Pete had killed our mum.

After the People's March, Pete left the building sites of the West Midlands and moved to London. The era of the great industrial disputes was coming to an end. The coal miners suffered a bitter defeat in 1984–85 and that was that, really. Thatcher's government pressed ahead with its anti-trade-union agenda, destroying those former industrial communities.

Pete took a job with the Communist Party and sided with the intellectual wing. The drive then was about modernising the left, making it relevant in a post-industrial world. It was a drive that would tear the left apart and ultimately lead to Tony Blair. Pete seemed to enjoy his new life, living in a fancy flat in Islington. Many of the old guard thought he was a class traitor.

After Mum died, I followed Pete to London. I doubtless had fantasies of reconciliation, but they never materialised. Pete was indifferent to me, often callously so. I never fully understood why. Yet I never stopped trying.

I got a job in advertising. I worked in Cannes and Paris and Milan. I bought a ridiculous cashmere overcoat with comedy shoulder pads that cost me a month's wages. And every time I went back to Birmingham, to visit friends and relatives, I felt increasingly like a stranger; contemptuous, ashamed even, of its scale, its lack of ambition, its provincialism. I worked hard to lose my Brummie accent. I didn't know then that there was a heavy price to be paid for leaving; that it might be impossible to find my way home.

When the Berlin Wall came down, and the Communist Party collapsed, Pete went back on the tools, living a peripatetic life, mostly doing building work on the houses of ex-party colleagues. But the building work was tough. He was always a heavy smoker, and now his drinking started to increase. He ended up in a council flat in south London, where heroin addicts sat shooting up in the stairwells. His bed was a mattress on top of two front doors nailed together. One day I got a phone call from King's College Hospital. After drinking a bottle of whisky, Pete had fallen asleep with his dinner in the oven and set fire to the flat. He was alive, but had inhaled a lot of smoke.

After that, Pete moved back to the Black Country, onto a narrowboat. He was still drinking heavily and later developed lung cancer. It was on the boat that his body was found. He had fallen over and smashed his head on a metal bin. Perhaps he was weakened by the chemotherapy; perhaps he was drunk. Probably both. By the time I got there from London, the body was gone. Only the bin remained, with my dad's head imprinted upon it.

When I'd got the phone call to tell me that Pete was dead, I'd felt nothing. Well, that's not quite true. I'd felt relief, freedom, a happiness even, as if some long, arduous battle was over; that the thing I'd spent my life trying to get, the thing that had driven me on, was now gone. I rarely thought about Pete in the immediate years after his death. I told myself that there could not be a dad-shaped hole in my life, because there had never been a dad shape in the first place. I told myself that any grieving for Pete must have gone on while he was still alive.

But then a crushing ennui descended and my ambition evaporated. There really didn't seem much point to anything any more. Though I carried on with my job at the *Guardian*, it was with little enthusiasm. Daily, I worked on stories about the increasingly spiteful and racist EU referendum campaign, our divided nation, the savage austerity measures that were attacking the poor, the growing sense of hopelessness among so many working-class people. What the fuck was happening to Britain? What had happened to the Britain that my father had promised me? After a particularly enervating commute one day, I started walking to work. It was eleven miles and I marched determinedly, furiously even.

In spring 2016, while having a clear-out, I came across a box of Pete's stuff. When we'd emptied his boat, I had taken that box, although I'd never examined its contents. Inside were papers and photographs and scrapbooks containing newspaper cuttings about industrial disputes from the 1970s. I found love letters from girlfriends and letters to Pete from me and my sister, and carbon copies of letters he'd written to us and to others. I found his old flat cap, and put it on. It was exactly like the one I'd recently bought for myself.

At the bottom of the box, I came across a commemorative mug from the People's March for Jobs. It was chipped and the handle was wobbly, but there it was, with the route printed on the side, all the towns and cities that the marchers had stayed in listed. I looked at the date the march had set off: 2 May 1981. In a few weeks' time, it would be thirty-five years to the day since those men and women had walked 340 miles to try to save their communities and their culture, and thirty-five years since I had turned down Pete's invitation to join them.

I called work and booked some time off. Then I bought a one-way train ticket to Liverpool.

2

THE GOOD COMPANIONS
(LIVERPOOL TO WIDNES)

At 9 a.m. on 2 May 2016 I stood on the steps of St George's Hall, Liverpool, as those marchers had done exactly thirty-five years earlier. The sky was dark. I was fifty-two years old, with a dodgy left knee and a pain in my right foot from a recent operation to remove a neuroma. I looked down at my feet. If I kept on putting one in front of the other, would I eventually walk into Trafalgar Square?

I pulled a sheet of A4 paper from my pocket. On it was an image of the original march poster, which I'd found in Pete's box alongside the chipped mug. The march had gone in a zigzagging fashion, heading for its first night in Widnes, before moving north-east across to Manchester, then south to Birmingham, south-east across to Bedford, and then the final push south to London. Liverpool to London as the crow flies was around 180 miles. This route was nearly double that.

You could see why Pete and the other organisers had chosen each host town at the end of a walking day: Salford, Stockport, Stoke-on-Trent, Walsall, Coventry, Luton – they were all part of the industrial heartlands back in 1981, the places beginning to feel the savagery of Margaret Thatcher's cuts and therefore the places where the march was likely to attract the most support. In the early days of the walk, in the industrial north-west, the walking days were shortish, anywhere between six and eighteen miles, with any number of suitable overnight towns available. After Birmingham, as the march crossed the green heart of Warwickshire and Northamptonshire, the days became longer, up to twenty-five miles, as the industrial centres were fewer and farther between.

I put the map away and shifted my pack, feeling the straps dig into my shoulders. I took a deep breath. Then I started walking.

From lampposts hung the scarves and flags of Liverpool Football Club. The week before, the Hillsborough inquest verdict in Warrington had finally vindicated the families of the ninety-six killed at the 1989 FA Cup semi-final, exposing the lies and cover-ups of the police, the media and the right-wing political class, who'd spent over a quarter of a century traducing not only those fans, mostly working class, but also the city of Liverpool and its people.

That traducement had been nothing new. It had found expression back in 1981, too, when the then Chancellor of the Exchequer, Geoffrey Howe, had privately suggested to Margaret Thatcher, after the Toxteth riots in July of that year, that Liverpool should be subject to a 'managed decline'.

Four days after the Hillsborough tragedy, Rupert Murdoch's *Sun* printed its verdict under the headline 'The Truth'. The *Sun* claimed that fans had picked the pockets of victims, urinated on the 'brave' cops and beaten up a police officer giving the kiss of life. The narrative had been set: drunken Liverpool fans had caused the disaster and were in effect murderers.

Liverpool fans and the city generally, already stereotyped as a hive of fecklessness and criminality, found that the accusations had great narrative traction in the wider world. The survivors and their families lived with that burden for the next quarter of a century. That's what a story can do.

As I carried on walking out of Liverpool, people scurried

past, umbrellas up, or hoods pulled tightly over their heads. It had started raining, gently at first, then a downpour. I dug into my bag, pulled out my waterproof trousers and jacket, and put them on.

A man asked me for some money. I shook my head, said sorry, I didn't have any spare change, and felt that flush of shame, making myself feel a little better by looking him in the eye while I spoke to him, as if that recognition, that human connection, was as valuable to somebody going hungry as something to eat. He stood there looking at me, with his hand out, as I walked away.

In almost every doorway there was a sheet of cardboard, on top of which there was a sleeping bag, usually stained and damp-looking, inside which I could make out a backside, or some shoulders, the person inside scrunched up in a foetal position. Sometimes the nose or tail of a dog poked out too.

I turned into Duke Street. Before I left Liverpool, there were a few people I wanted to see. I'd written a piece in the *Guardian* about my walk and had asked anybody who remembered the People's March to get in touch. Keith Mullin had sent me a picture of himself and three of his mates, all wearing People's March T-shirts. They had been twenty at the time they joined the march, young unemployed lads from Huyton who loved music and Everton FC.

In 1986 Keith joined The Farm, who went on to have hits with 'Groovy Train' and 'All Together Now'. In 2012 he joined up with other musicians, including Paul McCartney, Paloma Faith and the Royal Liverpool Philharmonic Orchestra, to form The Justice Collective, to raise money for charities associated with the Hillsborough disaster. They had the Christmas number one that year with a version of The Hollies' 'He Ain't Heavy, He's My Brother'.

As well as playing with The Farm, these days Keith worked as a lecturer at the Liverpool Institute for Performing Arts (LIPA), the college jointly founded by Paul McCartney in 1996, housed in the Beatle's old school in Mount Street. I found him there.

Like mine, Keith's dad was in the Communist Party of Great Britain. And, like Pete, Keith's dad was in UCATT, the building workers' union. It was Keith's dad who'd suggested he go on the march. We shared a similar background – similar age, an inner-city childhood, both unemployed in May 1981.

I asked Keith about the high level of homelessness I'd seen on the streets of Liverpool that morning. He told me how much worse it had got recently. For the last two years, he'd taken part in the *Big Issue*'s Big Sell event, going out on the streets to help sell the magazine. 'If I'm gonna talk to people about homelessness, I need to get close to it,' he said.

There were three types of people you encountered when selling the *Big Issue*, according to Keith. First, those who came up to you, acknowledged you existed, wanted to give you money, asked how you were. Then there were the ones who were ashamed. They averted their eyes, wouldn't make eye contact. 'Their shame is of themselves, because you exist, because they can't do anything about a society where you exist,' Keith said. Finally, there were the 'other type', the 'people who would like to expunge you from existence. I've had people shout things at me. And I've had people walk past who know me, yet looked straight through me as if I'm invisible.'

Keith told me about the crowds on 2 May 1981, about how they'd gone to Scotland Road to get their kit. 'You got a jacket, sweatshirt, T-shirt, everything with People's March for Jobs written on it. And new boots! Who sets off on a walk like that in brand-new boots!' he laughed.

He talked about the thousands of people marching with them, past Lime Street. 'I looked up at the shopping centre, and saw a group of lads I used to know from the football. They had their fists in the air, waving down at us, me and me footy mates, as if to say, "What are youse doing on that march? We didn't know youse were political." But they were there to see it, this great spectacle, almost like an act of respect.'

'You weren't on your own on that march,' Keith told me. 'Wherever you were, people would come out and march with you.' He talked a little about the spirit he'd met, the thousands of people cheering along the way, how he'd grown up politically, step by step. 'I went on the march a boy and came home a man,' he said. He told me how proud his family had been of him, especially his father. Keith asked me if I had gone on the march. I hadn't, I told him.

'Why not?' he asked.

'It's complicated,' I said.

And it was complicated. I had worshipped Pete, my dad, who championed the underdog, fought for the rights of working people. In the 1970 general election he had stood as a Communist Party candidate in Wolverhampton South West against the Conservative Enoch Powell. In 1968 Powell had made his infamous Rivers of Blood speech, warning of the consequences of mass immigration. The week before the election, Pete came back to our house in Aston, his face bloodied and swollen, one eye closed and blackened, claiming he had been beaten up by Powell's thugs. It was shocking, seeing my father like that. But it only made me worship him more.

'Carter was . . . the greatest working-class orator I have ever seen,' wrote one of Pete's obituarists. 'He could hold mass meetings of hundreds of people spellbound with his speeches, which were often peppered with quotations from Shelley and other poets.'

In his box, I'd found photographs of Pete speaking to those huge rallies. There was even one of him in the pulpit of a church, right fist clenched, with his thick, black curly hair making him look like Che Guevara.

My amazing father. And then he left us, and broke my mother, and me and my sister Sue too, and seemed to want little to do with us any more. When I did see him, it was in his new home, with his new middle-class lover and her middle-class children. I started drinking, fighting with the police, fighting with anybody really. Sue left home. I got expelled from school, my mother got cancer. So, yes, it was complicated. And, no, I wasn't going to go on his stupid fucking march.

Just across the road from LIPA was Liverpool's Anglican cathedral, the architect Giles Gilbert Scott's masterpiece, a vast, hulking Gothic silhouette that stood on a rise south of the centre of Liverpool and commanded views across the Mersey and the city.

I walked in. There to greet me was Myles Davies, the current vice-dean of the cathedral. Before setting off, the 1981 marchers had been addressed by the Anglican Bishop of Liverpool, David Sheppard, and other church leaders. Earlier that same year, as unemployment had rocketed, the Church of England had gone from being the Tory Party at prayer to one of the leading voices of dissent. All along the route, the Church had put up the marchers in their halls, fed them, raised money for them.

In 1981, Myles had been vicar of a small church in Seaforth, on the Mersey, a very poor area. 'Liverpool was hit very hard by the early years of Margaret Thatcher's government and at a stage where austerity was getting noticeably worse,' he told me. 'A number of projects which had been intended to get people back to work and regenerate the city simply had the plug pulled on them. Those people in places like Seaforth are still rather left behind.'

We paused by the cathedral's Memorial Chapel, where the Hillsborough Flame was being looked after during building work at Anfield. 'The Hillsborough experience is deep in the DNA of Liverpool people,' Myles said. 'The Church has had a long and ongoing relationship with the families of the victims.'

I'd heard a reporter on the BBC News say that, after the verdict a week earlier, the city seemed to be walking a little bit taller. 'I think it was a turning point for the city,' Myles said. 'People had felt their voices hadn't been heard for so long. For the families it was a moment when a certain amount of peace was restored. Not justice. I think that's still for the future. But they could finally lay to rest some of the memories and particularly the way their loved ones had been tarnished by what they were accused of being, and of having done. Thirty years is a very long time to grieve.'

Myles had noticed a huge rise in homelessness on the streets of Liverpool since 2010, but especially in the last year. 'It's all over the city. In a way, it had more or less disappeared, but it's firmly there now. You can't go into town without seeing that. People with drug or alcohol problems, congregating and not really sure where to go.'

He talked about the role of the Church in modern Britain, in looking after the most vulnerable. 'I think it's been felt there's been no choice but to do that. When the Archbishop of Canterbury came here last year for the opening of a food bank, he made it clear that this was great and very important work, but that it shouldn't be needed. It's wrong and unjust, and we need to be working towards a time when people are being looked after properly. If you are putting a plaster on a wound, you are also proclaiming that the wound needs something more than a plaster.'

It was time for me to say goodbye. Outside, in the car park, Myles shook my hand and wished me luck.

'Of course, unlike the original march, you are doing this alone,' he said. 'It sounds like a pilgrimage.'

I headed south-east, walking away from the glitz of modern central Liverpool, with its regenerated waterfront, Liverpool One shopping centre and Baltic Triangle creative quarter. I thought about the campaign to leave the European Union, and about how much Liverpool had benefited from EU money – the city had been the recipient of £2.3 billion of EU funding since 1994, with another £450 million due in the years up to 2020.

Among the schemes paid for in part or wholly by EU funding had been the new cruise ship terminal, the Echo Arena, the restoration of St George's Hall, investment in the upkeep of both cathedrals, and £285 million from the European Social Fund going into 1,260 projects to develop the skills of Merseysiders.

Of Merseyside's fifteen parliamentary seats, fourteen had been won by Labour at the general election in May 2015; one, Southport, had gone to the Liberal Democrats. Now the country was preparing to vote in a referendum on leaving the EU. The right-wing papers were cranking up the rhetoric about taking back control, about getting our country back. It was difficult to imagine all the EU money that had been spent regenerating Tory-phobic Liverpool coming from a Tory-controlled Westminster.

Within a mile, I crossed some kind of invisible line. Gone was the optimism and vitality of central Liverpool, replaced by boarded-up pubs and churches, derelict factories, and shops with graffitied metal shutters pulled down. Myles Davies had told me how the shutters had been an enduring legacy of the 1981 Toxteth riots. After shops had been looted, the owners had installed shutters and they'd never been removed.

Myles had also talked about the regeneration of Liverpool, about the city's year as European Capital of Culture in 2008 kicking it all off, how tourism and the huge increase in student numbers had transformed the centre. 'But you don't have to go far out of the city to find the "other" Liverpool, the left-behinds,' he'd told me. 'The prosperity that has come to the city hasn't permeated those areas at all. Those people feel forgotten.'

To my left was a small street of two-storey Victorian terraced houses. I walked along it. A few of the houses had grey metal panels covering their windows and doors, with notices pasted on them carrying a telephone number for a security firm.

Many of the houses had crumbling windowsills and peeling paintwork, but one, about halfway down, was immaculate, freshly painted, with a hanging basket outside the front door full of bright purple and scarlet fuchsias and busy lizzies. Further along, there was an 'I'm voting Leave' poster on one of the windows.

The next street was worse than the first in terms of empty houses, perhaps half being boarded up. I walked further and further into the estate. By now I was walking along streets with no occupied houses at all; no sign that anyone had ever lived there. No bins. No cars. If it wasn't for the grey metal panels, it could have been a Victorian photograph.

As I stood on the corner of one deserted street, a yellow coach pulled up and lots of cameras were pressed up against the windows before it drove away again. A black taxi pulled up about a third of the way along the street, and two people with cameras got out of the back and started taking shots. They were middle-aged, American, judging by their accents.

'It's over there,' the cabbie said, pointing across the road. The couple crossed, stopped outside one of the boarded-up terraced houses, and started taking pictures. I walked up and asked them what it was they'd come to see.

'Don't you know?' the man said. 'This is Ringo Starr's childhood home.'

'We love the Beatles,' said the woman.

About five miles east of the centre of Liverpool, I walked down a suburban side street and knocked on a door. It opened and there was Chris Jones, with a smile as broad as the doorframe.

Chris had also seen my piece in the paper. He showed me into his living room, and disappeared upstairs. A few minutes later he returned with armfuls of stuff, items that he held up one by one for me to inspect. There was a bottle-green People's March bomber jacket, with the yellow logo on the back now faded away to almost nothing. There was the march-issue sweatshirt, the T-shirt, and his identity pass, still on a loop of the original string, with a small black-and-white photograph of his twenty-five-year-old self.

'Marcher number 246,' he said, proudly. He held up his People's March commemorative mug, like the one I found in Pete's box. On one side of the mug was the iconic march logo, on the back an inscription that read: 'Determined never to return to the desperate days of the 1930s, people of courage have taken to the roads of Britain, confident that they can help arouse the conscience of the nation to end the scourge of unemployment. March for jobs! March with dignity! March for Britain!'

These days, Chris was a senior lecturer at Edge Hill University, teaching nurses who wished to specialise in heart and blood vessel care. Before that he'd spent most of his working life as a nurse. Back in 1981, he'd been a third-year student nurse. His dad, Bill Jones, of UCATT, again, had told him that there was a march going from Liverpool to London to protest against unemployment and that he should go on it.

'You've got to remember the context,' Chris told me. 'Unemployment had exploded. All of a sudden, the dole office moved to a big sort of hangar-type place that they had to open up as a sort of emergency thing, and hundreds and hundreds of people would be queuing up to go in.'

Chris had had four weeks' holiday due him and the march, his dad told him, was looking for a first-aid man.

'So I signed up. I marched it all as well. That was the other thing. I didn't want people saying to me, "You're just sitting in that van all day." So I walked it. The lot.

'Looking back, it was the biggest experience I ever had. Absolutely. A breathtaking experience. Just walking that far, you know, and seeing how your country fits together. It felt like a J. B. Priestley-type thing, where you're seeing a vision of your own country and in a way you never thought you would.'

I asked Chris why he felt so strongly about going on the march. He'd been a young man, sure, but he wasn't unemployed, he'd been on a career path.

'They didn't have any first-aid support and had no money,' he said. 'So it was either me or nottin'.' Besides, he was seeing first-hand the effects the government's policies were having on the city and the country, and couldn't sit idly by.

'You know, in 1981, for older people the 1930s were still in their minds,' he said. 'So "No return to the 1930s" was a slogan that still had a certain resonance for a lot of people. Here were all these people who looked poor – because the whole thing was done on a shoestring – marching from the north, again, against unemployment, again. It was not that unusual to see older people at the side of the road crying.'

Chris talked about the early days of the Thatcher project. 'It was still a novel idea back then, all this "you're all on your own, mate". There was a lot of pushback against it, people were resisting. But people are softened to it now. They're more or less "Yeah, but what are you going to do?"'

I asked Chris if he remembered my dad. His face lit up. 'My family was very active in the Communist Party; my dad died in 2010, and he was a committed socialist to the end. That's how we knew your dad,' he said. 'We all liked him. Lovely warm presence. He stayed at our house on numerous occasions. My mum is very small and vivacious. Your dad called her Twinkly Sally, and it was perfect. I still call her Twinkly Sally to this day – she's eighty-four now!'

Chris told me he'd joined the Communist Party as a young man. He asked if I'd ever been a member. No, I told him, I had never been a member of any political party. He looked surprised.

'Anyways,' he said, 'the CP was like going to university in a way. At a time when you heard dreadful racist filth spouted on the streets, there you were pulled up on it.'

Chris laughed, then shook his head. 'We were all committed to this dreadful idea [communism]. I mean, what were we thinking? As Alexei Sayle wrote, thank God the British people were sensible enough not to listen to us!' He laughed again.

Chris had recently joined the Labour Party. He had been to see Jeremy Corbyn speak in Liverpool and had been impressed. 'I've given out my last leaflet. But I wanted to be part of this wave,' he said. 'I stood there listening to him and thought, "I can see working-class Liverpool coming back for this."'

I asked Chris if he thought something like the People's March could happen today. No chance, he said, 'not even against zero-hours contracts. Socialism still made sense back in 1981, because there was a factory there, and an owner there, and if that factory closed and the work went elsewhere, it went more or less next door. But now nobody makes anything here, it's all gone to China. Organised labour has lost all of its power.'

Don't forget, Chris said, that it was not uncommon for people to organise work-ins. 'The whole premise of a work-in was that these are our jobs and you're not taking them,' he said. 'That's gone now. The idea of *our* jobs. Everybody's used to the idea now of "step out of line for ten seconds and it's all going to China".' This was one of the things he admired about Corbyn. 'The one side are saying we've got to do austerity, the other side that we've got to do austerity only not as bad. That's now the consensus,' Chris said. 'With Corbyn, he's saying that it's an ideological choice, not an economic necessity. And he's absolutely right.'

Had I spoken to Kim Laycock, Chris asked. She had been on the march, too, lived just up the road, they'd stayed in touch. She had an interesting story to tell. He texted her. She texted back. Yes, I could go and see her.

Chris saw me to the door.

'How come you weren't on the march?' he asked me.

'Come in,' said Kim.

Kim lived on the ground floor of a converted Victorian house. Over tea, she told me that in 1978 she'd had a son, Joe. She was twenty years old at the time, and a single parent. She'd scratched around for work, trying to balance the demands of raising a child and earning a living.

'But it was hard,' she said. 'It was hard to get a job that would give you enough money to afford childcare. So many of us were forced onto the dole because of it. And the dole was terrible, and we all knew it.'

After May 1979, with the election of the Thatcher government, everything seemed to get worse, and quickly.

'There were people leaving babies on counters in the dole office. Their money would be stopped every other week, back then just like today, for not looking for a job. But they couldn't afford the childcare, so if they had a job, they'd be forced to give it up. It was hard for everyone.'

Kim had grown up in a working-class political family, living in the poor terraced streets of the Dingle. 'My dad was in the unions and my mum fought tooth and nail for everything, and everybody. So I'd grown up with protest and kindness, helping others out in the community, back then when there were solid communities.'

Her mother, Olive Laycock Rogers, had died in 2014. She'd been a writer, 'doing a lot of poetry and prose, quite gutsy political stuff. Very feminist as well, but from a working-class woman's perspective. She'd gone around working-class areas doing workshops.'

At home, Kim said, her mum had always encouraged her, telling her she could be whatever she wanted to be.

At school, she'd told her teachers that she was going to be an architect.

'They said I should aim for a job in the canning factory. When I told Mum, she just said that I must find a way to fight it, that she would back me all the way.'

In 1981, Kim heard about the People's March for Jobs.

'I thought, "OK, I'm going to go on that",' she told me. Undaunted by the reality of being a single parent with a three-year-old son, she took inspiration from a film she'd seen about a woman who'd travelled across the Siberian tundra on her own in the 1920s. 'I thought, "If she can do that, no equipment, just a big coat, I can walk to London, because I'll just get myself a good little pram and da-da-da."'

The march organisers thought differently, saying it would be too hard on a baby, and blocked her joining. The march left Liverpool, and Kim wasn't on it. But her mum had taught her well – she wasn't going to be beaten.

'I said to the march guys, "Listen, how would it look if the *Liverpool Echo* found out that you'd stopped an unemployed single mum from going? And why are all these people marching anyway? I know they're losing jobs and industry's closing down. But they're marching for a future. Well, what's this child? This child is the future, and if we don't fight now, well he won't have a future."'

So, a week after the march had wound its way out of Liverpool, Kim and her three-year-old son joined up. Within three days, Kim knew she'd been fully accepted when the organisers bought her a brand-new pram to replace the old one with broken wheels that she had turned up with. 'They said, "That's not going to last till London. You're not walking round Liverpool now,"' she told me, laughing.

I left Kim and walked on, through the eastern suburbs of Liverpool, cutting through the vast and immaculate Allerton Cemetery, one of Liverpool's main burial grounds.

The rain had stopped, and I sat down on a bench close to Cilla Black's grave to remove my waterproof trousers and my heavy Gore-Tex boots. I hadn't done much long-distance walking, but I'd taken advice from a colleague who had. He had told me how important it was to take my shoes and socks off at regular intervals to stretch my feet and give them some air. I removed my socks and wiggled my bare toes.

It felt wonderful to have fresh air on my feet, if slightly disrespectful of Cilla, lying just across the way. After a brief pause, I put my socks back on and swapped my heavy boots for my lighter walking shoes. Puddles still dotted the walkways in the cemetery but the sun was drying them out. I stood up, pulled on my pack, tightened the shoulder straps and started walking again. The weight was always a shock at first, but my body and legs soon got used to the load and found the right pace and rhythm. My lighter shoes felt wonderful compared with the boots.

I headed east, out of the cemetery on its far side, and then along a busy dual carriageway before ducking back into residential streets, this time not terraced houses but smart Edwardian semis. The meandering nature of my walk felt good. What joy to just duck this way and that, following a rough course, not really knowing what I would find around the next corner. People were out in their front gardens, tending to flower beds or washing their cars. I wondered what they were making of a middle-aged man with a giant backpack marching along their quiet residential street.

I was soon out of the residential areas and onto a dual carriageway, cars and lorries flying past at seventy miles an hour. The world had opened up, a sweeping mackerel sky over that flat, expansive landscape of the north-west.

A road sign said left to Manchester and Southport, straight on to Runcorn and Widnes. The pavement disappeared. Ahead was just a narrow grass verge and hedgerows. I carried on, walking carefully on the uneven ground now, bracing myself as articulated lorries thundered past, their wake making me stumble as they passed inches from me. I continued for a few hundred yards but it felt too dangerous. This pattern would become familiar to me over the next month, trying to traverse on foot a country whose main roads were often not designed with pedestrians in mind.

I turned around and walked back to the last junction. The road that ran off it was so much better, quieter, with a pavement, flanked by fields of young wheat. Occasionally, I passed grand gates with a crest, and private driveways leading to houses in the distance. I stopped at a gate in a field to rest, took off my pack, gulped down some water.

Before long I was out of the countryside and back into a town, first walking through an industrial estate of warehouses and small units and a recycling plant, then terraced houses flanking the road. I passed a 'Welcome to Widnes' sign and I thought to myself, 'I've just walked from Liverpool to Widnes.'

Along the main shopping street, I stopped to sit on a bench and removed my shoes and socks once more. A group of young lads on BMX bikes held their noses as they rode past, crying, 'Your feet stink, mate,' in a distinctly Scouse drawl.

It was 7 p.m. I'd walked fourteen miles in total, with a heavy pack. It was the furthest I'd walked in one go for as long as I could remember. I hadn't done any training for this, figuring that the original marchers probably hadn't done much either, and had been powered by tea, fags and beer. But then most of them had been young.

After I'd finished massaging my feet, I put my socks back on – made of a 'smart' wool which, using technology from space travel, regulates the temperature of the feet and prevents soreness. That's what the blurb said anyway. I wasn't sure of the science, but I had bought them in a Liverpool outdoors shop the day before setting off, after watching an in-store video in which gorgeous young men and women were trekking in the Annapurna or some such place, clearly having triumphed over the elements owing to their choice of sock, and, if the looks on their gorgeous faces were anything to go by, just about to go back to their tents and have unbelievable sex. My feet were very sore. I felt as if I must not have been wearing them correctly. I was also pretty sure that, whatever else may or may not happen in Widnes that evening, unbelievable sex probably wasn't on the cards.

Ten minutes later I was standing in the reception of the Widnes Travelodge handing over £50 to the woman behind the counter.

'Is your car in the car park?' she asked.

'No,' I said, and took a little pause for dramatic effect. 'I have no car. I have *walked* from Liverpool.' I put a lot of emphasis on the 'walked'.

I stood there, waiting for the wide eyes and wonder. She carried on typing into the computer and then handed me my room card. I thought she must not have heard me. 'It's quite a long way,' I said, 'when you're walking.'

'What is?' she said.

'Liverpool,' I said.

'Oh,' she said. 'I usually drive. Great shopping there.'

There was a pause. Then I picked up my card and went to my room.

3

THE DESIRE PATH
(WIDNES TO WARRINGTON)

I lay in bed for a while, stiff from the previous day's walking, before getting up and making a coffee. I sat on the end of the bed and drank, free of distraction. Hotel coffees always taste delicious to me – in terms of bang for your buck, far nicer than a shop-bought coffee, even though in terms of flavour they're obviously not. Maybe there's something in the fact that you had to make it that enhances the whole experience; do we value something much more when some of our own industry has gone into creating it?

In America, just after the Second World War, the makers of Betty Crocker cake mix thought they were onto a sure-fire winner when they invented a mix that was effectively a complete cake in a box. When US housewives failed to respond to this, the puzzled marketing people turned to the ideas of Edward Bernays, Sigmund Freud's nephew, who had been a pioneering force in the advertising industry using his uncle's theories about what drove people's deepest desires.

The housewives, they deduced, felt guilty serving up a cake to which they'd contributed so little; so guilty, in fact, that they wouldn't buy it. The recipe was changed to require the addition of an egg, and the cake mix flew off the shelves. On one level, this might be an insight into how vulnerable we are to the manipulations of the advertising industry. But could it also carry an optimistic message? Perhaps another way to look at it is that we are collaborative, co-operative animals, at our best when working together.

I packed my rucksack, finished my coffee and went down to reception. The same woman from the night before was behind the desk.

'Have you worked all night?' I asked.

'No,' she said, she'd been home. But she was working double shifts, needed the money.

'Where are you off to today?' she asked me.

'Warrington,' I said. 'I am *walking* there.'

'Oh,' she said. 'Shops aren't as good as Liverpool's.'

Looking for breakfast, I headed out of the motel in the direction of Widnes Shopping Park. Negotiating the busy roads that stood between me and my destination was easier said than done with my heavy pack; the message that my brain sent to my legs, in terms of exactly what speed was needed to nip between the cars, didn't quite get through. It was like trying to accelerate with the handbrake on.

I walked through the car park and onto Widnes's pedestrianised old high street, relieved to be away from the cars.

There was a man selling the *Big Issue*. I thought of Keith Mullin, made eye contact, said hello, asked him where he was from, but he didn't seem to speak any English at all. I gave him £2, but I didn't take a copy. Keith hadn't told me what that felt like, when people gave money but didn't take the magazine. Was it a good thing, having money in your pocket and still having the copy to sell? Or did the seller feel patronised; was receiving money without giving something in return then effectively like begging, which the whole *Big Issue* thing was set up to avoid?

Widnes's old high street was busy. There were plenty of nail bars and beauty salons and hairdressers, most with a nod to some idea about American glamour – US Nails, Head to Toe US-Style Nail Bar, Star Nails. There were bookmakers and payday loan shops. And there was a travel agency, across two shop units, one of them taken up with a coffee shop called The Departure Lounge which, I could see through the large window, was doing a good trade. I walked in and a middle-aged man at the foremost desk asked me if there was anything he could help me with.

'I'm just having a look,' I said. And then, apropos of nothing, 'How do you manage to compete with the internet?'

He crossed his arms, sat up a little straighter, tilted his head to the left and looked me in the eyes.

'We have better buying power, *actually*,' he said, stressing the word 'actually', and then fell silent. I thought the conversation was over. But then he continued. 'People like the one-to-one, the personal service. I've just sold Malta at £199. Why would you do that on the internet?'

When he said the word 'internet', he'd tucked his chin into his neck and made a face like he'd sucked on a piece of fermented fruit. He pointed towards the coffee shop. 'The internet can't give you that, can it?' he said. 'People come and have a chat with us about their holidays, then go and have a coffee and a bit of cake and have a think about it.' I followed his finger. The tables were all full. People were engrossed in conversation.

'I guess not,' I said.

At the end of the high street I found a cafe. On a side table were copies of the newspapers. The *Daily Mail* had the headline 'Nice work if you can get it! Exposed: Ex-ministers and civil servants whose work in public sector opens doors to lucrative private jobs'.

I took a local paper, and found a table. The headline on the front page read 'Unemployment falls to record levels'. The number of people signing on in the borough had dropped by 23 per cent in the last year, and now only 2 per cent of the population was actively seeking work. A spokesperson from the Department for Work and Pensions was quoted as saying the numbers were a vindication of the government's policies and that the recovery was being driven by 'a huge growth in logistics', with a special mention for Lidl's major distribution centre, just across the Mersey in Runcorn.

A young woman brought my coffee and my breakfast. Around me, I could hear people chatting away, and everybody seemed to have a Scouse accent. I was about a dozen miles east of Liverpool. I wondered when accents would change as I walked through England. If you got on a train or an aeroplane, it was one of the first things you noticed on arrival, that people talked differently to those in the place you'd departed from. But what happened when you moved at three miles an hour? Would it be gradual, impossible to notice the subtle change? Or stark, from one major town to the next, as if by an act of collective will people decide: 'Here, we speak like this'?

I finished my breakfast and headed back outside. The sky was cloudless, the temperature around eighteen degrees. At the corner of an alleyway, there was a young woman playing a guitar. She was singing Ben E. King's 'Stand By Me', rather well. I stood listening, and when she had finished and was retuning her guitar for the next song, I went up and put a pound in the guitar case at her feet.

She thanked me and looked at the big rucksack on my back. For the first time it occurred to me that, especially in towns and cities, people seeing me walking around with a large pack might assume that I was homeless.

'On the road?' she asked me.

'I'm not homeless,' I said. As if to prove my point, I dug into

my pocket and pulled out another pound coin, which I put into
her guitar case. Looking back, this probably didn't prove to her
that I wasn't homeless at all, just that I was a bit weird.

'Can I ask you some questions?' I said. 'I'm walking through
England, trying to get a flavour of the country in 2016.'

'Sure,' she replied.

'How old are you?'

'Seventeen.'

'And if you could vote in the EU referendum next month,
how would you vote?'

'Probably out. Sounds like a stupid answer, but we should
have a go out.'

That threw me a bit. I had bought into the idea that the vote
would be split between young and old, with the young all about
Remain, for togetherness and internationalism, and older people
supporting the Leave campaign, for regained sovereignty and
a stop to mass immigration. Those were the battle lines being
portrayed by the media.

Before I could think what to ask her next, she launched into
'Good Riddance' by Green Day, which more sensitive souls than
me might have taken personally. At the end of the song I put
another quid in her guitar case.

'Thank you,' she said. 'You like that one? Dads tend to.'

'I'm not a dad,' I said.

'Oh,' she replied.

She was at LIPA, in Liverpool, she told me, a ninety-minute
commute each day on the bus from her parents' house. She was
studying acting, wanted eventually to do musical theatre.

Would she stay in Widnes afterwards?

'Nah,' she replied. 'Not much going on here. Probably move
to London.'

She told me the songs that bring in the most money, that she could make £60–£70 in a couple of hours, but that there had been a lot more people busking in the streets of Widnes recently, so making decent money had got a lot harder.

I said good luck, and walked away. The girl struck up 'Homeward Bound'. A nice touch, I thought. Not only because I was homeward bound, kind of, but because I knew that Paul Simon had been inspired to write the song while sitting at Widnes railway station during a tour of England in the mid-1960s. With a ticket to his destination (London) and lovesick for a woman he'd recently met, the lyrics had come to him. There was, periodically, a plaque commemorating this at Widnes station – periodically, because it kept getting nicked, apparently. Simon once told an interviewer: 'If you'd ever seen Widnes, then you'd know why I was keen to get back to London as quickly as possible.' Which seemed a bit harsh.

I walked back through the alleyway, into the mayhem of the car park of Widnes Shopping Park, where some cars were circling, looking for a space, and some were stationary, their hazard lights on, that code for 'I am here, waiting for a spot to become free', hoping everybody else would understand and honour the code. On the far side, I noticed a gap in the hedge, through which ran a dirt path that had been trampled through the lavender and the low shrubs. This 'desire path' would have saved anybody who took it the trouble of walking about thirty metres to the end of the hedge, where the official path went. The human need to cut corners in this manner is not necessarily down to laziness, but rather a need to defy, often unconsciously, the planners who dictate our built environment. The planners say, 'You will walk this way. We know best.' People say, 'I will walk whichever way I please, thank you very much.' Our paths are among the oldest imprints of man on the earth.

Pete's desire was always to be moving, free of constraints,

to leave my mum, leave us. Back then, I couldn't stop that, couldn't make him stay. He was making his own desire path through life, his needs much stronger and wilder than the pull of home. As we forge our desire paths, flowers get trampled, hedges get destroyed. My younger self couldn't see it, or accept it, but there is something rather wonderful and hopeful about it all that speaks of human defiance and resilience; people going where they go, despite the damage they cause. There was probably a lot more of Pete in me than I was willing to admit.

I took the desire path and walked across the car park of another large shopping centre, the warehouse units selling nest-building paraphernalia: homeware, DIY materials, garden supplies. Behind it, the streets got quieter, with modern red-brick office blocks surrounded by wire fences, and then came light industrial units and breakers' yards, where shipping containers were stacked up, rusting away, and weeds grew up the spiked metal railings and though cracks in the pavements. There were crumbling buildings there, half standing, overgrown with buddleia, and roads going nowhere, with traffic roundabouts built for some future that hadn't yet arrived. The air of desolation hung heavy.

I was looking for the St Helens Canal. My experience the day before had taught me that this whole expedition would be a lot more pleasant, and less likely to lead to my death, if I avoided main roads as much as possible.

I'd seen that the canal linked Widnes to Warrington, arrow-straight, a part of the Trans Pennine Trail. Some concrete blocks had been laid across the road. I slipped over them and a few minutes later I was on the towpath of the canal, which ran alongside the broad expanse of the River Mersey. To the west I could see the supports in place for a new bridge across the river, to be called the Mersey Gateway, and beyond that the glorious sweeping arch of the Runcorn Bridge, similar in design to the Sydney Harbour Bridge. When it was built in 1961 it had the third-longest steel-arch span in the world.

In the distance I could see the giant cooling towers of the Fiddler's Ferry power station, looming over the estuarine land-scape. On the far bank of the canal, in the reed beds, a swan sat on a nest, its partner patrolling the canal in front of it, surging in short, alarming bursts towards the coots and the Canada geese and the mallards, feathers raised. I looked out over the salt marshes of the Mersey, alive with wading birds. A large telecommunications mast had been decorated with steel petals at the top so that it looked like a giant dandelion.

It felt magnificent to be away from the traffic and the noise. In the course of a normal day in the city, I'm not sure we fully appreciate just how stressful our proximity to traffic can be. A German study recently found a correlation between traffic noise exposure and the risk of heart disease due to the psychological and physiological stress on the body. It activates the sympathetic nervous system that controls the 'fight or flight' response, rais-ing blood pressure and heart rate. Over time, this can damage the cardiovascular system. I didn't need scientists to tell me that. Just a few minutes walking along that silent corridor and I felt as if I was floating.

The towpath was deserted, so I started singing to myself, loudly. And as the last song I had heard was 'Homeward Bound', and as I was still in Widnes, that's what I sang.

A kestrel hovered, fluttering delicately, and then dived towards a reed bed on the edge of the salt marsh. A female jogger came past me, accompanied by a young boy on a bicycle, his helmet slightly too big for him so that it kept falling down across his eyes. The woman said hello.

I passed a lock that led from the canal to the River Mersey. Moored nearby were houseboats, just like Pete's. I'd bought one of my own just after his death – a death I'd convinced myself had had no impact on me, and yet there I was, living on a boat. It was a hundred-year-old converted Dutch barge, which I'd bought in east London and taken up the Thames to its new mooring, on an island in the river linked to the mainland by a footbridge.

There were twelve boats on the island, lived in by a mixture of dreamers and artists, musicians, therapists, and even a retired Navy man – the go-to person for all of us when we needed help with knots and repairs. We had barbecues and parties to mark the islanders' birthdays and anniversaries. We bought a communal chainsaw and had days where we'd all turn out to chop up the fallen wood on the island to feed our log burners. When someone was sick, we'd organise cooking rotas to make sure they were eating properly. Doors were left unlocked. It could take an age to get off the island in the mornings, as there was always somebody to stop and chat to. For a brief while, I was happy there. It was the closest I'd ever come in a big city to finding a human-scale 'village' to live in.

The only problem was the landlord, a property developer who'd picked up the island for a song and raised the mooring fees by an eye-watering amount each year, because he could. When your home is a ninety-foot-long, sixteen-foot-wide slab of steel, and moorings on the river are as rare as hen's teeth, you are not in a strong position to complain.

My fees went up from £8,000 a year when I arrived to £12,500 a year three years later, plus increases in the annual service charge. It all seemed so arbitrary, leaving everybody feeling precarious and exposed. The landlord imposed these increases without explanation and with, it seemed to me, some relish. New edicts came thick and fast: log burners, our main source of heating, were banned; he would fire off circular emails, complaining that some of the boats weren't clean enough, often threatening eviction if his will wasn't bowed to; he threatened to ban barbecues, music, pets, flowers in pots on the walkways.

Because we were 'offshore', our boats weren't liable for council tax and therefore we had no protection from the local authority. It was ironic that the very thing that had attracted all of those dreamers and idealists – the idea of living in a community – had delivered them straight into the hands of someone so ruthless.

The way people coped with the helplessness was fascinating. Some put their boats on the market, desperate to be away. But the landlord sent an email around saying that anybody selling up had to go through his appointed broker or else they could not sell the boat on the mooring (effectively making the boat worthless). Those who couldn't or didn't want to move – with kids at local schools, jobs nearby, unable to afford the prohibitive prices for property onshore – fell into two camps. Some went down the appeasement route, trying to keep onside with the landlord; bargaining, submissive. For others, myself included, that anger and impotency was channelled into violent fantasies; anger allied with impotency is a dangerous and toxic mix.

In my mind, I think he became the embodiment of so much else that was going on in London, and the country at large: the rolling back of protections and security for ordinary people. Unlike in 1981, when there was a sense that protest could still be effective, now there was a sense of inevitability about this loss of security; that it was as inevitable as the tides coming in twice a day and lifting my boat off the mud in west London.

I became quite ill with it all. I put my boat on the market. During the period I was trying to sell, terrified that any transgression on my part would see the boat and me evicted, I felt perhaps the most precarious I have ever felt in my life. All of which wasn't helped by the talk of redundancies at work. But there was something else, too: that somehow the primal anger I felt towards that landlord – a male figure of absolute power, showing cold indifference, with no duty of care – was tied in with my feelings towards Pete.

An *acte manqué* is a subconsciously deliberate mistake, an acted-out parapraxis. So show a French audience a drama where somebody driving to an appointment she didn't want to keep crashes into a tree, and they would probably understand. I wondered sometimes whether my subconscious had delivered me into the hands of that landlord – whether the death of Pete, with his indifference, and my life led trying to correct that, had left me needing a surrogate. No wonder that at times I wanted to kill that landlord.

It was in this period of insecurity that I'd first walked those eleven miles to work. I'd crossed the footbridge, turned right and headed towards central London. I was in control again and it felt magnificent.

At Hammersmith, I joined the hundreds of people waiting at the lights to cross the road, and got swept along with them until they disappeared into the tube station and I peeled off left along Hammersmith Road. I walked up Kensington High Street, north-east across Hyde Park to Marble Arch, and across that island onto Oxford Street. By that time I had been on the road for two hours, and had covered seven or so miles, my endorphins flowing; I had felt really connected to this city, myself.

As I walked along Oxford Street, I looked at the hordes of strangers and, whereas I would usually feel a desire to escape to a quieter backstreet, I felt something akin to communion.

I started making up stories about the people walking towards me. There was a woman rummaging through a bin, with stained clothing and odd shoes on her feet. I imagined her to be an eccentric paediatrician, fresh from Great Ormond Street Hospital, where only this morning, on the operating table, she'd saved the life of a baby with a hole in his heart. Behind her, a man in a sharp suit was screaming into his phone. I turned him into a pilot for the UN World Food Programme, on his way to a meeting to raise funds, trying to organise an aid drop for people starving in some far-off country. No wonder he was so animated.

It was a miracle to me how I could change my world by this simple process, how projecting goodness onto people transformed everything. I gave my boat landlord a backstory too, one that helped explain the greed and the spite, and consequently I felt more compassionate towards him. But when I thought about Pete, about his own upbringing, his fears, I was unable to continue the game. Back then, it was too soon, the wounds too deep, for me to be so generous.

I would finally walk up York Way, through some revolving doors, up an escalator, along a corridor and then sit down at my desk. My colleagues asked what the hell had happened, because my eyes were on fire.

'I have just walked to work,' I said.

'But you live in Brentford!' my boss said. 'That's . . . I don't even know where that is. How far is that?'

'Around eleven miles,' I said.

I did it every single workday for the next three months. Religiously.

At Sankey Bridges, I got off the canal and turned right onto the Old Liverpool Road. The return of the traffic made me feel under siege again. I stopped in a shop to buy a banana. The Asian man behind the counter looked at my rucksack. By now

I was convinced that people thought I was homeless; that unless they were conducting their own version of my Oxford Street experiment, that's what they would see.

'I've just walked from Widnes,' I told him.

'That's a long way,' he said, and his accent was distinctly Mancunian, as was that of the woman standing next to me buying some scratchcards.

'There's a bus, you know!' she said, and laughed. I now knew where the Scouse accent ended and the Mancunian one began: somewhere along the St Helens Canal between Widnes and Warrington.

I passed a church, the windows all boarded up, the grounds waist-high with weeds. On the opposite side of the road was a giant hand car wash. I'd noticed a few of these on my walk so far. They made sense in modern Britain: why invest in expensive machinery when there is an abundance of cheap labour available?

Soon I was in central Warrington, passing the council offices and lovely town hall, built in the Palladian style in 1750 as a private house, and declared by Nikolaus Pevsner to be the 'finest house of its date in South Lancashire'.

It was still early, so I was confident I could find somewhere to stay. But the first three places I tried were all full (or perhaps they thought I was a tramp). The third suggested I try a place down by Warrington Bank Quay railway station, and so I walked back across Bank Park, and got another chance to see Warrington's lovely town hall, though I was less delighted by its charms than the first two times I'd passed it, lugging, as I was, my house on my back.

Down by the railway station, loomed over by the giant Unilever chemical factory, belching yellow smoke into the otherwise cloudless sky, was a hotel: an old-fashioned-looking place that had probably once been the hotel serving passengers from the railway station. They had a room, and I was soon in it, looking at myself in the mirror. My face was bright red and my scalp tender from the sun. I liked that, the feeling that the walk was leaving its mark on me. It was leaving its mark on my feet, too. A blister had appeared on the heel of each foot, and my toes looked red and angry.

I showered and headed out into town, seeking first a cotton sun hat, which I found on a market stall, and then some plasters for my blisters and some sun cream, which I found in the big central shopping centre, Golden Square.

From there, I went in search of the offices of the *Warrington Guardian*. I had a theory that local newspaper offices would be good sources of information for me as I progressed through the country. Who knows an area better than local reporters?

A young woman, reporter's notebook in her hand, ushered me into a small office leading off the reception. I started my spiel by saying I was following the route of a march against unemployment that had come through Warrington in 1981. 'That's probably before you were born,' I said, and I think that was the first time I had ever uttered those words. But instead of feeling decrepit, I felt good, like an elder.

She summoned a photographer, and we went into the car park, where I was asked to walk up and down, staring moodily ahead past the camera, looking like a man walking through England in the footsteps of his father.

When we had finished, I asked her what I had intended to ask at the start, before I had become the story: whether there were any interesting people in Warrington I could talk to. Yes, she said, there was a local historian who was a mine of information and would be delighted to chat. Then there was a local councillor. What he didn't know about Warrington wasn't worth knowing. She scribbled two mobile phone numbers down.

'We'll run your story in the paper tomorrow,' she said.

I walked up the main street a little while before stopping at the River of Life, a memorial to the victims of an IRA bomb in Warrington in 1993. It had exploded on 20 March, at 12.25 p.m., in Bridge Street, where I was now standing. Three-year-old Johnathan Ball had been out shopping with his babysitter to buy a Mother's Day card. He died instantly as the bomb blew apart the metal bin it had been left in. Tim Parry, twelve years old, was gravely injured in the blast and died five days later. The memorial carried the two boys' pictures, in a composite that showed them seemingly sitting side by side, smiling for the camera, like two brothers, although they were strangers. Warrington would always be associated with that carnage, an indelible mark, joining the matrix of indelible marks that took in Enniskillen, Dunblane, Lockerbie, Hungerford, Whitehaven ...

I took out my phone and called the historian. A recorded voice at the other end told me that the number was not recognised. I tried again, looking carefully at the number the woman at the paper had written down, in case I had misdialled. But no. Same voice. I hung up and tried the local councillor. It rang a few times before a man's voice barked, 'Who's this?!'

'Hello,' I said. 'I was given your number by the local newspaper.'

'WHO. IS. THIS?!' he yelled.

'Erm . . . I am walking to London and, erm . . . I am in Warrington, and the paper thought you might be a good person to . . .'

'Fuck off,' he said, and hung up.

I wandered on, past a pub called The Looking Glass, and then doubled back, finding myself close to Golden Square shopping centre again, in the Old Market Place, thinking to myself what a sheer joy it was just wandering aimlessly around a strange town, trying to find out what its story was, what story it told about itself.

There was a long table and benches in granite, with brass plates fixed to the table. At one end of the table were sculptures of the Mad Hatter, the March Hare, Alice and the Dormouse, slumped asleep on the table, the other places left free for Warringtonians to sit a while. A plaque told how the sculpture was erected in 1984, in honour of Charles Lutwidge Dodgson, Lewis Carroll, born in a parsonage in the village of Daresbury, just down the road. So, this was one of the stories that Warrington told itself. Places need stories.

One of the stories told about our little island in the Thames where my boat was moored is that it was a location for the 1951 movie *The African Queen*. The production was based at nearby Isleworth Studios, and they allegedly took Humphrey Bogart and Katharine Hepburn down to the river to pick up some shots in the little creek that ran between our island and the next one. If you look closely, the story has it, in the background of many of the shots in the film are trees and shrubs that don't grow in Africa, interspersed with plants that do, borrowed by the production crew from Kew Gardens just across the Thames. The rose-ringed parakeets that have now colonised huge swathes of London are rumoured to be descendants of birds that escaped during the filming of *The African Queen*. When I lived on the boat, I loved telling the story of *The African Queen*. And people seemed to love hearing it. It didn't really matter whether it was true or not.

After I sold my boat, I moved to Brighton. Just down the road from the flat I rented was a plaque commemorating Lewis Carroll's many visits to Brighton to visit his sister. In the communal private gardens of Sussex Square there is a tunnel linking them to the beach. It is claimed that Carroll used that tunnel as inspiration for the hole through which Alice fell into Wonderland, yet investigation suggests Carroll didn't visit Brighton until 1874, nine years after *Alice in Wonderland* was published. Everybody knows this, but the story of the tunnel persists, perhaps because people want the story more than the truth.

Brighton was founded on the whimsy of young royals – first Prince Henry, Duke of Cumberland, and then his nephew George, Prince of Wales, who later became George IV – who came to 'take the water' on the advice of a Dr Russell from the nearby county town of Lewes and enjoy liaisons with their mistresses away from the prying eyes of the court in London.

Even today, Brighton still flags up its permissive, liberal credentials, shaped by its founding story. So, if a city's founding story is coal, or steel, or shipbuilding, what happens when that industry is stripped out? What story does a place tell itself then?

I walked through Palmyra Square, a lovely open green space surrounded by handsome, solid red-brick Georgian buildings. Just over the road was Warrington's Museum and Art Gallery, in a building it shared with the town's central library. The latter was established in 1848 as the UK's first publicly funded library. It was now under threat of closure, the local authority looking to find savings to balance the books against the backdrop of central government cuts.

On the main staircase of the museum was an oil painting of George Formby; the ukulele-playing star had lived in nearby Stockton Heath and was buried next to his father in Warrington Cemetery. There was a list of notables with local links: Joseph Priestley, Lewis Carroll, Pete Postlethwaite. In a glass case was a bust of a Buddhist monk, said to carry a curse as every museum staff member who had ever touched it had soon after been involved in a dreadful accident. There was a large botany section, arranged

45

around a lovely ornate iron balcony, below which were the fossils and the geology section. It was a gorgeous little museum.

I walked into the museum's industrial heritage section. Warrington had been known as 'The Town of Many Industries', growing rich in the Industrial Revolution through copper-smelting, shipbuilding, tanning and the cutting of heavy cloth known as fustian – industries all long gone.

There was a cabinet dedicated to the iron clipper ship RMS *Tayleur*, built in Warrington, which sank on her maiden voyage in 1854, just outside Dublin Bay, on her way to Australia. It had been thick with fog and the compasses had not been working because of the iron hull. In high seas, the ship hit rocks off Lambay Island and, of the 650 people aboard, only 280 survived. She was operated by the White Star Line, the same company that, fifty-eight years later, would suffer another, more famous loss on a maiden voyage. No wonder the *Tayleur* tragedy became known as Warrington's *Titanic*.

I walked back to my hotel room. Tomorrow I would be walking to Salford, seventeen miles away – an unnerving thought. My pack was weighing me down. My thighs were sore, my calves tight. I hoped that my blisters would not get worse.

I went down to the bar and sat on a tall stool. The only other customer was a man sitting four stools away from me, in his fifties, maybe, with greying black curly hair and spectacles. I thought about the People's March for Jobs, about what they might have been up to when they arrived in Warrington thirty-five years ago. Keith, Kim and Chris had told me about the nights they had on the road, the drinking, the music, the speeches, the warm welcomes from councils.

'You couldn't put your hand in your pocket if you went into a bar wearing your march T-shirt,' Chris had said. 'Everybody wanted to buy you a drink.'

I raised my hand towards the barman. 'Pint of lager, please,' I said.

The man four empty stools from me ordered a pint as well. I thought I detected a foreign accent.

'You're not from round here?' I said.

No, no, he wasn't, he said, he lived in Canada, in Manitoba.

'Here on business?'

There was a pause.

'Holiday,' he said.

The man picked up his pint and sipped it, and after putting it back on the bar, stared ahead. It looked as if our conversation was over. But I was curious. Warrington seemed an odd place to spend your holidays.

'Canada, eh?' I said. 'Been there a few times. Nice place. Never been to Manitoba, though.'

'Nothing special,' he said.

Another long pause.

'Holiday, eh? In Warrington,' I said. 'Long way to come.'

The man took another sip of his pint, slowly, then put it back on the bar, all at half speed. I imagined it was how everyone drank in Manitoba. He half turned to me, not quite making eye contact.

'I come here every year,' he said, quietly, as if telling me a shameful secret. 'My parents emigrated to Canada from Warrington when I was young. I just like being back in the old place.' He turned and stared ahead again.

Where was the 'old place' for me, I wondered? I was born in Ruislip, Middlesex, on the living-room carpet of a house my parents had been visiting. Not much of a founding story, really. We were always on the move. I went to nursery school in London, then schools in Aston, Perry Barr and Sparkhill in Birmingham, colleges in Solihull and Walsall, and then, since my mum had died, and her house had been sold, I'd been pretty much constantly on the move. By my reckoning, I had lived in nearly forty different houses in my life.

On my many foreign travels I'd come across a Spanish word, *querencia*, which can be translated in a few ways – it is the place you return to but also the longing for home, not so far removed from the nostalgia which, in Ancient Greek myth, drove Odysseus back to Ithaca from the Trojan War, almost demented with homesickness.

'Feels like home, that's all,' the man from Manitoba said, a few moments later, without turning his head.

4

THE BIG SELL-OFF
(WARRINGTON TO SALFORD)

My alarm went off at 7 a.m. I had a big day ahead, and was still nervous as I packed my rucksack and made myself a coffee with the little plastic kettle. I showered and got dressed, carefully putting my socks over the blister plasters, and then slid my boots on. There was a little pain that gradually subsided as my feet found their place in the boots.

The Canadian man was the only other person in the breakfast room. 'Morning,' I said. He waved his hand at me and immediately went back to lifting a spoonful of cornflakes to his mouth.

A young woman in a hijab came out of the swing doors from the kitchen.

'What would you like, love?' she asked me, in a thick Manchester accent.

'Full English, please, love,' I said.

I loved calling people 'love'. But I wouldn't have dreamed of doing it until a few years ago, when I became friends with a priest who had a parish in inner-city London. He called everybody 'love', or 'my love', and I had caught the habit.

Maybe it was one of those ageing things, like wearing a flat cap, or having a beard, or taking an interest in the obituary pages in newspapers. There weren't many joys to be had in ageing, but being able to call people 'love' and wear a flat cap without sounding like a sexist pig and looking like a giant twat are surely two of them.

The woman put my breakfast in front of me. 'Thanks, love,' I said.

'You're welcome, my love,' she replied.

Close to the hotel was a newsagent. I bought a copy of the *Warrington Guardian*, and then sat on a low wall outside the shop flicking through it. I wasn't on the front page. Fair enough, I thought, the main local story must take precedence. There was nothing about me on pages two and three either, just a story about the local police rearranging the parking of their squad cars because of obstruction concerns, and another about how a local stately home was to be used as a location for *Peaky Blinders*.

There was a story about a violent assault outside a nightclub in Bridge Street, and one about how Padgate Lane was going to be closed for roadworks. I carried on flicking through the pages. There was a spread of photographs of Warrington's 'bloomin' lovely' spring flowers, and a feature about how daydreaming was good for you.

On I flicked, past the death notices, and the small ads for cars and beds and wardrobes and used children's shoes, and then the horoscopes, and then I was into the sports section, and the latest news from the Warrington Wolves rugby league team.

I put the paper in the bin and started to walk out of Warrington. 'One always begins to forgive a place as soon as it's left behind,' said Mr Meagles in *Little Dorrit*. It was going to take me a little longer than that to forgive Warrington, I thought.

I meandered through the streets. I passed the Halliwell Jones Stadium, home of the aforementioned Warrington Wolves. I imagined that Halliwell Jones was a former player – a doughty prop forward, maybe – and a legend round these parts. While waiting to cross the busy roundabout, I asked the man standing next to me who Halliwell Jones was.

'A BMW dealership,' he said. 'Just up there.' He pointed up a main road.

'Oh,' I said. Perhaps sensing a little disappointment on my part, the man added: 'They do Minis as well.'

I walked along Orford Lane, the houses now red-brick terraces, past a Polish supermarket, charity shops selling second-hand furniture, and Babycakes & Roses, a 'cakecraft' shop, with the shutters down and a 'to let' sign pasted onto them.

The majority of the shops still open for business were nail bars and hairdressers and fast-food shops – eight of them in a short strip. One shop's facade simply read 'WE BUY GOLD' in capital letters. Opposite that was Bargain Booze. And then there was Betfred, 'the bonus king'.

I popped into a Co-op. There was only one person on the tills, and I joined a queue of about ten people; most were young mums, children waiting alongside them. It took a long time for the queue to go down. It was only when I got about five from the front that I saw what was taking the time. Every person, after having their shopping put through the till, was handing lottery tickets to the assistant behind the counter for checking.

'No good this time,' the assistant would say. Or 'yup, that's a tenner', in which case the young mum would ask for scratch-cards from the big displays at the front: 'One of those, please, two of those, one of those.'

I walked on, every so often coming to another cluster of shops, and every time a similar configuration: nail bars, hair-dressers, discount booze shops, fast food, bookmakers. And then I turned left onto the Manchester Road. I was walking to Manchester along the Manchester Road! I walked past the giant cemetery where George Formby and his father were buried;

the grass must have just been cut, that sweet smell hanging in the air.

The road broadened out, became a dual carriageway, and as the cars sped up and headed purposefully to some distant destination, so did I, my walking mode switching from an amble to a march.

As the lorries roared past, I thought about those young mums buying scratchcards in Warrington, and the ubiquity of betting shops, and the vast number of places selling cheap, calorie-rich fast food on our high streets, and of hundreds of channels on our televisions, and of the commuters staring fixedly into their phones on the train playing Candy Crush.

Towards the middle of the twentieth century, there had been two dystopian novels written by British cultural critics that offered a glimpse of our futures: *Nineteen Eighty-Four* (1949) and *Brave New World* (1932), by George Orwell and Aldous Huxley respectively. The west had fixated on the horrors contained within Orwell's book, of a state that censored information, watched over its citizens with ubiquitous surveillance and restricted the freedom and rights of individuals. This was perhaps understandable, as communism, and especially the communism practised by the Soviet Union and East Germany, seemed to run perfectly to Orwell's narrative.

Huxley's vision of the future took us to the same totalitarian place, but instead of being cowed and coerced by a powerful state, we would become willing participants in our enslavement, sedated by technology, a gorging on consumer goods (and cheap fast food), and instant gratification of all our needs. Soma, in Huxley's novel, was the drug we would all be taking to make life endurable.

The Berlin Wall fell, communism collapsed and capitalism didn't have a countervailing force any more. It was free to exert itself without any ideological counterpoint. Some, like the US cultural theorist Neil Postman, argued that in Orwell and Huxley's dual visions, we had the great twentieth-century debate between communism and capitalism pared back to their pure, essential characters: a Manichaean world of no choice, or of limitless choice.

In his 1985 book *Amusing Ourselves to Death*, Postman wrote: 'What Orwell feared were those who would ban books. What Huxley feared was that there would be no reason to ban a book, for there would be no one who wanted to read one. Orwell feared those who would deprive us of information. Huxley feared those who would give us so much that we would be reduced to passivity and egoism. Orwell feared that the truth would be concealed from us. Huxley feared the truth would be drowned in a sea of irrelevance. Orwell feared we would become a captive culture. Huxley feared we would become a trivial culture . . .

'An Orwellian world is much easier to recognise, and to oppose, than a Huxleyan. Everything in our background has prepared us to know and resist a prison when the gates begin to close around us . . . [but] who is prepared to take arms against a sea of amusements?'

Back in Liverpool Keith Mullin had told me about how many of the kids going through his college had low expectations but high aspirations, so that there's 'a real dissonance between what we're telling kids they can achieve and the reality'. It was fuelled mainly, he said, by TV talent shows and the mythos of the American/British dream, that there's 'some higher being who will find some skill or talent in you and take you away from all of this and offer you paradise'.

'That's exactly why people do the lottery in Britain every week,' Keith continued. 'They hope getting instantly rich will change everything for them. There's that hope there. But a better society is one where people can change their lives through their own industry, not making Camelot richer.'

He looked down at the floor and then back at me. 'We didn't have any of this shit back in 1981, did we?' he said. 'We were fighting for a fairer world, not for the right to get rich.'

The landscape was still pan-flat, the skies huge, the blue flecked with the tiniest wisps of white. Where the hedgerows at the side of the road gave way, there were almost endless fields of oilseed rape on either side, running to the horizon, the whole scene now a brilliant band of blue over a brilliant band of yellow.

There was a truck-stop cafe up ahead. I went inside and ordered a cup of tea.

'You could have left your bag in your car, my love,' said the woman behind the counter. 'It's safe.'

It took me a second to understand what she was talking about. 'I don't have a car. I'm walking,' I said.

'Walking? Where to?'

'London,' I said. 'But not today, obviously. I'm heading for Salford tonight.'

She looked at me, and there was a pause, and I thought she was going to ask me why I was walking to London, and I was trying to work out what I would reply – whether I would give the whole spiel about the march and about my dad, and how I'd wanted to get a look at England in May 2016, and try to work out what's changed in the years since the march passed by this way; or whether I would just say I fancied a long walk and how nice it was to be out and about in springtime.

The woman pursed her lips.

'Sugar, love?' she said.

'One please, love.'

54

I took my tea outside, where I'd spotted a little bench by the door as I'd entered. I removed my shoes and socks, and rubbed my feet. I reckoned I'd walked around four or five miles so far that day, roughly a quarter of the way to Salford, and I was exhausted.

Sitting there barefoot, I pulled out my phone, tapped the icon for Airbnb, and was soon looking through accommodation in Salford. I found a double bed in a family home that was available that night. I booked it.

The door to the cafe opened and the woman who'd served me my tea came and sat on the bench, still in her pinny, and lit up a cigarette. She looked at my bare feet, and I explained my friend's advice. She took off her shoes and wiggled her toes in her tights.

'Been on my feet since five this morning,' she said.

We sat in silence for a while, her pulling deeply on her fag, me sipping my tea.

'Worked here long?' I asked.

'A few years,' she said. 'I own this place. I used to work as a psychiatric nurse in a secure unit in Warrington. When I retired I used my savings to open this cafe.'

I asked her what it was like growing up in Warrington. She told me that her ancestors had come over from Ireland seeking work. 'The kids at school used to call us Irish "white niggers",' she said. She told me how she went off to The Gambia to volunteer as a nurse, how she loved it there, in Africa generally. Within a few minutes, my questions were stacking up like printouts in a printer tray. But she stubbed out her fag, stood up, tightened the strings on her pinny and said, 'Best get back to work, love. Enjoy your walk.' Then she was gone.

Five hours later, I was walking along the banks of the Manchester Ship Canal, passing distribution warehouses. In the distance I could see, rising like a forest, the glittering buildings of Salford Quays, built on the site of the docks that once served Manchester. The docks were abandoned in 1982, the year after the People's March for Jobs, and three thousand people were thrown onto the dole. Salford City Council purchased them in 1984 and a process of regeneration was started.

I passed through MediaCityUK, which opened in 2010 and is now home to a University of Salford Campus and production facilities for ITV and the BBC, making such shows as *Blue Peter*, *Dragons' Den*, *Mastermind* and the flagship BBC *Breakfast* programme.

I walked across the bridge spanning the former docks and stopped to look at the basin, the wharf cranes gone, replaced by new high-rise apartment blocks with convex fronts that make them look as if they are puffing their chests out.

It was by now late afternoon, and joggers were out, looking glossy. In modern Britain, the arrival of joggers to an area seems to be like salmon returning to formerly polluted rivers.

I wandered around The Lowry, a theatre and arts and restaurant complex, clad in stainless steel and glass, with a large and spectacular aerofoil canopy over its entrance. The Lowry had been described in the *New Statesman* as 'not quite "Salford's Guggenheim"', with the writer saying the building was ultimately too small and 'well behaved' to stand comparison with the museum in Bilbao. I thought it looked fantastic.

On the other side of the canal was Old Trafford stadium, home of Manchester United – in May 2016 the world's third-richest football club, behind Real Madrid and Barcelona (but only just), with a value of £2.3 billion. I always loved the old jokes about Manchester United fans. For instance, what does Old Trafford at 4.45 p.m. on a Saturday have in common with Wormwood Scrubs prison? They're both full of Cockneys trying to get out.

Or how do you confuse a Man United fan? Show them a map of Manchester. Boom, boom.

These days, the global nature of the English Premier League means that the Man United jokes are somewhat losing their currency. A few days after I was there, a bomb scare at Old Trafford meant United's game with Bournemouth was postponed. The TV news interviewed frustrated fans who'd travelled from France, the Philippines, the USA and India just to see the game.

Since the formation of the Premier League in 1992, TV companies, and especially Rupert Murdoch's Sky, have paid eye-watering amounts to televise games and sell them around the globe. The most-watched sports league in the world, it is broadcast in 212 territories to 643 million homes and a potential TV audience of 4.7 billion people. That Man United had won the Premier League a record thirteen times since its inception explained the fact that it claimed the biggest fan base in the world, with one 2013 survey saying United had 659 million followers. That's a lot of replica shirts to shift.

Premier League football clubs had attracted the world's money men too, who bought the clubs for investment purposes, but also for the kudos. In the 2015–16 season, thirteen of the twenty Premier League clubs were majority foreign-owned, with Manchester City – or 'the noisy neighbours' as Alex Ferguson used to call them – majority-owned by a billionaire from the United Arab Emirates, with the remaining 13 per cent of the club owned by the Chinese government. The electronic advertising boards that lined the pitch were now sometimes in Mandarin or Arabic.

In one of the strangest and perhaps most salient images of football in 2016, Leicester City players posed with a big framed photograph of the recently deceased Thai king, Bhumibol Adulyadej, wearing black armbands – presumably at the behest of the club's Thai owner. It was quite something to see a 132-year-old English football club acknowledging its new allegiances so explicitly. Not that many Leicester fans would have been complaining that year, of course, having won the Premier League title a few months earlier.

But did the idea of a global village, vastly accelerated under the deregulated hypercapitalism of the 1980s and the digital revolution that followed, really take into account humans' need for belonging and meaning and identity? Does the nationality of a football club owner really matter? A football club that's likely to have been in your family, and at the heart of your community, down the generations?

What happens when said foreign owner decides that Manchester United, with more Chinese fans than English ones, should be relocated to Beijing? It would never happen, right? Try telling that to fans of the Montreal Expos baseball team, or the Seattle SuperSonics basketball team, or the San Diego Chargers American football team, who, in the last decade or so, had moved, respectively, to Washington DC (six hundred miles away), Oklahoma City (two thousand miles) and Los Angeles (a mere hundred miles); the Chargers had spent fifty-six seasons in San Diego.

If our sports teams are much more to fans than simply businesses, but a core part of their identities, then what about other businesses that we use daily? Does it matter that three-quarters of Britain's railway franchises are run by foreign-state-owned or -backed companies? Or that four out of the Big Six energy companies supplying British homes are foreign-owned? Or that increasingly our National Health Service is being sold off to private interests, many of them overseas companies, as are our water suppliers, since privatisation in 1989, with twelve out of the twenty-three in foreign hands? Does it matter that key decisions about prices or jobs or investment are taken in boardrooms in Australia or Canada, as long as we get our water and gas, and our football team avoids relegation?

I travel to work on trains run by Thameslink and Southern, two of the worst-performing franchises on the UK rail network, owned by the same parent company, Govia, which is itself 35 per cent owned by Keolis, a French firm. They have a monopoly on my route to work. It is a daily occurrence that the trains are late, and often very late. In 2016, a National Rail Passenger Survey showed that Southern had the worst satisfaction rating (65 per cent) of all the train operating companies. Only 20 per cent of Southern trains arrived on time from April 2015 to March 2016.

If the trains are over thirty minutes late, you are entitled to apply for a small rebate. But because of the nature of the franchise awarded to Govia by the government, the train operator gets a ringfenced sum of £1 billion a year to run the service properly (or not), and the government takes any operating profits – and has to bear the costs of compensation. So there is no incentive for Govia to run a decent service. Its profits are safe whatever happens and David Brown – chief executive of Go-Ahead, which owns 65% of Govia – trousered £2.16 million in 2015, up from £1.9 million in 2014. So, when I am sitting in fury, late for work again, filling in my 'delay repay' form, it's actually me as a taxpayer stumping up the compensation. How brilliant is that?

Before privatisation, when the government was responsible for the trains, once every five years I would have had the opportunity to vote for a change. But then if a government was accountable to citizens in that way, they couldn't be so insouciant and indifferent.

Eventually, a diminished sense of personal control can lead to 'passive coping' and what the psychologist Martin Seligman has termed 'learned helplessness' – where we make an accommodation with the world, relinquishing our control or agency. We become simply too insignificant, the forces against us too powerful, to think we can muster effective protest and change. The only alternative is to get angry at the injustice of it all. But there are surely fewer things more destructive for mental health than to have that anger and for it to have no place to go. It was exactly the same feeling I had while living on the little island.

And there is a real human cost to all of this. Not that you would necessarily know it, as most things in modern life are refracted through the prism of the markets. When reports are released saying that the numbers of people presenting to their GPs with mental health issues are soaring (there were more than sixty million prescriptions for antidepressants issued in 2015, up from less than thirty million in 2005, and the figures for type 2 diabetes are just as shocking, up from 1.4 million people in 1996 to over four million today), you'd imagine the government might be curious as to why. But instead of questioning what might be making us sick in the modern world, the government and media tend to turn first to organisations such as the Confederation of British Industry, who talk about our mental health crisis or obesity epidemic solely in terms of work days lost and its effect on the country's gross domestic product.

To cope with this new reality, which extends to nearly every privatised service we have to use and might one day see our football clubs shipped off to the other side of the world, we are medicated with antidepressants – a market, incidentally, to talk a language business understands, that is now worth nearly £300 million a year in the UK. The annual cost to the NHS for treating diabetes is £14 billion.

I looked at my watch. My Airbnb host would be home from work by now. So I headed north, away from Salford Quays, across the M602. Within a mile I had entered a completely different world. This was a Salford that L.S. Lowry would still recognise, with a warren of tightly packed terraced streets of red-brick houses, many boarded up, as were many of the pubs and shops. This was the other story of modern Salford, where, in 2016, a quarter of all under-sixteens were officially living below the poverty line, 70 per cent of the population lived in areas classed as highly deprived and nearly 10 per cent of the working population were long-term unemployed. The number of people living there being admitted to hospital with malnutrition had doubled between 2010 and 2014. There had also been the re-emergence of Victorian illnesses such as rickets and beriberi.

Two kids, not even in their teens, raced up and down the road on scrambler motorcycles, helmetless, pulling wheelies. One boy had a microscooter and was smashing it against a lamppost, as if it were an axe and the lamppost a tree. I wondered how many of the people living here would be taking up the thousands of new jobs created by the BBC and ITV and Salford University, and using the posh restaurants and shops just the other side of the M602. In the windows were draped the flag of St George or posters backing the Leave campaign in the EU referendum.

I found the house where I would be staying and knocked on the door. Annie opened it, a young woman with a warm smile. She showed me in, made some tea, and soon we were sitting out in the nice little rear garden, with its pots of geraniums, at the end a wall, beyond which was a narrow cobbled alleyway that ran between the houses. I asked Annie about the 'for sale' sign in the front garden. She was selling up, she said, moving to a small town in West Yorkshire. 'Probably better for my little girl,' she said. We chatted about Annie's career as an artist, about her father who was ill with leukaemia in the nearby Salford Royal, about the nurses and doctors there and how they were working miracles, understaffed and overworked.

I asked Annie where I might find something to eat. She mentioned a pub on the Eccles New Road that she thought was OK, but when I got there it had closed down. Bright, modern trams ran along the road, heading for Manchester, and they might as well have been going to the moon. I found a corner shop, its window boarded up, and although there was a light on above the door, so that in the gloaming it looked like an Edward Hopper painting, it was difficult to tell whether it was open or not. I pushed the heavy, cell-like metal door, and it opened. Inside was an Asian guy standing behind the till, the tiny shop filled with bright artificial light in that windowless space. It felt like a place under siege.

'Do you have any sandwiches?' I asked, to which he just shook his head and, without saying a word, looked away.

Eventually, I found a Chinese takeaway, and took my food back to Annie's house. It was late and she'd gone to bed. I sat alone in the kitchen eating my special fried rice. From outside the window came the sound of children shrieking with excitement and things being smashed up.

*

Next morning, Annie had to nip out. There were estate agents coming round to show the house to potential buyers, she said. Could I let them in? I only had four miles to walk to Manchester, so I was in no hurry.

'Of course,' I said.

About fifteen minutes after Annie left, the bell went and I opened it to find an estate agent standing there. I explained who I was.

'Great,' he said. 'We're expecting a few people around to view.'

Shortly afterwards, the bell went again and the agent disappeared to answer it, before returning with a man in his fifties wearing a smart suit and a tie.

'Hello,' I said.

The man looked at me, but didn't seem to see me, because instead of saying hello back he started asking the agent a few questions about the place, but not many. He had a Home Counties accent.

'Do you want to see the garden?' I asked him. Annie had shown me where the key to the back door was.

'No,' the man said. 'I know what these gardens look like.'

He disappeared upstairs and was back down within two minutes. He said goodbye to the agent, but not to me, and then he was gone.

'How do you think that went?' I asked the agent.

'Quite well, I think,' he said.

'He didn't seem that interested in the house,' I said.

'You can't really tell. He'll probably call later and put in an offer.'

'Really? That easy?'

'At the moment, yes,' he said.

The doorbell went again. This time it was a couple, again in their fifties, and again with what sounded like southern accents. They had the same perfunctory attitude to the house, barely looking at it. Just ticking off a few things on their notepads, and not interested at all in seeing the garden.

'Are you sure?' I said. 'It's rather lovely.'

'No need,' she said. And then they were gone as well.

I asked the estate agent what was going on.

'Buy-to-let investors. Up from the south for the day,' he said. 'They make dozens of appointments and blitz the place, then make their offers.'

'Is that a thing now?' I asked.

'Oh, yes,' he replied. 'It's our main market. They've been

priced out of the south, so they're building portfolios here instead. Often they're part of investment syndicates buying up whole streets.'

There were three other buy-to-let viewers that morning who, like the ones before, walked around the house with a cold detachment. The last viewers were a young couple, she heavily pregnant. They actually seemed to look at the house, saw the place, as if they were genuinely imagining somewhere they would call home.

'It's lovely,' the young woman said, in a Manchester accent.

'Yes,' the young man said.

'Would you like to see the garden?' I asked.

'We'd love to,' the woman said.

As we went outside into the lovely little courtyard, with its geraniums, I asked them how they were getting on in their search. They said that every time they'd found somewhere they could just about afford, they'd been outbid.

'Buy-to-letters have cash and offer the best prices,' the woman said. She told me they were renting in the area, but the rents were going up quickly.

'I've got a child at a local school,' she said. 'I'm not sure how much longer we will be able to afford the area.'

They all left and I sat there alone in the house, in its silence. It was all like some huge fire sale taking advantage of the poverty. Outside the front window was the jingly sound of 'Greensleeves' being played from an ice-cream van.

I heard Annie's keys in the door and soon she was in the living room, asking me if I would like a brew. I wondered if she'd ask me how the viewings went, but she didn't. I was guessing that she'd seen enough in the short time the house had been on the market to know what was happening.

'They were nearly all buy-to-letters,' I said, when we were sitting down at her kitchen table with our tea.

'I know,' she said, wearily. She had friends locally who had been priced out of renting.

'This is a poor area, but there is a real community here. A lot of these families in this street, they've all been here for ages, they all know each other,' she said. 'But the sell-off of council houses has forced people into the private rented sector and the bedroom tax is forcing many from their homes. As more and more buy-to-let landlords move in, they don't care about people that might be struggling the way a council has responsibilities for them. Those landlords don't hesitate to evict people. Already, this street is changing. The community is being destroyed.'

Annie brought out some biscuits, and then poured me a top-up from the teapot. 'It can't last, can it?' she said. 'I mean, it's just not sustainable.'

She told me that the biggest housing association in Salford had made an operating profit of over £3.5 million last year, and that the highest-paid director had got a hefty pay rise and now earned nearly £170,000 a year. 'Look at the NHS, education, it's all the same thing,' Annie said. 'Selling it all off. Running everything for profit. How can poorer people survive in that world?'

5

THE TRIAL

(SALFORD TO MANCHESTER TO STOCKPORT)

I left Annie's, walked along her road, and then out onto Liverpool Street, which Annie said would take me all the way to Manchester city centre.

In the smaller communities along the road, there were more boarded-up shops, with metal shutters pulled down, and vast derelict areas where factories had once stood, grown thick with weeds, and hand car washes and small units offering MOTs. To my right, I could still see Old Trafford. I wondered how many families from this part of Salford would be able to afford to go and watch United play these days, with two adult tickets and two teenage tickets in the Sir Alex Ferguson Stand costing £152.

A pair of swifts darted past me and flew low, zigzagging over a piece of scrubland with their loud, shrill, screaming calls, picking up insects on the wing, before chasing one another at breakneck speed along a terraced street. A friend's daughter calls them sky dolphins, and that seems about right. The swifts were returning to our land from Africa, heading back to the exact same nesting spot as the year before. There was something about the swifts and the young couple at Annie's house that made me feel quite despondent. I wondered if either pair had far to go before they were home.

On the skyline ahead I could see Manchester – like Salford Quays before it, a forest of tall buildings rising into the air, as if suddenly the ground was fertile again. Everywhere there were tower cranes and buildings going up. Most of the men on the streets were wearing hard hats and high-vis jackets, as if that was some kind of traditional city dress. The cars seemed to have gone up a league, too. There were big, shiny new 4x4s and Mercs and Porsches everywhere.

Research published just before I'd set off from Liverpool showed that Manchester had received £136 million from the EU's structural funds programmes between 2007 and 2013 alone. That money has been spent on the Graphene Institute (making Manchester one of the world's leading centres for the development of the strongest and most conductive material known to man), the city's Royal Eye Hospital, its bridges, its tram network, regeneration of run-down districts and many of its fine museums. As in Liverpool, Greater Manchester's parliamentary constituencies were dominated by Labour, the party holding twenty-two of its twenty-seven seats. Just like Liverpool, it was hard to imagine any Conservative administration, after a possible Brexit, pouring as much money into the city as the EU had done.

One of the museums that had been a big beneficiary of EU funding was the People's History Museum (PHM), which opened in Manchester in 1990 after relocating from Limehouse Town Hall in London, where the collection had lived since 1975. The PHM was Britain's leading repository for the history of working people in the UK, appropriate given Manchester's leading role in the Industrial Revolution.

I knew that the PHM had some archive material from the People's March for Jobs, and I was excited to be dropping in. But I hadn't bothered to get in touch in advance, convinced as I was that as soon as I told the person on reception that I was walking in the footsteps of the 1981 march, exactly thirty-five years later,

I would be welcomed with open arms and, dare I say, probably treated as a bit of a hero.

When I also added, with some dramatic flourish, that I was the son of one of the organisers, then, well, they would probably give me the keys to the museum, or the freedom of Manchester, or at least some biscuits.

I approached the bespectacled middle-aged man behind the desk.

'Ahem. Hello,' I said.

'How can I help you, sir?' he said.

'Is there any chance I could have a quick word with the director or a curator, do you think?'

'What is the nature of your enquiry?' he asked.

'Well,' I said, taking my time, relishing this, wanting to tease out the great reveal. 'Do you remember the People's March for Jobs?'

'Jarrow?' he said.

'No, not that one,' I said. 'This one was in 1981. Kind of inspired by Jarrow. Against Thatcher and unemployment. Went from Liverpool to London.'

'No,' he said.

I wasn't expecting that. I felt myself literally moving onto my back foot.

'Well, it was a big deal at the time. Had lots of coverage in the press,' I said, starting to feel as if I was trying to sell him something. 'By the time they got to London, it had really caught the nation's attention. More than a hundred thousand people turned up in Trafalgar Square to welcome them.'

'Doesn't ring a bell,' the man said.

'Well, it was a big deal, this march,' I said, 'and here's the thing: exactly thirty-five years ago to the day, they were in Manchester. And here I am, thirty-five years to the day, in the same place.' I pointed to the ground to emphasise that I was indeed in Manchester. 'And I'm walking from Liverpool to London, in their footsteps, to honour their walk.'

The man was still looking at me indifferently. The dead-dad card was all I had left.

'But the most amazing thing about it all,' I went on, 'was that one of the main organisers of the 1981 march was my dad! He died a few years ago. So, I am honouring him, in a way, and also the struggle of working people, by walking every last step of the 340 miles myself.'

The man looked at me. I thought I saw a glimmer of something in his eye.

'Is this a charity thing?' he asked.

'What?'

'Are you doing a charity walk?'

'No,' I said. 'It's not for charity. Not at all.'

'Because you'd need to write in to the director about that type of thing.'

'Could I just speak to somebody in the office? Anybody,' I said. Apart from you, I didn't say.

He sighed and picked up the phone. I heard the words 'walk', 'charity', 'I've told him that we don't do this sort of thing'.

'Somebody will be down to see you soon,' he said, after putting the phone down. 'Why don't you wait in there?' And he pointed to the coffee shop on the other side of the reception.

I walked over to the cafe, ordered a coffee and a flapjack, and took a seat. Eventually a young man came in and introduced himself as Chris. He was the curator, he said, and asked how he could help.

I told him my story. The experience at the desk had shaken my belief in my project. But Chris's eyes lit up as I was explaining, and he said something along the lines of 'amazing'. I could feel myself growing again inside. How simple human needs were, our basic desire to be heard and seen.

'We have a lot of archive material on the People's March,' he said. 'While you have a look around, I'll dig it out.'

I walked past a map and display commemorating Wal Hannington's 1932 hunger march, when, with unemployment at nearly three million due to the Great Depression, about three thousand marchers from the poorest areas of the UK walked to London to be greeted by a crowd of one hundred thousand in Hyde Park. They were carrying with them a petition with a million signatures on it, demanding the abolition of the means test for unemployment benefit.

The marchers had been condemned in the press as a threat to public order and Ramsay MacDonald's National Government reacted by deploying seventy thousand policemen to control the marchers and their supporters, and prevent the petition from reaching Parliament. Violence erupted in Hyde Park, and seventy-five people were seriously injured.

There was also a display documenting the Peterloo Massacre of 1819, when the chronic economic depression following the Napoleonic Wars had seen workers thrown into ever-deeper poverty. On 16 August 1819, a demonstration of eighty thousand people gathered in St Peter's Field, Manchester, to demand parliamentary representation for ordinary people. Shortly after the meeting started, local magistrates called upon the military to arrest the organiser, Henry Hunt, and disperse the crowd. The cavalry charged into the masses, sabres drawn. Soon, eighteen protesters were dead and between four hundred and seven hundred seriously injured.

I walked through an exhibit on the miners' strike of 1984–85, with photographs of the Battle of Orgreave, where, on 18 June 1984, at a coking works in South Yorkshire, mounted police rode through crowds of striking miners, raining baton blows indiscriminately upon the protesters. The historian and Labour politician Tristram Hunt later described the confrontation as 'almost medieval in its choreography . . . a brutal example of legalised state violence'.

By the end of that day, 123 people had been injured. Of the ninety-five pickets arrested, seventy-one would eventually be charged with riot, a crime that was at the time punishable by life imprisonment. All of the subsequent trials collapsed when evidence given by the police was deemed 'unreliable'.

In 1991, South Yorkshire Police had paid £425,000 in compensation to thirty-nine miners who had sued for assault, wrongful arrest and malicious prosecution (though the out-of-court settlement was made without any admission of liability or wrongdoing). In 2015, the Independent Police Complaints Commission reported that there was – in the words of a *Guardian* summary – 'evidence of excessive violence by police officers, a false narrative from police exaggerating violence by miners, perjury by officers giving evidence to prosecute the arrested men, and an apparent cover-up of that perjury by senior officers'.

As with Hillsborough, by the time the state had been forced to investigate, a quarter of a century had passed. Lives had been ruined, the protesters traduced, survivors traumatised. The effects of the miners' defeat can still be seen in former pit towns and villages up and down the country today, in the poverty and the hopelessness, and in the widespread alcohol and drug use.

I looked at a display about the Bryant & May match girls' strike of 1888, when workers walked out to protest against fourteen-hour days, poor pay, lack of security, terrible working conditions and the arbitrary dismissal of a young female worker. The sepia photographs made it seem like a world familiar to my great-grandparents' generation but inconceivable today.

But at that very moment, just across the Pennines, at Sports Direct's warehouse in Derbyshire, Mike Ashley, a man with a fortune estimated at £2.5 billion, was presiding over a business empire where 80 per cent of the staff were on zero-hours contracts, where workers suffered harsh deductions from their pay packets for being just one minute late, and where, according to a union spokesman, a pregnant woman had been so afraid that she might lose her job if she missed a day's work that she'd given birth in a toilet. A parliamentary committee compared Sports Direct to a 'Victorian workhouse'.

I continued on through the museum into a gallery displaying trade union banners, the double-height ceiling allowing them to be shown off in all their epic glory. Among them were the Liverpool Tinplate Workers' banner from 1821 (the oldest trade-union banner in the world), and the White Lion Lodge banner from 1830 (the oldest surviving miners' banner). The colours were gorgeous: rich reds and blues, fringed with gold or silver trim.

Looking at all of them brought back powerful memories. As a child, in Birmingham, I'd marched behind the banner of my dad's union, UCATT, during the campaign he'd helped organise in 1972 against the building firm Bryant's use of casualised labour – the seventies equivalent of zero-hours contracts. The dispute had quickly escalated into a national building workers' strike. One of the things I'd found in Pete's box was a letter from Bryant warning him to stay away from its sites.

UCATT's banner was a scarlet red, with a scene of two men laying bricks in the middle of it, inlaid with gold filigree, and the words 'Unity is Strength' across the top. I'd watched the two men holding high the poles on either end, the banner rippling in the strong breeze. Even at that young age, I'd felt acutely the sense that here were my people – that they could do anything, that in unity was an unbreakable strength.

I remembered that the march had come to a halt in Birmingham's Victoria Square, where Pete got up to address the thousands gathered, denouncing Bryant, pledging to fight, exhorting all of these people to stand firm in the fight for a thirty-five-hour week and better pay and safer conditions.

I looked up at all of these adults, towering above me, and as my dad started his peroration, I could feel the crowd, as one, grow somehow, until the final thumping words came from the podium and the crowd let out a roar and raised their clenched fists into the air. It was impossible for my eight-year-old self to imagine that those people could ever be denied.

A year later, on 24 July 1973, I stood outside the courtrooms in Birmingham, again under the UCATT banner, with four hundred protesters. This time it was without Pete, though; he was inside, having being charged with unlawful assembly and conspiracy to trespass.

Earlier that year, Pete and seven others had occupied the offices, inside Birmingham's iconic Rotunda building, of a company suspected of collaborating with the big building firms to supply 'lump' labour. The occupation had ended peacefully, but it was widely believed at the time that central government, through the office of the Director of Public Prosecutions, had pushed for prosecution, determined to make workplace occupations illegal.

Trespass was a civil wrong, or tort; you could be sued for it, but it was not a crime. But conspiracy to trespass was a different ballgame, the addition of the conspiracy turning a civil offence into a criminal one.

According to the defence, the conspiracy charge brought against the trade unionists almost amounted to a new offence. Only one other instance of a similar prosecution was known in all legal history.

In the end, the case collapsed and the workers walked free. I remembered that feeling, of standing outside and seeing the scenes of jubilation. I remembered my dad standing there, fist clenched in the air again, telling those gathered that they would never be defeated.

That victory would be short-lived. The battle lines between the state and the workers were being drawn. The year before, in February 1972, the miners had won a strike over wages, humiliating Ted Heath, the Prime Minister. Later that year, the government was further embarrassed by the case of the Pentonville Five dockers – shop stewards who were jailed for refusing to stop picketing despite a court injunction but released after widespread protests and the threat of a General Strike.

It was with that background, and with the very real prospect of a full-scale workers' revolt on the cards, that the state started the fightback. In October 1973, just a few months after the Rotunda trial, a series of proceedings was enacted against a group of twenty-four men who came to be known as the Shrewsbury pickets, accused of violent picketing and intimidating workers during the building workers' strike in Telford in 1972.

Among them were two building workers, Des Warren and Ricky Tomlinson, later to become an actor. Like in the Rotunda case, they were prosecuted for conspiracy and, as if during the Birmingham trial the authorities had learned what not to do, the men were convicted and sent to prison.

Tomlinson, speaking in 2012, and calling for the sentences to be quashed, said, 'We have maintained our innocence for forty years. We have always known that there was political interference by Ted Heath's Conservative government in respect of the charges brought against us.'

He added that a lack of evidence clearly did not matter to the government: 'They decided to throw the conspiracy charge against us, which was a way of getting around the evidence problem.'

Des Warren had died in 2004 from Parkinson's, a disease he attributed to the long-term effects of the treatment he received during his time in prison, including the 'liquid cosh', a cocktail of tranquillisers administered to 'awkward' inmates.

Many of the other jailed pickets ended up on blacklists and never worked in the building trade again. The campaign for their exoneration continues to this day.

The state's campaign to crush organised labour would find ultimate expression in the defeat of the miners in 1984–85 and the steady erosion of union power under the Thatcher and Major governments. And now, not only was the trade union movement greatly imperilled, but the only museum dedicated to telling its story was too.

In 2010, under the coalition government, it was announced that funding for the People's History Museum was to be slashed, and stopped altogether in 2015. There was a one-off £100,000 payment to the museum in 2015, to plug the shortfall in its budgets, but after that the future was uncertain, and at the time of my visit it was exploring other funding options.

I met up again with Chris, the museum's curator. He took me into the archives, where he'd dug out the file on the People's March for Jobs. I sat there for an hour, going through all of the correspondence, reading letters between the organisers and members of the Parliamentary Labour Party, maps of the march and flyers listing prominent supporters, including showbiz figures such as Julie Christie and Spike Milligan; from football there was Billy Bremner, Brian Clough and Jack Charlton; Dorothy Hyman, Yorkshire miner's daughter and Olympic athlete, was also there, as was the playwright Arnold Wesker.

At the bottom of the list were the grandee politicians – Eric Heffer, Harold Wilson, Tony Benn – and the rising stars: Patricia Hewitt, Ruth Lister and Peter Hain. And there, prominent on the flyers, was the name and address of Pete Carter. In 1981 he had still been full of the fight.

*

The next day I started walking out of Manchester, the city looking magnificent in the spring sunshine. I sat for a while in Piccadilly Gardens, watching the trams run around me like a giant train set, as people sat on the grass eating their sandwiches, or walked through the square with shopping bags carrying the names of expensive boutiques.

I walked along Piccadilly. In almost every shop doorway there were blankets and sleeping bags, some occupied, others just lying damp and limp. I passed Piccadilly station and under a bridge carrying railway tracks, and onto London Road. On the opposite side was a strip of grass, and on that grass were tents, maybe two dozen of them, of all sizes, from little one-man jobs to family-sized tents you could stand up in.

Behind the tents, black bin bags spilled their contents onto the grass. Slung between trees were makeshift washing lines. According to Manchester City Council's annual rough-sleeper count, the number of people sleeping on the streets had doubled between 2015 and 2016; the city was now the north-west's homelessness hotspot. The reasons for the huge rise were complicated, Jenny Osborne, the local authority's strategic lead for public health, told the *Guardian*. The rise in EU nationals with no recourse to public funds had been one factor, she said. But the cumulative impact of welfare reform, and the conditionality of the benefits system, where jobseekers were required to spend their days searching for jobs on the internet or face sanctions, had been huge. The introduction of the bedroom tax had also played a big role, Osborne said: eight thousand people in the city were deemed to be 'under-occupying' their properties, but a chronic shortage of one-bed flats meant there was nowhere for them to move to.

Looking at that pitiful sight of tents, with hollowed-out people sitting outside them, like shell-shocked troops returning from the trenches, I thought about the much-vaunted Northern Powerhouse of George Osborne, Chancellor of the Exchequer, with cities such as Liverpool and Manchester at its core, and the old mantra of neoliberal capitalism that 'a rising tide lifts all boats'. Walking through those two cities in the spring of 2016, with the posh boutiques and the luxury flats going up everywhere, it was apparent that, yes, there were many winners. But the losers could not be airbrushed out. They were everywhere I looked.

There was a line of thinking about this, that the very visible presence of the losers – whether on the streets, or in our newspapers, or in the many TV programmes that seemed designed to humiliate the poor – was quite deliberate, a warning of what could happen to the rest of us.

It was fast becoming orthodoxy that anyone who was unemployed or homeless or disabled, or who had mental health issues, was a feckless shirker or a liar. That 'othering' has permeated through to the belief systems of many of those on benefits too.

During research on welfare reform spanning four years, Daniel Edmiston of Oxford University found that there is now an expectation in jobcentres, with their punitive use of sanctions, of users being 'subservient, compliant and grateful'. Many of those Edmiston interviewed said they were so worried that their benefits depended on the caprices of jobcentre staff that they were consciously moderating their behaviour to please them.

Examples abounded in his research of claimants standing up to the system and finding themselves sanctioned, with all of the potential horrors – homelessness, hunger, children taken into care – that a total loss of income might entail.

Witness the neologism 'precariat', which had emerged to describe not just those on the bottom rungs of society, but many people still just about managing. That sense of precariousness was not just material but psychological too.

'All the people like us are We, / And every one else is They,' wrote Rudyard Kipling in the poem 'We and They'.

I hadn't walked far out of Manchester's glittering city centre before the boarded-up pubs and shops reappeared. A few of the houses had Leave posters in their windows. A teenage boy in a hoodie was on the pavement crouched over his BMX, and asked if I could help him. The chain was jammed, he said; did I know how to fix it? I had a horrible feeling that I was about to get mugged. I took off my rucksack and knelt on the ground, levering the chain out of the gap between the cassette and the frame with my penknife, and put it back on the teeth of one of the sprockets, all the time hypervigilant that this boy might run off with my bag or that his accomplices would run around the corner and attack me.

'Thanks, mate,' the boy said, spinning his back wheel with obvious joy. Off he rode, and I was left there, feeling happy that I had been able to help, and also ashamed of myself.

After a few more miles, sitting in a little valley, the town of Stockport was before me; to my right was the Stockport Viaduct, built in 1839–40, with twenty-seven brick arches, carrying the railway from Manchester towards the south, and serving as a template for rail bridges in L. S. Lowry's paintings.

I found a hotel, dumped my bag and set off to explore. I wandered around Stockport's lovely Old Town, with its gorgeous Merchants House and Produce Hall, opposite which was a covered market – a Grade II listed building dating from 1861 that, with its glass and steel frame, looked like one of the giant plant houses at Kew Gardens. Soon after it had first opened, it was affectionately nicknamed the Glass Umbrella. I walked around, past stalls selling model railways, and children's clothes, and bed linen. A plaque on the wall declared that the hall had won the Best British Small Indoor Market prize in 2015.

I walked across a little bridge. In the background, looming over the town, was the Unicorn Brewery, founded by the Robinson family in the mid-nineteenth century and still run today by its fifth and sixth generations. From the bridge, I looked down at Little Underbank, a narrow cobbled street that looked as if it could be a film set for a Dickensian drama.

I had lunch in a place called Lord of the Pies – because who can resist a pun-based pie shop? – and afterwards went into a nearby newsagent. While I waited in the queue I scanned the newspaper headlines. 'Greed of Loan Shark Banks' screamed the *Daily Mail*. The *Telegraph* splashed with 'Gove: We will make Britain safe after Brexit'.

Ahead of me, a man in a tracksuit was handing a little plastic card to the woman behind the till. Once he'd handed it over, he stood there, shuffling from one foot to the other, with his hands jammed in his pockets. She looked at the card and shook her head.

'We've not got enough money, lovey,' she said, and handed the card back. The man took it, put it away in his pocket.

The woman then said to him, with softness in her voice, 'You could try the place down the road.'

'They've got nowt either,' the man said, and turned and shuffled out of the shop.

'What was that?' I asked the woman.

'Simple Payment,' she replied. She said the government had introduced the system so that people without bank accounts could access their benefits payments from local shops.

'But if we've got no money, we can't give it out,' she said.

'Doesn't seem very dignified,' I said to her, 'going around shops trying to get your money.'

'No,' she agreed.

I arrived at the town's hat museum, the Hat Works, located in a former cotton mill. Hats had been made in Stockport since the seventeenth century, but it wasn't until the early nineteenth century, and mechanisation, that the town became a world centre of hat-making. The last two hat factories in the area, Wilson's and Christys', had closed down in 1980 and 1997 respectively.

I wandered around the exhibits. There were the hat blocks of the royal milliner Philip Somerville, and hats he'd made for the Queen and Princess Diana. On the wall was a press cutting from the *Stockport Express* about Aileen Plant, who had died in 2014 at the age of one hundred, and whose family had played a leading role in the town's hat industry.

The museum was delightful, with a section about Stockport County Football Club (nicknamed the Hatters, of course) and collections of cricket and football caps, the fedora worn by Harrison Ford's Indiana Jones, John Steed's bowler from *The Avengers*, Tony Hancock's homburg and Fred Dibnah's oily cap.

There was a section about the town's long tradition of making hats for the military, with a feather-strewn hat once belonging to the Duke of Wellington, and the Pathfinder, a hat made for policewomen containing a hard shell that was rolled out for the 1984–85 miners' strike.

In a glass case was a Native American headdress, and underneath a quote from Oscar B. Jacobson, a US painter from the early twentieth century who'd become a champion of Native American people. It read: 'The Anglo-Saxon smashes the culture of any primitive people that gets in his way and then, with loving care, places the pieces in a museum.' I thought how that quote needed updating for the twenty-first century, now that it wasn't only 'primitive people's' culture that seemed to exist largely in museums.

On my way out, I saw a group of Chinese visitors entering the museum. 'They're a long way from home,' I said to the woman behind the reception desk. She explained how a Chinese TV documentary about British traditions had been filmed at the museum, and how visitor numbers from East Asia had soared as a result.

There was a display of hats for sale. I tried a few on.

'Any of these made locally?' I asked the woman.

'Not any more, love,' she said. 'Some of them are finished here, but they're all made abroad, mostly in the Far East.'

She paused. Then: 'It's very sad, when you think about it.'

6

HAPPY VALLEY
(STOCKPORT TO MACCLESFIELD)

I was up early the next morning. I would be heading for Macclesfield, some eighteen miles away. My body was sore, but felt as if it was getting used to the demands I was placing on it. It had only been a few days earlier that I had gone to bed in Warrington, gripped with fear and apprehension about walking the seventeen miles to Salford. But I was becoming more confident about the distances now.

I had guessed that the People's March for Jobs would have gone south on the A6 and then along the A523, which, as it approached Macclesfield, became the Silk Road, named after the industry the town was once famous for. Tempting as it was to walk along the Silk Road, and be in Cheshire, not China, the route looked as if it would be busy with traffic.

There was a walking trail, the Middlewood Way, which followed the trackbed of an old railway line all the way to Macclesfield and which started about three miles south-east of Stockport. It would mean adding a few miles on to my day, but the prospect of getting away from the traffic convinced me that it would be worth it.

I walked along the Marple Road, as the tight Stockport terraced houses gave way to semis and then detached houses and then, finally, wide expanses of green. I had the felt sense – one that can only really come with the tempo of walking, the default speed of our ancestors until yesterday – that I had left a place and was on my way to the next one. 'The soul travels at the speed of a camel,' goes an old Arab saying.

I saw a little public footpath sign, hopped over a stile and headed cross-country. Following the edge of a field, I came down by a brook, and then through a dense wood, the ground carpeted with bluebells, clambering over fallen, rotting trunks.

I thought about those desire paths I had seen, those ancient markers of humans' determination to follow their own way. Why did they seem so powerful to me? Was it that they spoke of human resilience, innovation and sheer contrariness? The very attributes that have taken our species to the remotest points on the planet, have driven our quest to cure diseases, to attempt to map the human brain, even to take us into the dark, lonely void of space? Lost in my walking reverie in those dense woods, the fact that I was creating my own desire path in walking from Liverpool to London, cross-country, gave me a sense of being a pioneer; I was eschewing the roads, I was ancient man, I was . . .

'Fore!'

. . . I was walking across a golf course.

'Sorry,' I shouted to a man in the distance dressed as Rupert Bear.

I hurried across the fairway, around a manicured green, back into woodland, and eventually out again, past a little fishing lake, where two men sat on creels, staring out on the water. I asked one of them if he knew where the Middlewood Way was. When he pointed in roughly the direction whence I'd come, I determined that if I was going to continue my cross-country pursuits, it was probably wise to buy some Ordnance Survey maps.

Eventually I found the Middlewood Way, a straight line in a tunnel of trees. The trackbed had once carried the line of the

Macclesfield, Bollington and Marple Railway, which had operated from 1869, transporting cotton, coal and silk as well as passengers. It closed in 1970, before being redeveloped fifteen years later as a human superhighway.

Within minutes of joining it, I was being passed by horse riders, joggers, and an old man in a mobility scooter, with a little Yorkshire terrier sitting in a wire basket on the handlebars. There were whole families out on bicycles, the kids either pedalling their own bikes or, in the case of the very young, sitting on those single-wheel affairs attached to their parents' bikes, their little legs turning frantically for no practical gain but to learn how to contribute to the collective effort. It was so instantly noticeable how, as soon as people are away from roads, everyone relaxes and seems to shed their guardedness, saying hello, or waving.

I was now firmly back in my reverie, happier than I'd been since the start of my walk in Liverpool, just putting one foot in front of the other, my breathing easy, my footsteps light, my mind free to wander, untroubled by anything at all. The birds were in full-throated spring chorus. If there were times on my walking days that I would be counting down the miles until I could stop, then that section wasn't one of them. I felt like I could have walked forever.

The trail passed through Higher Poynton station, the space in between the two old platforms now covered in grass, with picnic tables laid out at intervals, on which some of the families who'd cycled past me earlier sat eating their sandwiches.

Just past the old station, I saw a man walking towards me and waving. It was David, the older brother of one of my work colleagues. David had kindly offered to put me up in his home in Macclesfield for the night. Being a keen walker, he'd also come up the trail to walk with me.

David was a teacher at a further education college in Macclesfield. At fifty-nine, after thirty-four years in the profession, he was coming up to retirement. He had lived in Macclesfield for thirty-six years now, with his wife Rachel. 'We're not quite accepted as locals yet!' he laughed.

It made a welcome change to share part of my walk with someone, and David was excellent company. He explained how Macclesfield was known as Treacle Town, after a perhaps apocryphal story that told of a horse and cart going down one of the town's steep hills, carrying a couple of barrels of treacle, when the cart overturned and the streets were running with the stuff. 'We've got the Treacle Market once a month, a combination of farmers' market, artisan foods and bric-a-brac,' David said. 'Ironically, just about the only thing you can't buy there is treacle.'

Seeing as he'd lived in Macclesfield since the People's March had come through the town, I asked him what changes he'd seen there in his lifetime.

One of the biggest was the loss of all the heavy and traditional industries. 'Back in the 1980s, there were still silk mills,' he said. 'Bollington, which we'll be walking through in a bit, was a cotton town, but Macclesfield became a silk town. That's why our football team is nicknamed the Silkmen.'

After France's silk-making industry was hit by the upheaval of revolution in the eighteenth century, David explained, Macclesfield had seized the opportunity to turn itself into Britain's silk powerhouse, with most of the town making a living from its production. Now, with production mostly having moved to China and India, Macclesfield's silk industry was reduced to two companies.

'When we first came here, there were lots of people who'd never left town, but that's changed a lot as well,' David told me. 'Macclesfield is quite a cosmopolitan place now. It's a lovely place to live.'

He told me how a lot of people commuted to Manchester for work, and how some even commuted to London. He also explained how Macclesfield had the good fortune, after the decline of the silk mills, to attract a big ICI Pharmaceuticals facility, which in 1993 became part of Zeneca and in 1999 part of AstraZeneca, an Anglo-Swedish company and one of the pharmaceutical industry's biggest players.

In 2013 AstraZeneca announced that it was closing its nearby Alderley Park facility, with the loss of 1,600 local jobs, and moving its operations to Cambridge. But in December 2015 the firm announced a £75 million investment in the Macclesfield site, building a state-of-the-art packing and warehouse facility, and thus securing the future of 3,500 jobs at the site.

'ICI were the pathfinders, if you like,' David said. 'You need a big player to come in and then lots of other employers in support businesses – like medical writers and marketing people – will follow. There's a big Siemens plant just outside the town now as well.'

Because of the arrival of ICI and the companies that followed it, Macclesfield never went through the period of high unemployment that other mill towns experienced, David said. 'In the last twenty years, it's been transformed from a typical slightly decaying textile town into a thriving place. The older industries were replaced at just the right time, and the jobs that came in tended to be well-paid. Maybe Macclesfield just got lucky.'

Maybe it had. But AstraZeneca's closing of its Alderley Park facility might act as a cautionary tale about a town's economy relying so heavily on a modern global corporation.

In May 2014 the US firm Pfizer, the world's largest research-based pharmaceutical business, finally admitted defeat in its attempts to buy AstraZeneca for £69 billion, after opposition from politicians, scientists, trade unions – and from within

AstraZeneca's boardroom. Pfizer had promised that the take-over would result in more scientific breakthroughs and more skilled UK jobs.

People in Sandwich, Kent, had plenty to say about those promises. In 2011 Pfizer had closed its sixty-year-old, world-renowned research laboratory in the town – site of the discovery of Viagra – with the loss of thousands of jobs.

Mark Moorhouse, a Sandwich town councillor, told the *Guardian* that the decision to close the site had been 'like a death sentence' for the town. 'You are talking about 2,500 well-paid scientists, who spent a lot of money. There aren't a lot of well-paying jobs around here.'

Moorhouse estimated that some three thousand people not employed by Pfizer relied indirectly on the firm for the lion's share of their income, from cleaning contractors to restaurants, taxi companies and pubs. And that wasn't taking into account the part that Pfizer employees played in local community and civic life, in the sports teams and amateur dramatic societies, the choirs and the churches. When Pfizer upped sticks and left, the cost to Sandwich had been enormous.

We came to a sweeping viaduct, where the former railway was once carried high over the River Dean and its wide valley on twenty-three magnificent sandstone arches. There were plans to demolish the viaduct after the railway had closed, but a petition from the people of Bollington had saved it. From the bridge, there were spectacular views over the town, and the wooded hills beyond.

'This place is known as Happy Valley,' David informed me.

Far below us, on a field, there was a cricket match going on. The sun was strong, the air warm. 'Fancy going down to watch a few overs?' David asked. 'There's a nice pub next to the ground.'

And so we found ourselves in Happy Valley, sitting on the grass just beyond the boundary rope with our pints of cold lager, watching Bollington Cricket Club trying to defend their not-so-happy innings of sixty-seven all out. The opposition were making a bad fist of it, though. They were fifty for six and struggling to get the ball off the square.

I was curious about what David had told me, about the fact that the area seemed to be thriving. On my walk so far, the centres of Liverpool and Manchester had a buzz about them, but the outskirts of those cities and the towns I'd walked through had all appeared to be struggling.

'Well, we have a Tory-controlled borough council,' he said. 'And they are always trying to save money, and trying to keep council tax down as much as possible. They have privatised some of their departments, but they have not gone as far as other local authorities. They're not ideologically mad, like some are. One of the reasons they can have low rates is because we've got high business-rate payers.'

David talked about the local hospital, about how the accident and emergency department was under threat of closure.

'I think an A&E department is deeply symbolic,' he said. 'It speaks to how much a country is willing to look after you. Even if you don't use it, having it there is like having an umbrella in the hall even if it's not raining.'

There was a loud shout from the middle. The umpire's finger went up. Bollington had taken a wicket. The batsman trudged back to the pavilion. The opposition was now fifty-five for seven and Bollington scented blood. The next batsman started walking out to the middle. Blond hair tumbled out from under his helmet. From the way he carried himself he looked about twelve, and very nervous.

David had mentioned his Christianity while we were walking,

and I had told him about Myles Davies's comments back at Liverpool Cathedral, about how the Church was stepping in to help society's most vulnerable people. David said that this was the case in Macclesfield, too, that although homelessness wasn't on the scale of, say, Manchester, his church ran a weekend refuge for the homeless in the winter.

'It's been forced on the churches to some extent,' he said, 'because the authorities are stepping back from their responsibilities. One church runs a food bank, another provides a meal every Saturday for people on their own. The NHS is a great bulwark, because people still get free healthcare. But how long will that last?'

David went off to the bar to get another round. The young man at the crease was playing and missing a lot. David came back, sat down on the grass. 'Did I miss anything?' he said, pointing to the middle.

'Not really,' I said. 'It's all very tight. This young lad could make a name for himself here.'

David talked about nearby Prestbury, where a lot of players from the Manchester football clubs lived, and where mansions costing millions were being built.

'They'll have two or three people living in them, or they'll be empty and owned by Chinese property investors. It's shocking,' he said. 'Within our constituency, there's a huge amount of wealth, but it's just more and more inequitably distributed. That's probably the biggest change in our lifetimes, I think.'

David told me that there was no council housing left in Macclesfield, that it was all now run by housing associations. Again, he said, the Church was playing a key role on one of Macclesfield's poorer estates, where a community of Christians lived, and where they ran football and music clubs, among other things.

'You've got a lot of people living there who are very disillusioned, especially young people,' he said. 'Macclesfield is a great place to live, but it has quite a high level of youth unemployment. That's the way it's gone, hasn't it? Work that was available to young people with no qualifications has more or less disappeared. It's stacking shelves or nothing. To get an apprenticeship at somewhere like AstraZeneca you need A-levels. So there is a subclass of unqualified young people who would have worked in the mills, where they would have had a chance to find their feet. That has largely gone.'

Another wicket fell. It was now sixty-six for eight, but the young man with the blond hair under his helmet was still there, and in the very next over he nicked a ball though the slips, ran two and jumped in the air as if he had won the Ashes.

It was tough getting up off the ground after the day's walking and three pints of lager in the sunshine. But we still had a few miles to go before reaching David's home, and soon we were climbing the steps back to the viaduct and walking across it, over Happy Valley. After an hour or so, we crossed a footbridge over the Silk Road, from where we could see the main source of Macclesfield's new prosperity: the AstraZeneca plant sprawled before us like a giant university campus.

We walked through a graveyard and shortly afterwards arrived at David's house; his wife, Rachel, was there to greet us. After a week of staying at hotels and Airbnbs, it felt great to be in a family home. David showed me to my room, and I kicked off my boots and lay back on the bed, before running a deep bath with bubbles and feeling the warmth of the silky water caress my tired muscles.

Over a dinner of chicken stew, garlic mash and green beans, Rachel asked me about my walk so far, and I told her what I had seen, about the feeling you got when you connected towns through the simple expedient of walking, the sense that you really began to understand at some deep level how a country is put together geographically and emotionally.

We talked a little about living in Macclesfield. Rachel said that for middle-aged, middle-class people like them, it was a lovely place to live. 'There's a lot of music, concerts every weekend, and arts, and orchestras and am-dram to a high standard,' she said.

'And a very good football team!' David added.

'But the last commercial cinema in town closed in 1997, and so you have to go to the multiplexes in Stoke or Stockport,' Rachel continued. 'A lot of the shops in the centre have closed because of the out-of-town shopping malls, where people can drive and park for free, so the town centre is slowly losing its identity. It's tough for people who don't drive or can't afford the trains.'

We talked a little bit more about their faith. As a Christian, what did David make of what was happening to the poorest and most vulnerable in society – how it seemed to be them paying the highest price?

'It's true. The people with the least are being made to pay for the mistakes of the politicians and those who have a lot more,' he said. 'Maybe capitalism has these inevitable consequences, I don't know. It's maybe a trite cliché, but you have the situation where directors of companies have to be paid exorbitant salaries and bonuses because that's the market rate and they won't be attracted to do the job otherwise. Whereas if you're a Deliveroo driver, or somebody working for Sports Direct, you make them work harder by reducing their wages or employing them on zero-hours contracts. For the have-nots, the greatest incentive they can have to work hard is to keep their job. As a Christian, I can't see that the system is sustainable, morally or otherwise.'

David was just about to turn sixty, and would be receiving his full teachers' pension then; I asked how he would have felt having to teach for another seven years, like any young person entering the profession today. He rolled his eyes.

'I couldn't have contemplated working full-time beyond this age,' he said. 'Don't get me wrong, I love teaching. But it is much tougher than it used to be.'

He said that when he started out, further education (FE) was 'like the golden ticket . . . nice students, relatively low numbers of teaching hours, maybe only twenty hours a week. Exhausting, but civilised. We used to have a staffroom with a little chess club in the corner, go to the pub every Friday afternoon. There's not even a staffroom now where people can meet, no suggestion that anybody should go to work to socialise as well. It's all just work now.'

It had all started to change, David said, in 1998, when all FE colleges became independent corporations, thus bringing the market into education. Colleges were told they were no longer part of the local authority, were told to 'stand on your own two feet, you'll get a budget from central government'.

But the long-term effect of such centralisation, he said, was that it enabled the government to cut funding year after year. Of course, he continued, the government was also desperate for everybody to be in full-time education until eighteen. And so many of the kids who went on to further education had no desire to be there; back in the 1980s and before, they would have left school at sixteen and gone on to do apprenticeships or decently paid work in the mills or factories. It didn't take a huge stretch of the imagination, he said, to believe that governments would be keen to keep young people in education for as long as possible simply to keep them out of the unemployment statistics.

So the government paid FE colleges for every student they

attracted. And the colleges, because they were now run as businesses, packed in the students. 'So now,' David said, 'there are some very large classes in FE.'

The result of all this pressure on teachers, David told me, had been catastrophic. They had become much better at teaching to the exam specifications, but that had taken a lot of the spontaneity and excitement out of education. Teachers were more frightened now, desperate to get good results; they were routinely working fifty or sixty hours a week, including all of the unpaid preparation.

'Because they're exhausted, their lessons aren't terribly exciting, and this has huge implications for the students as well,' David told me. All of this was enforced with a rigid system of observation.

'There's much more supervision of what you do, people peering over your shoulder. And that means lessons become much more uniform. To a great extent the spark's gone out of teaching. It's a huge generalisation really, but . . .' and he paused, as if not wanting to condemn the career to which he'd devoted his life and for which he had such obvious passion, '. . . but I think many teachers are just going through the motions now. They don't see it as a profession any more. It's just a job. If you feel you've got a vocation for teaching, and you come to the job full of excitement and passion, within two or three years that passion's gone. Turnover is huge. You're just living for the next holiday, or for the weekend. It's not good for anybody.'

Given what David had said, it was no surprise to read that nearly 40 per cent of newly qualified teachers quit the profession within a year.

But there was one more consequence of the marketisation of further education that David described as 'the biggest tragedy of all'.

'Do you remember that slogan in one of Tony Blair's administrations: "lifelong education"?' he asked me. 'Well, FE colleges provided that: facilities for anybody at whatever age to follow their enthusiasms. For some it was learning how to cook a curry or flower arranging. But for mature students it was another chance to take their A-levels or get some qualifications because they'd screwed up at school.

'That was a big part of the beauty of FE for me: teaching people of all ages. I've had students in their eighties who were there to learn because they just loved learning. That's mostly gone now. Because funding for FE has been cut so much, you can only run these courses if they're self-financing. That means colleges have to put their prices up. A lot of these courses were free, or cheap. Now an A-level has risen from maybe £50 to £750 a year – that's what an over-18 student would have to pay. Because you're charging £750, you don't get the students, and because it is market-driven, if you don't get the students, the course doesn't run. It is almost impossible now for an adult to go to college to do their A-levels.'

I thought about my mum. She'd left school in Birmingham at sixteen without many qualifications. When I was eight and she was in her mid-thirties, and working as a typist, she went to night school and took A-levels for free. She went on to take a degree, and afterwards worked as a teacher for a few years before retraining to become a social worker. She'd also taught adult literacy at the college at the corner of our road.

Her life had been transformed. Mine, too: for how much easier it would later be to reimagine my future and ambitions with somebody in front of me who'd made that journey. I'd gone to university, the second person in my family ever to do so. I doubt I would have done so if my mum hadn't done it first. It made me feel sad to think that my mum, today, would never have been able to do what she did. Sad, too, to think about all of the future wasted potential, especially among poorer people.

7

BEARTOWN

(MACCLESFIELD TO CONGLETON)

I walked through the centre of Macclesfield. It had its fair share of 'to let' signs hanging outside office blocks, and a few shop units were empty, as Rachel had described. It also had the pay-day loan firms, bookmakers and charity shops. But among these were businesses anchoring themselves to the town's story, from a chip shop called Silktown Fryer to a dentist's called Silk Dental Care. Even the local radio station was called Silk 106.9. I wondered whether, if I came back in twenty years' time, I might see the Zoladex Chippy, or the Diprivan Dentist, places named with a nod to the products of Macclesfield's largest employer today. Macclesfield seemed a lovely little town. It had been the only mill town in England not to be bombed in the Second World War. Maybe, as David had said, it was just a lucky place.

I walked past a little shop called The Corner Plot. David had told me it was opened in 2012 by a husband-and-wife team to sell fruit and vegetables. Run as a not-for-profit organisation, it employed local people with learning difficulties. Much of the produce it sold was grown at a local horticultural centre, which also employed people with learning difficulties. In 2013 the shop had joined a local delivery network so that Macclesfield residents could order their food from a variety of local independent stores, such as fishmongers and butchers, and have it all delivered together.

'It's such a good initiative that I think it's making money now,' David said. 'The whole thing has become a positive feedback loop. Lots of people are benefiting. But they are thriving despite the system, where high rents are seemingly devoted to getting all the independent stores closed down. We're fighting hard here in Macclesfield.'

David thought that the little shop provided some grounds for optimism, perhaps as a pointer to a more sustainable future. 'We have to develop a concept of sufficient and what's enough. The story we've had for the last thirty-odd years, of continual growth, is unsustainable for many reasons,' he said. 'The planet can't sustain it; we as human beings can't sustain it. It does seem as if globalisation is coming to a halt and economies are going to have to be more protectionist. But what effect will that have? Less power for the big multinationals, perhaps, and that's maybe a good thing. But how it impacts on the average person, that's critical. If we are going to change anything as big as an economic system, there are going to be a lot of casualties along the way and that's a frightening prospect.'

I passed a newsagent. The local paper was declaring that Macclesfield was set to be hotter than Ibiza that day. I wondered if the local paper in Ibiza was declaring that the island was set to be colder than Macclesfield.

I walked back across the Silk Road, and then up a steep little lane until I came to the Macclesfield Canal, which runs high above the town. After a mile or so, I met a man walking along the towpath with a lurcher. He had a long pointed stick in one hand and a bin bag in the other.

'Who's this, then?' I asked, pointing to the dog.

'That's Boy,' said the man.

The man told me that he'd given up work and these days lived on a narrowboat, travelling all over the country with Boy. 'I'm moored just up there,' he said. 'Every time I stop somewhere, I walk up and down picking up the litter. It's disgusting what people chuck on the ground.'

'My dad used to live on a canal boat,' I told the man.

'Used to?' he said.

'He died.'

'Oh,' the man said.

Since turning fifty, I'd noticed that people's response when you said your parent had died was not 'I'm sorry to hear that', but rather just 'oh', acknowledging it, but accepting it as an entirely natural state of affairs for a middle-aged man to have lost his dad.

It was all a bit of a relief. My mum had died when I was twenty-three and I'd spent a lifetime dreading questions about what I was going to do for Mother's Day, or whether I'd be going home for Christmas. When she died, and with Pete long moved away and uninterested, there'd been no home to go back to at Christmas. A person in their twenties without a mother, or a partner, was the object of pity. I'd hated that, and all the explanations that would have to follow: what did she die of? How old was she? That must be awful for you.

I didn't want to be different, marked out as a tragic case. But there it was. So now that I had got to the 'oh' stage, I was back into the natural swing of things. It was as if a burden had been lifted.

I said goodbye and carried on along the towpath, the far bank covered with yellow flag irises and delicate water forget-me-nots, among which beautiful demoiselle damselflies with aquamarine wings flitted. In a meadow on the far bank, a swan was chasing some Canada geese around, driving them away from the nest I could see among the reeds, on which the partner swan was sitting; on the bank itself, a crow was dive-bombing a heron, presumably for getting too close to its eggs. The world was getting ready to take delivery of new life, and its actors were fighting and scrambling to defend and protect.

Beyond the meadow, a Virgin Pendolino train hurtled past, heading south, a red streak of streamlined grace. It brought back memories of my own family holidays on narrowboats, when I was a teenager. We'd moor up at night and, train nut that I was, I'd go off to find a railway line, to sit there quietly, just to watch the trains fly by. One summer, they'd been testing the Advanced Passenger Train, known as the APT, a train developed and built by state-owned British Rail, whose revolutionary tilting mechanism enabled it to travel faster around the many curves of the West Coast Main Line, with a top speed of 155mph. I would sit there mesmerised as that futuristic train with a streamlined nose flew past, like Concorde on wheels.

The APT project had been beset by problems and delays, and Margaret Thatcher immediately alluded to cutting its funding upon her election in 1979. The train was finally introduced into public service in 1981, but those early runs were plagued with technical issues, the press deriding the APT as a white elephant – a further example of British Rail's incompetence, the narrative of nationalised inefficiency versus privatised efficiency gaining momentum. For the next few years, the train struggled to overcome its teething problems, and with the government and press hostile to it, it was finally abandoned in 1986.

I thought about the APT as another Pendolino screeched past, using tilting mechanisms developed by an Italian firm, but based partly on the APT prototype. The trains were made by Alstom, a French multinational. The original batch of Pendolinos had been made in Alstom's factory in Washwood Heath, Birmingham. In 2005, that plant closed down and Alstom switched production to Italy, where it now made trains for many of the world's rail networks.

In the financial year 2014–15, Alstom had a record €10 billion worth of orders, sales of €6.2 billion, and a group net income of €719 million. The original ATP, meanwhile, sits rusting on tracks outside a railway museum in Crewe. You can see it from the windows of your Pendolino as you go past.

It made me wonder what British Rail might have achieved with the APT if it had received more support from Thatcher's government. And what some of our former railway engineering towns – Derby, Doncaster, Crewe, Swindon, in their heyday employing 40,000, 3,500, 20,000 and 14,000 people respectively in train-building – might look like today if we were still making and exporting trains.

Arguably, Britain has one major train manufacturer left: Bombardier in Derby. I say arguably, because Bombardier is headquartered in Montreal, Canada, and listed on the Toronto stock exchange.

In many ways, Bombardier is a fine example of how globalisation rendered redundant ideas of sovereignty and the story a nation told about itself. Since state-owned British Rail Engineering Limited was privatised in 1989, it had been run by a consortium led by a Swiss-Swedish firm, passed on to a German company, and then sold off to Canada's Bombardier. In 2011, Sukhdev Johal, an academic at the University of London, had likened the company to 'a foster child, passed around from home to home'.

In 2011, Bombardier lost out on a £3 billion contract to build 1,200 new carriages for the Thameslink line. The Canadian giant immediately announced that 1,400 of the Derby plant's 3,000 workers would be made redundant.

'We regret this outcome,' said Francis Paonessa, head of Bombardier's UK passenger division, 'but without new orders we cannot maintain the current level of employment and activity at Derby.'

That contract had gone to Siemens, a German company, with the trains to be built at Krefeld in North Rhine-Westphalia. Gerry Doherty, leader of the TSSA rail union, called on the government to reverse the decision. 'No German or French government would be so foolish as to award such a vital contract to an overseas manufacturer, threatening thousands of domestic jobs,' he said.

The then Transport Secretary, Philip Hammond, told BBC Radio 4's *Today* programme that reversing the decision was 'not an option', but added, 'I think we have got to look at how we manage these things for the UK in the future.'

Ministers had argued that the British government had its hands tied by EU rules stipulating that member states could not favour their own industries in the tendering process without risking a referral to the European Court of Justice. Critics asked how it was, then, that French, German and Spanish companies always seemed to win the bidding process for manufacturing contracts in their own countries.

'The British tend always to go for the lowest bid,' said Chris Bovis, professor of European business law at the University of Hull, speaking to the rail expert Christian Wolmar for an article in the *Guardian*.

Bovis claimed that UK politicians fail to understand the finer points of European legislation, pointing out that there was room in the bid process to consider many other factors, including quality, security of supply, industrial policy, aesthetics – and social cohesion. By largely ignoring these factors and focusing on price, successive British governments had presided over the continuing decline of large-scale manufacturing. Good for the short-term balance sheet; disastrous for those eviscerated communities – and for the taxpayer, who pays the welfare bill that comes with failed industrial policy.

In February 2014, three years after Bombardier lost the Thameslink bid, it won a £1 billion contract to build new rolling stock for the Crossrail project in London, creating 760 new jobs at the Derby plant, in a decision that some have described as deeply politically motivated. Maybe we are finally becoming better at seeing the bigger picture.

I should imagine that this would be scant consolation to all those previously laid-off train-building workers of Derby, the chemists of Sandwich and Alderley Park, or the shipbuilders of Portsmouth and Glasgow – where, in 2013, BAE Systems announced the loss of 1,800 skilled jobs, in the case of Portsmouth closing its yard and ending five hundred years of shipbuilding in the city – and all of the other communities vulnerable to the vicissitudes of the global market who have either recently lost their jobs or live constantly with the fear of that loss.

And it isn't just the train-building industry in this country that has largely been lost overseas. The fact that a majority of the franchises on our privatised railways are now owned and operated by state-owned foreign companies shows up the shocking contradiction at the heart of our government: that it isn't opposed to state ownership at all, as long as it isn't our state. The profits from these franchises go back to their owners' countries of origin, funding public transport and spending across Europe.

Defenders of the rail franchising system tend to trot out the same justifications: that private equals efficiency while state-owned was inefficient and a bad deal for the taxpayer. But Action for Rail, a union-run campaign dedicated to exposing the myths of the benefits of privatisation, points out that over 90 per cent of new investment in the railways in recent years has been financed by the public-sector body Network Rail, and comes mainly from taxpayer funding. Further, it says, between 1995 and 2015 the price of tickets increased by an average of

117 per cent, or by 24 per cent in real terms, making ours some of the highest rail fares in Europe; and despite this, UK railways are slower and more overcrowded than publicly owned railways in Germany, France, Italy and Spain.

Official figures, Action for Rail says, showed that all but one of the private train operators received more in subsidies than they returned to the government in franchise payments. In 2013–14 the government contributed £3.8 billion to the UK rail industry. The top five recipients of public subsidy alone received almost £3 billion in taxpayer support between 2007 and 2011, allowing them to make operating profits of £504 million, over 90 per cent of which (£466 million) was paid to shareholders.

'These privatisations, they've made rich people significantly richer,' Keith Mullin had said to me back in Liverpool. 'And they've done it with industries that were paid for with our taxes, my parents' taxes, your parents'. It's theft, plain and simple.'

Incidentally, in 2014, figures from the Institute for Public Policy Research showed that over half of infrastructure projects involving public funding benefited only London and the southeast. Each and every Londoner had £5,426 spent on them annually, the figures showed, compared with £223 per person in the northeast. Was it any wonder that, as a nation, we seemed so hopelessly divided?

I sat down on a bench and removed my boots and socks, as usual, wiggling my toes in the warm air. Digging into my backpack, I retrieved a paper bag Rachel had given me. Inside was a big square of flapjack. About fifty yards away from me, next to a little stone bridge arching over the canal, was a woman with long grey hair. A Dalmatian dog was at her feet, sniffing around. As I ate my flapjack, I wandered up to her, feeling the soft grass under my bare feet. As I got closer, I could see that she was filling bird feeders that were nailed into the masonry of the bridge. I asked what her dog's name was.

'Josh,' she said. 'He's a rescue.'

Josh looked at me with some suspicion.

'He's OK,' the woman said. 'He's just a bit nervous.'

I asked the woman what she was doing. 'I've been filling these feeders for the last ten years,' she said. 'Recently, people have started nicking them. Can you believe it!?'

We chatted for a while. She used to live nearby, with her father. A year ago he'd gone blind, and had to be moved into a home. The house was sold to pay for his care. 'But I still come back to do this,' she said. 'It keeps me connected to the area.'

I went back to the bench where my socks and boots were, sat down, put them on. Then I walked back past the woman. Josh seemed less nervous.

'Here,' the woman said, holding out some bread. 'Take this to feed the ducks just along the canal. There's a mum with eleven chicks. Eleven!'

I got off the canal and headed west towards Congleton along winding country lanes, before joining a public footpath that ran close by a magnificent viaduct carrying the main-line railway. In the distance, looming over the otherwise flat landscape, was The Cloud, a sandstone ridge that lies close to the edge of the Peak District National Park. I remember sitting on the train going up to Liverpool to begin my walk, and looking out of the window at The Cloud. It seemed as if I'd been on the train for ages by that point, England speeding past at a hundred miles an hour. Although I now had eighty miles in my legs, seeing The Cloud made me realise just how far I still had to go.

I walked into Congleton, with its pretty Georgian and Tudor houses and well-kept park, bursting with spring flowers in neat beds. A sign on the railings announced that the town was a finalist in that year's Britain in Bloom competition. Nearby was the town hall, a handsome, imposing Victorian Gothic building with street-level arched windows and a sturdy clock tower.

Behind the town hall, in the old market square, was the museum. There I discovered that, like Macclesfield, Congleton had been built on the silk trade in the eighteenth and nineteenth centuries. By the mid-nineteenth century the town had more than fifty mills, and the Old Mill, built in 1752, was at the time one of the largest industrial buildings in the world. As the textile industry contracted in the UK, Congleton moved into ribbon manufacturing. Today, Berisfords, in the town since 1858, still produces 75 per cent of the UK's ribbons.

There was a bronze statue of a bear, alongside which a panel explained that in the early seventeenth century, when bear-baiting was popular, Congleton's bear had died just before the annual wakes fair. The large crowds that flocked to towns to see such spectacles were essential to the local economy. So, lacking in other funds, Congleton used the sixteen shillings it had saved to purchase a new Bible to buy a bear instead, and replenished the town's coffers with money from the larger crowds.

The twentieth-century folk song 'Congleton Bear' includes the chorus 'Congleton rare, Congleton rare, sold the Bible to buy a bear.' The town became known as Beartown, its foot-ball team nicknamed the Bears. Congleton also has a Beartown Brewery, and pubs called the Beartown Tap and the Beartown Cock. In 2011, seventy five-foot-tall fibreglass bears formed a trail around the town, and the proceeds from that project had gone to rescue an endangered moon bear from a bile farm in Vietnam and paid for it to live in a sanctuary. It seemed a nice touch that, four hundred years after Congleton's town funds had been used to torture a bear, its citizens had made amends.

I popped into the offices of the *Congleton Chronicle*, published weekly since 1893 and one of only a handful of independently owned newspapers left in the country. Its current editor, Jeremy Condliffe, was only the fourth editor in the paper's history.

A spate of takeovers in recent years meant that fewer than twenty publishers now accounted for almost 90 per cent of the thousand or so regional press titles in Britain.

In the reception area, I explained what I was doing to a woman behind a counter and asked if there was anybody around that I could have a quick chat with. While I waited, I looked at the national newspapers lying around. 'EU vote: now PM warns of war and genocide,' reported the *Daily Mail*.

A young man came out from the office and introduced himself as James, the paper's senior reporter. We sat on a sofa. James had been working at the *Chronicle* for four years, after getting his qualifications from the National Council for the Training of Journalists. Now twenty-seven years old, he had lived in the town his whole life. His daily beat covered court reporting, local crime and stints in the press seats at the council chambers.

'It's a great use of my local knowledge,' he said. 'The *Chronicle* is probably a different experience to most moving into local journalism because it's an independent paper – not many of those left – so we work to the whims of our editor only. They train you up very well and you get involved. The paper likes to hire locally because you understand the local vibes better.'

I asked James what Congleton was like as a place to live. He laughed.

'It's a very gossipy town,' he said. 'Readers often say they jump straight to the obituaries and then to the letters page. That's all they really care about – seeing who's died and what the local gossip is.'

I told James that, for the last four years, I had been working part-time on the letters page at the *Guardian*. I loved that section. It was like eavesdropping on a national conversation.

James told me about some of the serious issues exercising Congleton's letter writers. 'We've recently seen a lot of cuts, to healthcare, to adult services, things that affect a lot of people,' he said. 'And they're always cut with a smile on the face. You know, "Don't worry, we're changing the system, but it will be better." There's talk about closing Cheshire East's only inpatient mental health ward. And that's madness, isn't it? People feel that they're not getting the correct care and it's making them feel exposed and afraid.'

Congletonians were also worried about the decline of the town centre. 'People are always complaining about the high street. There's nothing there really. Mostly hair salons, nail bars and charity shops.' If you took away the supermarkets, there'd be nowhere for people to shop, James said. 'People are watching the town changing so that it's not a community any more. They always complain about the decline of the high street – and then they go to Morrisons because it's easy.'

Congleton these days was very much a commuter town, he said, following the demise of its heavy industry, and with its great links to London and Manchester. This had led to a house-building boom, another source of grumbling on the letters page. 'You would hope they would be for local people. But these new houses are very expensive and people my age can't afford to buy them,' James said. 'They're miles out of my price range. I live with my parents, which allows me to save money. It's the same with most people my age here. Some live independently, but it's always renting.

'It's annoying when you get to my age and you work in a time-consuming job, which doesn't pay very well – which is fine, you don't go into journalism for the money – and yet you end up through renting just putting your money into someone else's pocket. I'd like to think I'm a stoical person who takes it all on the chin. This is my time and I need to just make the best of it. But it would be much better if it were not this way. Everybody would be a lot happier if we didn't have to worry about these things and we could just . . .' James paused, trying to find the right words, '. . . if my generation could just have a slightly bigger slice of the cake.'

I asked James whether he saw his future in the town. He took a sip of his tea, thought for a minute. 'It's expected of me to go, to move away,' he said. 'If I didn't people would look at me weirdly, say, "Why didn't you go, bloody townie, you never left."' James told me about a friend of his. 'He said to me, "Look, I've never left Congleton. I've got to go." I said, "What are you looking for?" and he said, "I don't know. I've just got to get out of here. I'm not going to be in a small town like this for the rest of my life." People of my age, they think to themselves, or other people make them feel, as if they have to go.'

It was as if aspiration was now wholly framed in terms of moving away from where you're from, that you couldn't be happy where you are, that happiness always lay elsewhere. James was, in many ways, I said to him, living the dream, a home-town guy working on his local independent newspaper. Being part of the community. What more could anybody want?

He looked away for a moment. Then he turned back and said, 'I've been getting quite down recently, because, Christ, I've been here four years. I need to move on. Because when I go to the next job, they'll say, "What, you've just been working on your home-town paper, you weren't doing anything else?" That's not dynamic. They'll employ the person who went off to Malta and worked on a paper there, or worked for a charity over in New Orleans or whatever, because look how much experience that person has.'

I had heard this kind of talk a lot from younger people – the constant restlessness, a need to be always improving, moving on, building a narrative into their CVs, a narrative that showed ambition, momentum. Younger people I knew often made decisions about the jobs they applied for or accepted more in terms of how they would look on a CV rather than the personal satisfaction they might derive from doing the job. Or perhaps the two were these days inextricable.

I wondered whether all of this was part of the modern orthodoxy, where what you had was never enough, where sitting still for too long only meant falling behind in the race. Whatever it was, being young these days sounded exhausting.

James told me about people he knew in their mid-thirties, who'd left Congleton and had now come back. 'They go, "I've seen worse. This is fine." You go out there and realise, actually, I had it good. I might be the same when I go away. This might all be just a poisoning of the way people feel, an idea that has been forced into people's heads, breaking bonds with family and community – the thought that you can't actually be happy where you are.'

I asked James what he thought might be driving this ceaseless quest for advancement among his generation. He thought a large part of it was to do with tuition fees and the drive to get 50 per cent of young people to university.

'There's a sense of quiet annoyance when you consider how much money you're having to pay for education,' he said. 'In many ways you're forced into it. My headmistress was very angry with me because I hadn't finished my UCAS form on time. Because obviously schools want you to go to university because it looks very good for them.'

I thought about David back in Macclesfield and the way further education was now funded.

'So you go to uni, and many kids don't have much direction at that stage, so they do, like me, something like an English degree,' James continued. 'I mean, what the hell's an English degree!? So you come out after three years, you've done your liver some damage, and you're £20,000 worse off, and much worse for kids going now. And because half the country is going, a degree is much less valuable than it was. So, yes, coming out of university, you do feel a sense of betrayal. It's like that scene from *Fight Club*, where he says everyone's been made to believe that they're all going to become actors and celebrities, and now we know they were lying to us and we're all really pissed off about it.

'It's got to be helpful to the government, hasn't it,' James continued, 'having this steady flow of money from every graduate. All these young people so in debt and having to service that debt for much of their working lives.'

I asked James whether, if he'd been twenty-seven back in the 1970s or 1980s, he would have been so desperate to leave.

'Probably not. People generally worked locally,' he said. 'We had the mills, which are now going, going, gone. Maybe I would have found a local job. Maybe I'd be working at the *Chronicle*. But the fact that you'd have more local employment and cheaper housing would mean you'd be happy because you'd have all your family and friends around you.'

I walked through Congleton, past the giant Morrisons in the middle of town, and up a steep hill to my B&B. I'd been told to call the owner when I arrived, which I did, and then waited until a woman turned up to let me in and introduced herself as Pat.

'We spoke on the phone,' I said.

'No, love. You would have spoken to the other Pat,' she said. 'Pat's at her house in France, so I take over.'

It was in most respects like any other suburban semi, apart from the 'what to do in case of fire' notices and the racks holding leaflets telling visitors about things to do in the area. Pat showed me upstairs and let me into my room. 'Just give me a call, love, if there's anything you need,' she said, and was gone. I put my rucksack on the bed. There was a fridge, which contained a little jug of fresh milk. And in the corner was a sliding door, which I assumed was a wardrobe, but when I drew it back, there was a tiny shower behind it.

I sat on the bed and took out my photocopy of the original People's March for Jobs route, by now very creased and worn. I looked at how far I had come, and at how far I had to go. My body now felt walking fit and, like a dog bred for plenty of exercise, I relished the prospect of getting up and hitting the road each day. I looked in the mirror on the wall. My eyes were sparkling, alive. My skin looked less grey and saggy than it usually did. I had colour. My posture was strong, powerful somehow.

I dialled a number in Stoke-on-Trent. After a few rings, a woman answered. I asked if they had any rooms for tomorrow night. 'Is that just for the one night, shug?' she asked. Shug. Short for sugar. It's a Stokie thing and utterly lovely.

'No, two nights,' I said. The original marchers had had a rest day in Congleton back in 1981, but I wanted to press on to Stoke and have my rest day there. It was a slight infidelity to the march, but Stoke was much bigger than Congleton, and over the past few years had become something of a political touchstone, an archetypal post-industrial city.

In 2002, Stoke-on-Trent had elected its first British National Party councillor. By 2009, it had nine. Since then, the BNP had been wiped out, but Stoke's reputation as a right-wing, racist city had somehow endured. I was interested in spending as much time there as I could.

'Hang on a sec, shug,' the woman said. In the background I could hear paper being rustled and a fruit machine whirring and pinging. The room I was after was in a pub – and very cheap.

'We've got a room for two nights.'

'Great,' I said. 'Do you want my card details?'

'Oh, no, shug,' she said. 'Just pay us when you get here.'

I squeezed into the wardrobe for a shower and then headed back into town to find something to eat. On the old high street I found an Indian restaurant, but like no curry house I'd ever been in before. The dining room was lit with purple neon strips and on one wall – above a banquette of the deepest, lushest purple velvet imaginable – was a giant glass panel running the length of the room, behind which vast blooms of bubbles rose up, creating a spectral shimmering effect, the colours changing from green to purple to red. It was like watching the Northern Lights.

To my right, behind a purple rope, was a VIP room, encased in a semicircle of purple velvet padded walls rising to the ceiling. Around me, the other diners all looked about my age. Unlike me, sitting there in my scruffy walking trousers and T-shirt, they were all well-dressed and affluent-looking.

The waiter brought me a menu. There was a chocolate korma, a caramel korma, a prawn McCartney and a Tina tuna. For the more daring there was a suicide curry, with a line of little red chillies next to it like exclamation marks. Sundry options included a helicopter naan and Anneka rice. It was like being in a Bollywood version of a Mike Leigh film. I ordered a prawn McCartney and, although it was delicious, I couldn't really tell what part of it could possibly have been inspired by the Beatle. The waiter didn't know either. He seemed to think it was just a play on words.

'But it doesn't really work, does it?' I said.

'Not really, no,' he said.

I looked around again at the well-heeled clientele. A group of businessmen in suits had just sat at the table next to mine, and were clinking together bottles of Cobra, talking animatedly about a seminar they'd just been to. I thought about something else that James of the *Chronicle* had said to me – how many of the new pubs and cocktail bars and restaurants opening in Congleton these days were for the mature middle classes, the out-commuters, who had extra money to spend. 'Those places do really well,' he'd told me.

I finished my prawn McCartney and went next door to the pub, where I ordered a pint of Beartown Bearly Literate and sat down. There was a quiz going on, and the seven participants were the only other people in the pub.

'Fancy joining in?' asked the quizmaster, a man with a huge white beard and a big stomach. I declined the offer, owing to the fact that the curry and the beer and the walking in the sunshine had suddenly made me as exhausted as I can ever remember feeling.

'Number five,' the quizmaster said. 'Which word means school for naked exercise?'

'Gymnasium,' I said to myself.

'Number six. Which is heavier? Gold or silver?'

But that was the last thing I heard as I drifted off. By the time I woke up, the quiz was over and I was sitting alone in the otherwise empty pub.

8

GOD AND MAN
(CONGLETON TO STOKE-ON-TRENT)

The sky was leaden. It looked likely that it would rain at some stage, so I put the contents of my rucksack into drybags, and stuffed my waterproof trousers and jacket into the external pouch on the front of the pack.

I sat down for breakfast. Before starting my trip, I'd assumed that I would be constantly ravenous, and that consuming enough calories for a daily march with a heavy backpack would become a necessary obsession. But the more I walked, the less hungry I became. It was as if my body was undergoing some form of recalibration, letting me know just how much food it needed for the demands I was placing on it, my usual triggers for eating, set by the clock, now weaker and fading into the background.

I wondered if many of us ate so much these days because our brains needed that fuel to power the electrical impulses that are constantly stimulated by the demands of modern living. Driving a car on busy roads, trawling the internet with its infinite information, the threat of terrorism, insane working hours, financial worries, the gossip and envy fuelled by magazines, websites and social media leading to dissatisfaction in our own lives – perhaps these numerous extra brain tasks have created an almost permanent hypervigilance, our central nervous systems maxed out.

Perhaps the peace found in long-distance walking in nature, just like meditation, allows the brain to grow quiet, so that large parts of it are not needed. That morning, I couldn't eat the full English put in front of me. I did empty the fruit bowl, though.

I walked through the backstreets of Congleton, snatches of conversations drifting through open windows, so that I fleetingly felt part of the community's morning routine. I asked a young woman if she knew how to get to the Biddulph Valley Way, my day's route to Stoke, some eighteen miles away. She did, she said, and would show me where it started. As we walked together I felt that sense of instant intimacy with which I was growing familiar; snatched conversations and encounters were becoming things of substance and sustenance for me. The more I found, the more I wanted.

She asked me where I was going, and as usual I said the place at the end of that day's walk, and then, also as usual, added 'but eventually I am walking to London'. Her eyes grew wide and she asked me why. I told her, and her eyes grew even wider. I wondered if a person wandering across a landscape was some ancient archetype, speaking to our atavistic desires. 'All the Great Teachers have preached that Man, originally, was a "wanderer in the scorching and barren wilderness of this world" . . . and that to rediscover his humanity, he must slough off attachments and take to the road,' wrote Bruce Chatwin in *The Songlines*.

The woman was a one-to-one teaching assistant for children with special needs. 'I have a five-year-old today,' she told me. 'He has the brain of a two-year-old. It's difficult. If he has a good day, I have a good day. But if not, he's a two-year-old with a five-year-old's body.'

She pointed to a narrow alleyway between two factory warehouses. If I walked down there, at the end I would find the start of the trail. Soon enough, just as if C. S. Lewis had been on the town planning committee, I had left Congleton behind and was walking along a trail carpeted with yellow archangel and the delicate lilac flowers of wood sorrel, through a corridor of ash and silver birch, hazel and oak, from which burst spring birdsong.

The former railway ran high above the rooftops of Biddulph and then back out into glorious wooded countryside. I was lost in that walking reverie, just putting one foot in front of the other, my brain on its lowest alert, feeling happy and alive. The rain started to fall. I put on my waterproofs and carried on walking, splashing in the forming puddles like a child.

Through gaps in the trees, I spotted the pithead wheel and crumbling buildings of an old colliery. Chatterley Whitfield had been the largest mine in the North Staffordshire coalfield, and at its height, in the 1930s, was the first colliery in the UK to produce a million tons of coal in a year, employing four thousand people and fuelling Stoke-on-Trent's potteries and iron industries. By the late 1950s cheap oil from abroad had led to severe contractions in the UK coal industry, and by 1976 Chatterley Whitfield had been shut down.

The North Staffordshire coal industry, which had once employed twenty thousand people, began its final terminal decline after the miners' strike of 1984–85, and the coalfield's last deep mine, Silverdale, closed on Christmas Eve 1998. Today, Chatterley Whitfield, now a country park, lay ghostly quiet, the slag heaps and the deep wounds in the ground covered with grass and saplings, or filled with water.

I walked across a little bridge over a stream; at each end were security cameras sitting in nests of razor wire, the first cameras I'd seen for a while. I followed a desire path that cut straight across the grass, and was soon walking through tunnels under busy roads. I stopped in one, to shelter from the rain, and sat down on the floor to rest.

A couple of lads with two Staffordshire bull terriers came

trip-trapping through the underpass, and I suddenly felt vulnerable, sitting there on the floor with my big pack by my side. Perhaps it was just middle age, but I'd noticed that I'd become a lot more afraid of situations which, ten years before, would not have bothered me in the slightest.

The lads stopped for a chat and we talked about the weather. They asked me where I was headed and I couldn't be bothered with the whole 'to London' spiel, so I just said Stoke. One of them put his hand in his pocket and pulled out a half packet of biscuits and offered them to me. I didn't know whether that meant they thought I was homeless, or he just wanted to share his biscuits, but I figured that it didn't really matter either way.

'Thank you,' I said.

I got off the walking trail and onto the towpath of the Caldon Canal, which would take me on a winding journey through Stoke. From somewhere below me, the acrid smell of acetate wafted up from a factory. The far bank was thick with bluebells, and beyond the bank were the backs of houses, where I could see people hanging out washing on lines in their gardens, and factories and warehouses, where forklift trucks ferreted about and lorries were being unloaded. I loved the glimpses you got of big cities by walking along their canals, seeing parts not meant for general consumption. It was as if you got to see a place's inner workings, like peeling off the back of a watch.

I had a stand-off with a pair of Canada geese and their half-dozen goslings, who blocked the towpath and spread their wings, hissing at me terrifyingly every time I tried to inch past. I remembered the biscuits in my bag, broke off a few pieces and threw them in the water, and the goslings dived in after them, followed shortly by the parents.

I saw my first pot-bank soon after, by the side of the canal.

It was just standing there like a Brobdingnagian termite mound – obsolete now, surrounded by a modern housing complex, but as sure a sign that I was now in Stoke-on-Trent as passing the pyramids would be on the way to Cairo.

I got off the canal and headed into the centre of Hanley. The geography of Stoke-on-Trent can be bewildering for the unini-tiated. A polycentric conurbation, it was formed in the early twentieth century by a federation of six towns – Hanley, Burslem, Longton, Stoke, Tunstall and Fenton – now commonly known as the Potteries, with Hanley as its primary commercial centre.

The rain stopped, although the clouds still hung low and lugu-brious. I stood in the main square of the pedestrianised centre, watching the people of Stoke mill past. There was a preponder-ance of people on mobility scooters and using walking sticks, and others being pushed in wheelchairs. And maybe it was the greyness of the day, but people looked battered and tired, their faces lined.

In the central square, a man with a microphone and loud-speaker was haranguing the passers-by in a soft Scottish accent.

'Why is God punishing you? Maybe you've let him down. You're all sinners,' he was saying. Sensibly, most people seemed to be ignoring him.

'Sixty million people perished in the Russian Revolution. Because they forgot God. Many of you live in fornication. Many of you made marriage vows. How many of you are divorced? God hates divorce!'

I wasn't sure what church numbers were looking like in Stoke-on-Trent, but I was sure that particular recruiting sergeant was going about it the wrong way.

Thirty-five years previously, Kim Laycock had stood in that same square listening to people speak after the People's March for Jobs had reached Stoke. But the speeches back then had been defiant ones about communities fighting back. The march's organisers had latched onto Kim, pushing her three-year-old son all the way to London, and seen her as a poster girl, gently persuading the then shy young working-class woman, from Liverpool's deprived Dingle area, that her voice needed to be heard. As she stood in Stoke that day, she knew she was to be next on stage.

'Somebody said to me, "Guess who's on after you?"' Kim had told me. 'They went "Tony Benn",' and I said, "Right, I'm not doing it." And they all went, "Listen, Kim, you've got to. And you're getting up there with the kid." So I had to get up, and I was very, very nervous. And then, as I came off, Tony Benn says to me, "Wonderful, wonderful speech." And I went, "Arr, eh." It felt amazing that a man like him had listened to me. To me!'

In Liverpool, Kim had explained to me how Tony Benn had been a hero to her. Seeing him on the TV, she had always stopped and listened. 'I didn't agree with everything he said, but he made you listen when he talked about people's rights and the need to fight. For a young woman just starting her political and cultural life, to have Tony Benn say that to me . . . I knew he'd listened because he said it with sincerity. It really boosted my confidence. Little moments like that teach you a lot about how you deal with people. That march gave me great confidence for the rest of my life.'

Back in the same square in 2016, the evangelist with the microphone was still going strong. 'How many of you have dumped elderly parents in a care home? You want an easier lifestyle for your own selfish needs,' he said. 'So you abandon them. Maybe that's why God is punishing you. You're all going to hell.'

I walked along the high street, past the statue of Sir Stanley Matthews, the most revered son of Hanley and Stoke-on-Trent. Between 1932 and 1965, Matthews played outside-right for

Stoke City in two spells totalling nineteen years, and on the way won fifty-four caps for his country, becoming the only footballer ever to be knighted while still playing. Nicknamed the Wizard of Dribble and the Magician, Matthews was the first winner of both the European Footballer of the Year award – the Ballon d'Or – and the Football Writers' Association Footballer of the Year award.

After retirement, Matthews travelled the world, coaching amateur players. In 1975, in South Africa, despite the apartheid regime at the time, Matthews established an all-black team in Soweto known as Stan's Men. He played his final game in 1985, aged seventy, for an England Veterans XI against a Brazil Veterans XI, damaging his cartilage. 'A promising career cut tragically short,' he'd written in his autobiography, with characteristic dry humour.

Matthews died in February 2000, and the city came to a standstill as a hundred thousand people lined the streets to watch his hearse pass by. 'For all his fame, [Matthews was] as down to earth as the folk who once adorned the terraces in the hope of seeing him sprinkle gold dust on to their harsh working lives,' the journalist Les Scott wrote.

Matthews' ashes had been buried under the centre circle of Stoke City's ground. On the day I was there, sixteen years after his death, there were still fresh flowers under his statue. Not bad for a Port Vale fan.

I came to a stunning Grade II listed early nineteenth-century building with Roman Doric doorways and columns, and a cupola above the main entrance. Built as a slaughterhouse and meat market, it had been from here that people from the Potteries had drawn lots for tickets to escape to what they hoped would be a better life in the New World.

These days, the building housed a Waterstones bookshop and

a Wetherspoons pub, called the Reginald Mitchell. If Stanley Matthews is the Potteries' most famous son then Reginald Mitchell is arguably number two. Mitchell, born in nearby Kidsgrove and educated at Hanley High School (renamed Mitchell High School in his honour in 1989), started an apprenticeship aged sixteen with a local engineering firm, studying mathematics at night school. In 1917, aged twenty-two, he joined the Supermarine Aviation Works in Southampton, and within two years, such was his prodigious talent, he had become chief designer. Mitchell would eventually go on to design the aeroplane that saved Britain in 1940: the Supermarine Spitfire.

Outside the pub, sitting at tables drinking pints of lager in the late-afternoon gloom, were groups of middle-aged men and women. In a nearby doorway were two inert bodies wrapped up in blankets.

Standing outside a shop was a man in a smart Salvation Army outfit, selling copies of the *War Cry*. A few feet away from him was a young woman selling the *Big Issue*. For a while, I stood and watched the two vendors selling their magazines. I heard her ask him, in broken English, how many he had sold.

'Ninety,' he said. 'And you?'

She just shook her head.

The man told me that the Salvation Army had posted him to Stoke-on-Trent four years ago, moving him from Birmingham. Officers, he told me, were appointed to a town, not a church, and that was a big difference. I asked how he'd found the people of Stoke-on-Trent.

'It's a lovely city,' he said. 'Just the nature of folks round here. They don't mess about with artificial politeness. If people here want to say something to you, they will say it, whether it's good or bad. If it's a positive thing, you feel brilliant. If it's a negative thing, well OK . . .'

An elderly woman came up, popped some money in his hand, took a *War Cry*. 'God bless you,' he said.

'I'd do anything for the Salvation Army,' she replied.

He talked about the high levels of unemployment since the steel, coal and potteries industries had shut down, and about the recent rise in food banks.

'There's a growing need in this city for physical feeding,' he said. 'The food banks are so, so busy. And our hostel over in Stoke is always full. People with drink, drugs and mental health problems. You see the same people time and time again. They just keep going round the loop. They can't keep a tenancy by themselves. They just can't cope.'

A man came up and handed over some coins.

'Hello, sir. *War Cry* for you? God bless you. Nice to see you.'

The young woman selling the *Big Issue* had still not sold a single copy. She looked over at us.

The Salvation Army man talked about the rise in the number of asylum seekers turning up in Stoke-on-Trent, part of the government's dispersal programme. 'A while back, the council was selling off homes for a pound. Housing is cheap in Stoke and the government is buying up some of the cheaper housing and using that for asylum seekers and refugees while they're getting their papers,' he said. 'We've helped quite a few. There are a lot of Albanians and also a lot of people from the Middle East who have come through recently.'

Had that caused problems with local people?

He took a deep breath. 'Look, this is an area of high unemployment, and there's just a general discontent with the way things are going, and people feel forgotten and left behind. I don't think it's a racist thing at all. Most people round here are lovely, among the most tolerant folk I've ever met.'

An elderly woman came along, handed over some money and

started having a chat to the Salvation Army officer.

While they were talking, I walked over to the *Big Issue* seller. She seemed defensive, guarded.

'How are sales?' I asked. And she shook her head. In very broken English, she told me she was from Bucharest in Romania and had been in the UK for seven years. She lived in Manchester and travelled to Hanley every day to sell the *Big Issue*. She had a little girl in Manchester. She didn't want to go back to Romania. 'I very scared about that. I don't like it. Want to stay here. People here good, friendly.'

I went back to the Salvation Army officer. The elderly woman was putting a *War Cry* in her shopping bag.

'I enjoy standing out here on the street because people will come up, tell you their problems,' he said. 'This morning, I had an older gentleman whose wife died quite recently, and he is struggling. He is very isolated. His wife had been his whole world.'

I asked the man how old he was. Sixty-two, he said. I asked how society had changed in his lifetime. He thought for a while. 'Maybe society has moved on too far. We're no longer the people we were fifty years ago,' he said. 'When I was young, my parents lived within a few yards of their parents, families were all closer, invariably only one adult would go out to work. People now work a lot further from home. There are fewer and fewer links to our home community. Community has moved away from community, if that makes sense.

'We don't plant roots in the same way. If you are living among people most of your working life, in similar industries, you develop a community, through church, through going down the pub, the local working men's club. Now, we don't get that same contact with the people we work with. You clock off, go home, close the door on the world.'

'Hello, my love. God bless you. Are you keeping well?'

Opposite us were a bookmakers and a payday loan shop.

'Lot of those around these days,' I said.

'Well, our old charity shop in Blackheath was replaced by a William Hill,' he said. 'But these payday loan companies are a greater issue. It's just usury writ large. Targeting poor people. I deal with people in supported accommodation whose lives have been ruined.'

But his sympathy for people getting into debt was limited.

'We had this couple, couldn't afford a church wedding so we did one at the Salvation Army. Six months later, they're jetting off to Mexico. There is the expectation that you must have a forty-inch plasma TV, whether you can afford it or not. People are getting into terrible debt.'

I asked him about the upcoming EU referendum. 'The Leave campaign is very negative, quite racist,' he said. 'Politicians need to be sure of the facts before they speak.'

He told me about his Polish daughter-in-law, and the racism she'd encountered where she and his son lived in the West Country, and about how they had been considering emigrating to Canada.

His mobile phone beeped.

'That's my wife saying that my dinner is ready,' he said. And with that he packed away the few remaining copies of the *War Cry* and headed off. The *Big Issue* seller was still there. I waved goodbye to her and she smiled back, without any great enthusiasm.

Opposite the Stanley Matthews statue was a van with a sign above it that read 'The Staffordshire Oatcakes Sensation'. I joined the long queue and waited as those before me ordered their fillings. 'One cheese and bacon, one sausage, cheese and mushroom,' I could hear the woman behind the counter say to a man who poured batter mix onto a sizzling hotplate, placed the fillings on top and then rolled them up into a wrap.

I got to the front and ordered a bacon and cheese.

I stepped aside so that the couple behind me could order, and asked the woman behind the counter why Staffordshire oatcakes, this most iconic Stoke staple, had failed to travel beyond the county's borders.

'We're baffled, to be honest, duck,' she said. 'Because obviously other foods have gone all over, like the Cornish pasty, or crepes or whatever. Originally it was just a very cheap and nutritional food for farm labourers.'

I asked what was in the batter mix. 'Oats, flour and water,' she said. 'And a secret ingredient. I can't tell you that, can I?' And she turned to the man, who was her husband, and they both laughed.

Her husband had worked at Royal Doulton for twenty-five years. When that factory closed down and moved production to East Asia, he had used his redundancy money to buy the van. They'd been selling oatcakes in Stoke ever since.

'You could see it was going to happen,' he told me. 'Like with the rest of the potteries.'

'Inevitable, weren't it?' his wife said.

'But you didn't think a company like that could ever close,' he said. 'The only question I asked at the meeting when the announcement was made was, "Are they going to get the union rate?!",' and he laughed again. 'I mean, all these people want to do is feed their families, don't they?'

'The good old days have gone, haven't they?' his wife said. 'Quality's gone out of the window. It's all about maximum money for minimum outlay. The morals have gone down. Stoke lost all its industry: pots, steel, coal. We had the soul ripped out of us. But people are coming to terms with it and bouncing back. Is this yours, duck? Cheese and egg?'

GOD AND MAN

The man threw another giant bowl of batter onto the hotplate.

The woman talked a little about their three children – two sons, aged twenty-seven and twenty, and a daughter, twenty-three. The eldest still lived locally, and her daughter was still at home.

'She loves living at home,' she said. 'And we love to have her at home.' Their youngest had recently moved away to university, on the south coast. 'He's studying law and an "ology",' she told me. 'Not sure what. It's got a very long name. Wants to do criminal investigative practice. We're so proud of him. But we do miss him dreadfully.'

My oatcake was ready and I said farewell to the couple and walked through the streets of Hanley eating it, grease and melted cheese running over my fingers. It was delicious. I have no idea why Staffordshire oatcakes haven't taken over the world either.

I went into an estate agency. Since Salford and my experience of the buy-to-letters moving into deprived areas, it had become an obsession of mine. A woman behind a desk asked if she could help me, and I told her about Salford and wondered if the same thing was happening here. She nodded.

'People from out of town hear that the area is quite deprived and they make low offers, or outbid the locals,' she said. 'It's increased a lot over the last five years. They come to the area, want advice, contact us for half a day's viewings.'

I asked her what she thought of it all.

'Obviously, it is very good for my business. But long-term, how can it go on? Macclesfield people are priced out by Manchester people. Macclesfield people go to Leek and price locals out there. They come here, but are priced out by people coming from richer areas in the south. Where does all that end? That's on top of the loss of all those jobs round here and the way the town's been run into the ground. People just feel let down.'

I walked out of the city centre, through the bus station. At the end of the row of bus stands was a shimmering sculpture, maybe twenty feet high, made in the form of a giant lump of coal, and covered in thousands of discs, meant to replicate the tags that miners wore underground. I thought it was there to commemorate all of the miners of the North Staffordshire coal mines who helped make Stoke-on-Trent a one-time powerhouse.

But I was wrong. For although the statue was there to commemorate miners, it was not those of Staffordshire, but the miners of a small town in Czechoslovakia called Lidice, who – along with their families – had been slaughtered, imprisoned or displaced by the Nazis in 1942. In June that year, SS troops entered the town, seeking revenge for the killing in late May of the Nazis' Reich Protector of Bohemia and Moravia, Reinhard Heydrich, whose car had been ambushed by members of the resistance. Believing erroneously that Lidice had been harbouring partisans, the Nazis executed 173 men – every single male over fifteen years old. The women and children were rounded up and mothers separated from their offspring. The women were transported to Ravensbrück concentration camp in northern Germany. The children were sent to Łódź in central Poland. Those suitable for 'Germanisation' were adopted by SS families. The other eighty-two children were driven into the countryside and gassed.

The Nazis set Lidice on fire and blew up any buildings still standing. The river that ran through the town was diverted. Salt was poured into the soil so that nothing would ever grow there. The name of Lidice was removed from any maps. The place was literally wiped off the face of the earth. Or so the Nazis had thought.

In Stoke-on-Trent, the Labour MP Barnett Stross was deeply

moved on hearing about the tragedy. He addressed the miners of the Potteries, proposing the reconstruction of Lidice after the war. 'Hitler said "Lidice shall die"; the miners of Stoke-on-Trent declare that "Lidice shall live",' Stross told them.

Collecting from Staffordshire miners, many themselves impoverished, the fund raised £32,000 – over a million pounds in today's money. In 1947, work began on building a new Lidice overlooking the site of the old town. In 1949, the women who had survived the concentration camps, and a few of the children, returned and started to rebuild their shattered lives.

Standing there in May 2016, looking at the sculpture, it was a strong reminder of what ordinary people could achieve when bound by a common narrative. The relationship between Stoke and Lidice was in stark contrast to the newspapers' daily head-lines about foreigners and their exhortations to turn our backs on the EU – a body that has, whatever else, helped preserve peace in Europe since darkness almost completely engulfed it.

9

THE PENITENT PILGRIM
(STOKE-ON-TRENT)

I threw back the curtains. Below me in the car park was a skip full of stained mattresses and, alongside a row of leylandii trees, a hedge festooned with beer cans, under which broken glass sparkled like diamonds in the early morning sunshine. I had a full day and evening in Stoke-on-Trent and had arranged to meet a few Stokies prominent in the local community. After my eighteen miles the previous day, I was looking forward to the rest.

Just a few hundred yards up the road, I knocked on the door of a terraced house. A man opened it. He had thick black eyebrows, a bushy grey goatee beard and long grey hair, and on his head was a trilby with what looked like a peacock feather tucked into the hatband.

'Mike?' he said. 'Come in, lad.'

Alan Barrett was a local historian, writer and activist, and lifelong resident of the city. He went into the kitchen, came back with two cups of tea. My mug was rather beautiful, decorated with tiny exotic birds, and Alan, seeing me looking at it, said, 'That's nowt special, just everyday ware.'

Pottery was a passion of Alan's. Now sixty, he'd worked at Royal Doulton back in the day. He told me about the backstamp, the mark on china that tells you where it was made, and how most Stokies of a certain age will always look at it. 'It's called the Turnover Club,' Alan said. 'Always the saucer, because the cup's full. Wherever you are, you turn it over to see where it was made.'

He told me how he and his wife, Lyn, were members of the National Trust, liked travelling around the country looking at historic sites.

'We were at Blenheim Palace, Churchill's home, and it's got Churchill china,' he said, his eyes sparkling with the thought of it. 'Upton House, beautiful place to visit, that's got Churchill, too. They've got Dudson china in Tatton Hall. We were at a B&B once in Cleethorpes. Nice place, and the owner had all this Emma Bridgewater stuff on display. But the stuff we were served with was bog-standard.'

Just like the oatcake man, Alan had been made redundant when Doulton moved most of its operations to East Asia. 'I've worked for Spode and Doulton and they both died. I'm a bloody jinx!'

The loss of a well-paid job had forced him and Lyn to move to the small terrace they'd lived in ever since. And, just like the oatcake man, Alan had no problem with the people of East Asia having work. 'Everybody's got to live, haven't they?' he said. 'But they [the pottery firms] are on record – written record, mind – as saying no jobs in Stoke-on-Trent will be affected. Now excuse me. Common sense dictates that if you're paying a man £300 a week, and another man £300 a year, that's where you're gonna put your money. We lost thirty thousand jobs. That's a lot of jobs for one city to lose to outsourcing.'

We talked football. Alan was a lifelong supporter of Stoke City, one of whose most famous recent managers, Tony Pulis, had gone on to manage my own club, West Bromwich Albion. The two clubs have a sometimes fierce rivalry and historically both were known for their flowing, attractive football, something that, whatever else he brought to the party, Tony Pulis was not.

Alan told me about an interview Pulis had once given where he'd described Stokies as working-class folk who appreciated hard work.

'And we do,' Alan said to me. 'But I bumped into Pulis once, and I said to him, Tony, we have also given great beauty to the world: Stanley Matthews, Alan Hudson, Peter Dobing ... We've seen art on the pitch. Tony Waddington was our manager in the 1970s and he described it as the working man's ballet.

'I said to Pulis, we've given the world Clarice Cliff ceramics – not my cup of tea, but a lot of people like it – Cooper, Josiah Wedgwood – he was an abolitionist, great bloke – Doulton. James Brindley, engineer, who perfected the double canal lock, Arthur Berry, one of the world's greatest artists, he was from Stoke. Gertie Gitana, one of the greatest music hall stars of the early twentieth century. I said to Pulis, "Don't patronise us. We've given more to the world than just bloody hard work. We're not just cannon fodder for the wealthy classes, you know."'

Alan told me that there had been a lifting of mood in the city in 1997, when Tony Blair came to power.

'There was hope. "Things are going to be OK." But it didn't last long. There was a brilliant clip on the telly. It was live, so Blair couldn't do anything about it. It was in his constituency, and a young lad said to him, "Here, Tony, why's the Labour Party like a Newcastle United shirt? Cos you've both sold out before Christmas!"' Alan laughed. 'Stoke got itself a reputation as a far-right, racist place, but it isn't. The BNP hasn't been here for years. We're a strong Labour town. But if you kick people often enough – the Tories don't bother with us and Labour takes us for granted – then eventually people will disengage.'

Alan told me about how things had got considerably worse since 2010, how any vestige of hope that many people in Stoke might have had was being slowly extinguished.

'We aren't a militant people in Stoke-on-Trent. And that's becoming a problem for us,' he said. 'Our strength is that we don't like show-offs. We're a modest people. But our weakness is that we're a modest people. We aren't very good at standing up for ourselves. Many people are now totally apathetic. They've just given up. I love my city, I would never decry it, but . . .' and he trailed off, shaking his head.

He told me a story about a young woman he and Lyn had recently taken under their wing.

'Young lass,' he said. 'Severe mental health problems, on her own. We took her to apply for her employment and support allowance and she only scored nine points when you need ten, so she got turned down. We did some research and it seems that most people only score nine points. We eventually won the appeal and it's supposed to take eight weeks for the money to come through, but it took fourteen months. Fourteen months with virtually no money and no family support. How she didn't fold is beyond me. But you can understand why some people have killed themselves.'

I asked Alan what Stoke-on-Trent needed, what would begin to undo all of the damage visited on the city in the last thirty-five years.

'Flipping heck!' he said. 'What a question. Well, I'll tell you what we don't need and that's more bloody shopping. They've only got one idea and that is that retail is God. It isn't. We've got a workforce here on shitty, low-paid, zero-hours contracts. And they're willing, able and, quite frankly, desperate to have decent, secure employment. We've got a beautiful city here. Let's invite solar-panel people, wind-turbine people to come and manufacture here. Let's turn Stoke into a green manufacturing centre of excellence. We've got to do something. Anything.'

Alan took a deep breath.

'We all live in the same country,' he said. 'It should be about coming to a mutually compatible agreement. How about if we all just took a step back and looked at the bigger picture, stopped charging at each other like mad bulls. All we're doing at the moment is fighting nonsensical battles, which are wearing us all out, and those at the top of the tree are just laughing at us.

'If I look back to see how life has turned out over the last thirty-five years, I can't say I'm any happier than I was back then. Don't get me wrong, I have five grandkids that I love dearly, and another on the way. I'm looking forward to retirement, if we can ever afford it, and taking the grandkids to the match, and me and Lyn growing old disgracefully, with any luck. But, to be honest with you, Mike, I would have expected to be happier.'

I walked up the street. In the windows of many of the houses were Vote Leave posters. I carried on back into Hanley, past rows of terraces with cobbled alleyways between their backs. I came to a statue of Reginald Mitchell and then one of a steel-worker – a stainless-steel casting, on a steel plinth, proudly holding out a thermal lance, just like an infantryman carrying a pike walking towards the enemy.

The statue commemorated the battle of the Shelton Bar steel-workers to save their jobs in the 1970s. That fight had been lost in June 1978, when the last blast furnace was shut down and two thousand people were laid off. Shelton Bar's rolling mill contin-ued until 2000, when the works finally shut. At its height the steelworks had employed ten thousand people. The inscription on the plinth read: 'I believe in the dignity of labour, whether with head or hand; that the world owes no man a living, but that it owes every man an opportunity to make a living.'

I went into the Potteries Museum and Art Gallery. In the

entrance hall, a plaque declared that the building had been opened by the Prince of Wales on 3 June 1981, just three weeks after the People's March for Jobs had passed through and eight weeks before he'd married Lady Diana Spencer. In 1981, as Margaret Thatcher's policies were ravaging the industrial heartlands, we were already turning our industries into nostalgia.

In one room was a Spitfire, donated to the city in 1972, in honour of Reginald Mitchell. In the next were glass cabinets everywhere, full of the most exquisite ceramics from all over the world, following the evolution of the craft, from the Neolithic to Greek to Roman, funerary jars from China, fourteenth-century border tiles from Persia with raised Kufic inscriptions, and Italian Renaissance maiolica.

Alongside all of that was the finest collection of North Staffordshire pottery in the world. There were Josiah Wedgwood's neoclassical black basalt vases, eighteenth-century pearlware figurines, salt-glazed stoneware, Toby jugs, collections of the major Staffordshire factories such as Doulton, Spode and Minton – and less well-known ones such as that of William Greatbatch – and ceramic art masterpieces from the likes of Bernard Moore, Ruskin, Pilkington and Bullers. It was a spectacular display.

As recently as the late 1970s there had still been over sixty thousand people employed by the pottery industry in Stoke-on-Trent. By 1991 this was down to just over twenty-two thousand, and by 2016 only eight thousand people still made their living from it.

Alan Barrett had talked of a mini-revival in the industry, through small independents such as Mathew Dimbleby, Denise O'Sullivan and, most famously, Emma Bridgewater. These firms concentrated on handmade, high-end ceramics, and were benefiting from the burgeoning market of the newly wealthy of China and other East Asian countries, for whom the cachet of the 'made in Stoke-on-Trent' backstamp was irresistible.

Therein was the topsy-turvy narrative of globalisation and neoliberalism encapsulated perfectly: you outsource manufacturing to low-wage economies and thereby immiserate your domestic workforce; certain sections of those new manufacturing countries become wealthy; the newly wealthy don't want to buy the cheap stuff they produce but desire the high-status products stripped of their cachet by the outsourcing and mass manufacturing; small independents in the original manufacturing country start making goods of high quality and high price, stamped with the all-important 'Made in Stoke', to supply the new markets.

One of the things that tends not to return is mass employment for skilled and unskilled manufacturing workers, the very jobs that made Stoke-on-Trent such a powerhouse in the first place. Those remain in East Asia. Emma Bridgewater employs 280 people in Stoke.

The loss of those jobs in Stoke-on-Trent was taking a terrible toll. A 2015 Hardship Commission report on the Potteries area found that 38 per cent of the households in Stoke were living on less than £16,000 a year, 'the minimum amount required to access basic goods and services in Britain'. Three thousand households were dependent on charity food, and council tax arrears in North Staffordshire stood at £25 million.

I left the ceramics galleries in the Potteries Museum and walked into the next room. On the wall was a memorial to the miners of the 1984–85 strike, a stunning frieze made from coal drawn from the local Hem Heath colliery, two Davy lamps hanging from it, and flanked by busts of Joe Green and David Jones, both killed on picket duty. 'Lest we forget,' read an inscription in a stone tablet. '966 miners sacked, 200 imprisoned, 20,000 injured and two killed on picket lines.'

The North Staffordshire coal mines had been in the forefront of that bitter dispute, precipitated by the Thatcher government's reduction of state subsidy to the mining industry, which left most of Britain's pits under threat of closure. Some historians have called the twelve months of the strike from March 1984 to March 1985 the catalyst that accelerated the decline of industrial Britain.

The Conservative government had been preparing for the dispute, mindful of its defeat in 1981, when it had proposed closing twenty-three pits and had had to capitulate when, within days, half of the country's coalfields were hit by unofficial strikes.

It has been suggested, too, that the Tories were out to avenge their humiliating 1974 defeat to the miners, who'd gone on strike for higher wages at a time of rampant inflation. That dispute led to blackouts and the introduction of a three-day week to conserve electricity.

Two days into the strike, Ted Heath, then Tory Prime Minister, called an early election, believing that the British public sided with the government on the issues of strikes and union power. Heath got it wrong. The election delivered a hung Parliament as the Tories lost their majority. Heath failed to secure enough support from Liberal and Ulster Unionist MPs, and Labour's Harold Wilson returned to power in a minority government. In the second general election of 1974, held in October, Wilson's Labour Party won with a majority of three seats.

But by 1984 the Tories were ready for the miners. They had been stockpiling coal and converting power stations to burn heavy fuel oil; they had held briefings with senior police officers and recruited fleets of road hauliers to transport coal in case railway workers joined the strike in support of the miners. In July 1984, a few months into the strike, Thatcher famously called the miners 'the enemy within', saying that giving in to them would amount to surrendering the governance of parliamentary democracy to the rule of the mob.

In August, miners in Nottinghamshire sued the National Union of Mineworkers, claiming that the strike was unofficial without the ballot that the union's president, Arthur Scargill, had refused to hold. The High Court ruled that the NUM had breached its own constitution and fined it £200,000, which it refused to pay. By Christmas, ten months without income was having a catastrophic effect on mining communities up and down the country. As the miners became more desperate, violence on the picket lines escalated. On 3 March 1985, the NUM convened to debate the situation. Delegates voted ninety-eight to ninety-one to end the strike. On 5 March, the miners returned to work, many following behind their marching bands and pit banners.

Immediately, the mines began to shut. There were seventy-four closed between 1985 and 1989 alone. The last pit in Stoke-on-Trent, at Trentham, shut in 1993. In the mid-twentieth century, the mining industry had employed seven hundred thousand people. Official figures from the Department of Energy and Climate Change showed that in 2001, for the first time, the UK imported more coal than it produced – and that has remained the case ever since.

The year after the miners' strike ended, the Public Order Act clamped down on picketing and many other aspects of the right to protest, with greatly enhanced and sometimes unaccountable powers for the police. Section five of that act stated that a person was guilty of an offence if he or she '(a) uses threatening, abusive or insulting words or behaviour, or disorderly behaviour, or (b) displays any writing, sign or other visible representation which is threatening, abusive or insulting, within the hearing or sight of a person likely to be caused harassment, alarm or distress thereby.'

That 1986 act could be seen as a piece of pre-emptive legislation, designed to curtail protest from an increasingly angry population living increasingly insecure and precarious lives. The academic John Brewer, in the 1988 book *The Police, Public Order and the State*, wrote that the police had gone from 'policing the margins' of society to 'controlling large blocs of the population'.

In January 2014, in the House of Commons, the Labour MP for Wigan, Lisa Nandy, called upon the Prime Minister, David Cameron, to apologise on behalf of Margaret Thatcher's government for its programme of mine closures and the consequent devastation of communities. Cameron was unrepentant. 'I think if anyone needs to make an apology for their role in the miners' strike,' he'd said, 'it should be Arthur Scargill for the appalling way he led the union.'

But Cameron – educated at Eton, lest we forget, with its annual fees of over £30,000, and the man who, the month before my walk, had finally been forced to admit, after dodging around journalists' questions for days, that he had benefited from his father's Panama-based company Blairmore, which had paid zero UK tax on its profits in thirty years – had form for refusing to apologise to working-class people.

In 2011 he had told a gathering of local journalists in Liverpool that the relatives of the Hillsborough victims, as they continued to seek justice, were 'like a blind man, in a dark room, looking for a black cat that isn't there'.

My next appointment was with Danny Flynn, the fifty-one-year-old chief executive of the city's YMCA, who had the sharp, rapid-fire patter of a stand-up comedian. About the same age as me, Danny had seen first-hand the changes in Stoke over the past thirty-five years. 'I remember standing there in Hanley watching the People's March for Jobs come through in 1981,' he said.

Back in the early eighties, he'd left school and started an

apprenticeship as a diesel fitter. 'There were loads of us on apprenticeships; you dropped on where you could. Often through mates' dads. That was normal – everyone working and jobs for life.'

Seeing the writing on the wall following Thatcher's election, Danny had left for London. He'd returned in 1989, 'just really wanting to come home'. He'd been amazed at what he saw. 'Heroin had come whistling in around 1984,' he told me. 'Because I was living in London I escaped it, but loads of my mates that stayed got into it. Some are dead now. Went to a funeral last year of a mate who drank himself to death. Same age as me. Great lad. He got dragged into that scene. He just sat around bored all day, no work, waiting for his dealer. That's what they were doing in the eighties, just sitting around, watching telly, turning giros over, buying heroin . . . there are now people in Stoke who have never worked. People just collapse and get stuck, and so you get communities that have just turned in on themselves in terms of drugs, the black market, how the estates work.'

Danny explained how Stoke's six-town polycentric layout had worked against it after the loss of industry. 'These estates and towns were built on the back of the industries they served, so you had mining estates in the north of the city, steel estates in the middle, and pottery estates in the south,' he told me. 'In the 1980s, this all got killed, goodbye, and you ended up with these workless estates that are estranged from the other towns.'

After coming back to Stoke, Danny had worked in care homes for a while 'because I couldn't get a job anywhere else. But I really enjoyed that. Great Stoke working-class women, brilliant women.' He then worked in a night shelter dealing with 'the acute end of homelessness'. In 2003 he was appointed as chief executive of the YMCA, looking after some of the city's young and vulnerable people, with 138 in accommodation at the centre. That's where I'd found him, at the YMCA on the northern edge of Hanley Park.

'I'd pissed around at school, was told I was a bit of a dick, a bit stupid,' Danny told me. But one day he'd walked into a careers office, and a man working there had told Danny he was bright. 'You just need somebody on your side, don't you?' he said. 'That's what I'm trying to build here at the YMCA, getting these kids to step out of the culture of low expectations they've grown up with. God, I sound like a poncey sociologist now, don't I?'

Danny talked about homelessness in Stoke-on-Trent today, how it was a major and growing problem, with family break-up the single biggest driver of young people coming to live at the YMCA. 'I reckon 80 per cent of them come from challenged families,' he said. 'Blood isn't always thicker than water.'

What did Danny think was behind the break-up of these families? 'Financial problems, unemployment, it just causes family break-up because you get sick of looking at each other, don't you?' he said. 'Research from Staffs Uni about ten years ago found a higher proportion of young homeless in Stoke than other towns. Why? My view is that, in working-class towns, you're expected to go to work at sixteen. It's like "bring some money in or fuck off". Still a bit of that around, in Stoke, in tougher families.'

Danny didn't have a lot of time for what he saw as middle-class reformers, who came into Stoke with good intentions but preconceived ideas about the people and what they needed. 'I was talking to a mate recently, former miner, now a councillor. We were reminiscing, talking about how great Stokies are. This woman at the council, an "import", heard us and said, "You two make it all sound as if Stoke is really positive. When did it all go wrong then?"

'We just laughed. "It went wrong," we told her, "when they

ripped out all of our jobs. It went wrong when that traditional working-class city that had it pretty sussed, that was a pretty ordered, proud, conservative Labour kind of place, had its heart ripped out. We might not be the richest people in the world, but we are the warmest, friendliest and kindest people in the world." That's what we told her. About five years ago they measured community reciprocity, and Stoke came second in the country, just after some leafy place in Scotland. Stoke's development came from our own organising, not middle-class philanthropists coming here and making us better people. Social justice comes from the working class. It has to. But everything is top-down now.'

I asked Danny what needed to be done to help Stoke-on-Trent.

'Well, there's a lot of the negative side of the welfare state in Stoke around dependency. It's in many ways a disempowered culture now,' he told me. 'There's an ingrained idea, after years of being broken, that there needs to be a white charger coming over the hill to fix us, from Westminster or wherever.

'It's partly the trauma of loss of industry, but more about the sense of powerlessness that pervades everything now. There's a lot of research on leadership, but not a lot on "followship". How do you empower a group of disempowered people in a culture where they are used to having it done for them? It worked up to the 1980s, but then most people had a job.'

That disempowerment was being starkly reflected at the polls. In 1950, voter turnout for Stoke-on-Trent Central, a once-proud Labour stronghold, had been a record 83 per cent. At the 2015 general election, it had been just 51 per cent, the very lowest in the UK.

I was interested in Danny's take on the buy-to-let phenomenon I had seen on my walk. In 1981 there had been over five million council houses in England. By 2014 the number was down to

1.7 million, and was set to plummet further. The main reason for the sharp fall was the Tories' right-to-buy scheme. This policy had done two main things: it had transferred state assets into the hands of the private sector; and it had forced tenants into the unregulated higher rents of the private rental market. The housing benefit bill, paid for by UK taxpayers, had soared as a consequence. A few months before I set off, the Local Government Association had called it a shift in spending from 'bricks to benefits'.

'Yes, we've got all those buy-to-let investors coming up here from the south.' Danny told me. 'I've just had a woman down-stairs, family wrecked, two sisters very poorly, welfare-dependent, powerless, basically been shafted for the thirty-eight years of her life. She's living in one of these [buy-to-let] properties in Fenton. She's got mould and damp coming through the floor, and the land-lord is charging her £80 above housing benefit level, the robbing bastard. Silverdale, the former mining estate, that's all buy-to-let. It's disgusting. Did you know that back in the day Stoke built more council houses than any other city in the UK?

'Something like 65 per cent of all properties bought under right-to-buy are owned by an absentee landlord – they're not owned by the people who buy them, who quickly sell them on,' Danny continued. 'You didn't need the gift of prophecy for that one, did you? I still can't believe what bastards these Tories are now. I think back then there was a bit of one-nation Toryism that kind of balanced it a bit. They were not so com-pletely obsessed with the free-market liberal economics that's become established in the last twenty years. These bastards now, they're attacking people, hurting people, with a kind of malice. That's quite new.'

I walked back across Stoke-on-Trent to the pub I was staying at, the pavements slick with the rain that had fallen while I was at the YMCA. I thought about what Danny had been saying about middle-class 'do-gooders'. Here I was, a *Guardian* journalist, living in a Regency flat in Brighton overlooking the sea, with a fancy Smeg fridge and an expensive coffee machine, enjoying as middle-class a life as it was possible to imagine, wandering through the country like an anthropologist, trying to understand what had happened to working-class communities in the past thirty-five years. Could I possibly understand?

Danny and I had both been working-class lads with few prospects who'd headed off to London. But Danny had gone home, walked the walk, working at the heart of his community. I had thrown myself into advertising and then journalism, dropped my accent, and never really looked back. Well, not until recently, when the damage being caused to those working-class communities was getting impossible to ignore. And so I'd set off on my walk. But there was more. On some level, I had always tacitly known that there would be winners and losers in post-industrial Britain, and I knew that the price for my upward social mobility was being paid in places like Stoke-on-Trent, had secretly accepted it as a price worth paying for the benefits that capitalism had delivered to me. I was part of the problem. This was no pilgrimage. It was beginning to feel more like a penance.

I walked back through Hanley, past the memorial to the people of Lidice, and then through the centre, past the Stanley Matthews statue, where a group of men stood around drinking strong lager and shouting at each other, and then along Piccadilly, with its boarded-up shops. I walked past the statues of Reginald Mitchell and the man with the thermal lance from the Shelton steelworks, and then past the site of the steelworks itself, now a sprawling retail park. I thought about the poem

'Cloud Weavers', written by Tom Wyre, son of the Potteries and Staffordshire poet laureate in 2013–14:

Iron clad heritage,
Grasps the hill's smog filled lungs to gasp in the sky,
And catch wind of the Potteries.
Proud peoples, diamonds pressed from carbon seams,
Inventive brows,
Spark with the kiln and wheels,
Through smoke and weaving clouds,
To work the cogs and flywheels with steel strewn
Through coal hollowed veins.
Garnet blood, sweat and tears,
Mark the hours and echo along cobblestones,
Aloud to follow in the footsteps and glimpse a distant year,
Pioneers of clay, planes and steam machines,
A cast iron legacy, everywhere to be seen.
Early dreams made fact by labours of steadfast people,
My people and our history of which I am duly proud.

10

THE BIRDS AND THE BEES
(STOKE-ON-TRENT TO STAFFORD)

In the pub, I ate oatcakes for breakfast, with a bacon and sausage filling and a little puddle of melted cheese. I headed off soon afterwards. Again, the sun was shining and my legs felt strong, fully restored after my day off. I tried to imagine the day when I would walk into Trafalgar Square and I wouldn't have to move any more. It was inconceivable. I never wanted to stop. I crossed over the A500, six busy lanes of traffic that sliced the city in two, and then walked past Stoke City's ground, formerly called the Britannia, now named the Bet365 Stadium.

Bet365 was a rare success story in modern Stoke. One of the world's leading online gambling groups, with nineteen million customers in almost two hundred countries, the firm had three thousand staff in the city – it was the largest private employer in Stoke. In 2015 alone it had generated £1.5 billion in revenue. The company had been founded in 2000 by Denise Coates, the daughter of Peter Coates, who was himself the Stoke-born son of a coal miner and chairman of Stoke City FC. Peter had had business dealings in catering, radio, and a chain of betting shops, but it was with the founding of Bet365 that the family's fortunes really took off. By 2016 the *Sunday Times* Rich List had put their combined wealth at £3.8 billion.

Bet365 developed alongside and has contributed to the meteoric growth of gambling in the UK since 2005, when, through that year's Gambling Act, New Labour deregulated the industry and allowed online sports betting companies and online casinos to advertise on TV. In 2016 the Institute for Fiscal Studies estimated that the gambling industry contributed £2.6 billion to the exchequer annually. Before the Gambling Act, only the football pools, the National Lottery and bingo premises had been allowed to advertise. Between 2007 and 2012, according to research by Ofcom, the number of gambling adverts on TV grew by 500 per cent, to 1.39 million; in 2012, the average UK adult saw 630 of them, while the average child – aged four to fifteen – saw 211.

In 2004, the year before the act, the Coates family had made a donation to the Labour Party of £50,000, followed by £100,000 in 2005 and £150,000 in 2007, the year that the act came into force. Between 2009 and 2011, according to accounts filed in Gibraltar – a British overseas territory where non-resident companies can perfectly legally take advantage of offshore regimes to reduce taxation – a subsidiary of Bet365 based there had paid a 10 per cent rate of corporation tax, compared with 28 per cent in the UK, saving itself £13 million. In 2010–11, Companies House Gibraltar records showed that one of the Coates family companies, Hillside (Gibraltar) Limited, made profits there of £36.5 million, yet still received a tax rebate of £668,000.

A report by the Gambling Commission showed that in the twelve months to September 2015, around the time that gambling advertising hit an all-time high, British gamblers lost a record £12.6 billion; their losses had risen every year since 2011. The report also showed the rise of a relatively new phenomenon in UK gambling: fixed-odds betting terminals (FOBTs) in high street bookies. These machines allowed punters to stake up to £100 every twenty seconds – bank cards accepted! – on electronic versions of casino games, and have been called the 'crack cocaine of gambling'. They accounted for a £1.7 billion loss by players in the twelve months to September 2015.

It was in the nation's poorer areas where these machines had spread like a cancer. In 2013 research showed that in the fifty parliamentary constituencies with the highest unemployment levels there were 1,251 betting shops, where £5.6 billion was poured into FOBTs. By comparison, the fifty constituencies with the lowest unemployment had 287 betting shops and saw £1.4 billion gambled. East London's Bethnal Green and Bow had forty-five betting shops, while Henley in Oxfordshire hadn't issued a single licence for one.

In 2016 a report by the Institute for Public Policy Research found that problem gambling was costing the UK up to £1.2 billion a year, with the burden falling largely on the health service and the criminal justice and welfare systems. That the figure didn't eclipse the £2.6 billion of revenue to the Treasury from taxes on the gambling companies might lead cynics to the conclusion that the government had carried out a cost-benefit analysis.

'There are mind-numbing numbers of betting shops in places like Moston in my constituency,' the Labour MP for Manchester Central, Lucy Powell, told the *Guardian* in 2013. 'I think it is a moral question to ask whether it is a good thing that betting companies are targeting the poor and whether government lets them. According to these figures, there's more being spent on gambling than by the council in my constituency on services.'

John Redwood, the Tory MP for Wokingham in Berkshire, which had just three betting shops, was less sympathetic when approached by the paper. 'I put it down to the fact that poor people . . . put getting rich down to luck and think they can take a gamble,' he said. 'They also have time on their hands. My voters are too busy working hard to make a reasonable income.'

The online betting firms had seen an effective way to get to those struggling communities – for what better represented the heart of a place than its football club, handed down through the generations? The first football club to have a gambling company shirt sponsor was Fulham in 2003. In the 2015–16 English Premier League season, seven of the twenty teams had shirts sponsored by betting companies. So even if your team didn't have such a firm emblazoned across their shirts, the chances were high in any game that they'd be playing a team that did. Every single Premier League club had an official gambling partner.

The YMCA's Danny Flynn, lifelong Stoke City nut, had talked to me about the Coates family and their prominent role in the city's economy. 'Decent, benevolent family, the Coates family,' he'd said. 'Labour people to the core. And they've helped Stoke a lot.'

I'd asked Danny how he felt about that money coming from an industry that tends to make its greatest profits from poorer people in society.

'I've no moral position,' he'd said. 'I'll have a go on the Grand National, and the FA Cup – we all do, don't we?'

He paused.

'But would I rather have a steelworks and potteries than a betting company? Of course I would,' he continued. 'But Bet365 gives the place hope, because you can see they've made a difference. One of the estates is rammed with their workers. Better than having an estate full of people on the dole. If that's the only show in town, then we need it to regenerate. Stoke's got to find positive markets that will grow the place and attract others.'

Past the Bet365 Stadium I found myself on a series of new roads with mini-roundabouts, all linking together a cluster of distribution warehouses. There were no pavements, so I walked in the road, dodging the trucks. According to my OS map, there was a footpath there somewhere, which would take me down to the towpath of the Trent and Mersey canal. I saw two men sitting in a hut by an electronic barrier to one of the warehouses, and stopped to ask if they knew where the path was; but they just shook their heads, looking a little confused to see anybody walking on that industrial estate.

I climbed over a little fence and around a boggy area fringed with reed beds, with the sound of a brook somewhere off to my right, the air full of chiffchaff song. I found the footpath, barely navigable through the waist-high nettles, and shortly afterwards I emerged onto the towpath of the Trent and Mersey canal – my 'road', straight and broad, the veritable superhighway of its day.

Any sense of panic I'd had while lost among the concrete and the roads evaporated instantly, and – freed of the need to find my way – my brain slowed down, as it always did when all I had to do was put one foot in front of the other, and the birds and the sough of the wind in the trees and the muffled horns of faraway trains beyond the trees became my soundtrack. Somewhere that morning, the hundredth mile since leaving Liverpool passed under my feet.

At Barlaston, there was a signpost pointing away from the towpath to the World of Wedgwood. In 2009, Wedgwood had moved nearly all of its production to Jakarta in Indonesia. Today the famous factory site at Barlaston employed a few ceramicists making high-end artisanal pottery, but it was essentially a heritage experience, with a museum and restaurants – and, according to their website, a nostalgic chance to 'celebrate the very best of British craftsmanship'.

The original nostalgia, a compound of the Greek words *nostos*, meaning 'homecoming' and *algos*, meaning 'pain' or 'ache', is less the looking back to the past as used in the Wedgwood brochure and more a concept of homesickness. Pro-Brexit newspapers were infused at the time of my walk with that Wedgwood nostalgia: 'taking back control', 'a once-in-a-lifetime chance to shape the destiny of our country', 'freedom', a return to some prelapsarian paradise. I walked past the World of Wedgwood. I didn't want to look back, be caught in the stasis of that. What was the point?

I got off the canal towpath at Burston. On my OS map was a footpath that would cut through fields to Stafford, my destination for the evening. I crossed a little footbridge over the River Trent, little more than a stream at that stage, and was soon hopelessly lost in fields of young wheat, walking along their margins, thick with cloying mud, trying and failing to find a stile in the hedgerow, now full and dense. I walked the entire perimeter of a vast field, up a steep slope, where I sank up to my knees in the bog.

I'd run out of water, and was now tramping in the midday heat. I scrambled over a fence, not noticing the barbed wire, which caught my trousers. I fell head first into the dirt, to the sound of ripping fabric. I looked at my leg, at the flesh through the foot-long tear, and could see the blood beginning to rise out of the scratch on my inner thigh. As a travel writer, I had trekked in some of the most inhospitable terrain in the world, in Sudan and Yemen in the summer heat, in Siberia and Mongolia in the frigid winter, on the summits of some of Nepal's highest mountains. And here I was, lost and bloodied in a Staffordshire field in May.

I emerged from the field eventually, and on to a road that rose gently, from the crown of which I could see the prison and the rooftops of Stafford a few miles away. Ahead of me there was a car parked in a layby, and next to it was a man leaning on a farm gate. I said hello.

'How do,' he said back. The tailgate of his car was down,

and on it were two big baskets of pigeons. He saw me looking at them.

'I'm just waiting to release the hens,' he said. 'When they're safely home, I'll release the cocks.'

'Where's home?'

'Stoke,' he said.

I told him I'd walked from there that morning, that it had taken me about six hours so far. The birds, he said, would do it in ten minutes.

'This will be their final training session before the big race tomorrow, Yeovil to Stoke, 142 miles.'

I asked whether all the races he took part in ended in Stoke. He looked at me like I was an idiot. 'They're homing pigeons,' he said.

His name was Dave, and he was in his late forties. He'd been racing pigeons since he was born, more or less. His mum and dad had been doing it all their lives – and his grandparents before them. His birds had had a good season. A few first places. He told me that pigeons can live up to seventeen or eighteen years, that most people only raced them until they're five or six, but not him.

'Got one that was racing last year and she's twelve,' he said. 'And she were beating some of the young 'uns. Keeps 'em fit. I'd never put 'em down. No, no. They get looked after in retirement better than most people do. Reward for good service.'

Dave spoke about his birds with tenderness and wonder. He told me how tough they were, how even if they'd broken a wing they'd somehow manage to find their way home.

He looked at his watch. It was almost time to release the hens. His dad was at the other end, waiting. Once the hens were released, he'd call his dad to let him know. Three rings for the hens. His dad wouldn't pick up. That way they saved the cost of the call. And then three rings on Dave's phone from his dad when the hens were home. Then it was safe to release the cocks. The hens, he said, would sit in the pigeon loft waiting for the cocks.

It made me feel a bit sad, hearing how Dave and his dad shared this thing they both loved. I couldn't really remember ever doing anything with Pete that brought us together like that. Pete had his politics, of course, and as a child I had spent many hours with him on demonstrations and at meetings. But when I was an adult we couldn't seem to find a common currency. He had this thing where he would allow me to get within a certain touching distance, emotionally, and then he would slam the door shut, put up the walls, as if terrified by love and the vulnerability it entailed.

'The cock knows the hen is there waiting for him,' Dave said. 'He's thinking, "I'm on a promise here, I better get a wriggle on." It's like being in the pub and getting a text message from your missus. You're thinking, "I better have a half and not a pint then." Everybody knows what's going on because you're on the halves!'

I asked Dave how pigeons found their way home. Nobody really knew, he said, but there were a lot of theories. Some people reckoned it was smell, or magnetic pull. Others thought they followed motorways. Dave's dad, 'being old-fashioned', kept a copper strip in his shed, convinced that would bring them back.

Dave showed me the screen of his phone. On it was an article with the headline 'New study shows that pigeons can read words'. 'People thought I were barmy when I used to say that pigeons read road signs, but there you are,' he said, smiling. 'It made me think, now that the Britannia has been renamed the Bet365, are they flying past, thinking, "Well, that's not the Britannia, we'd best keep going!"'

He lifted the basket of hens onto the top bar of the farm gate and pulled open the lid. There was a flurry of wings and then the hens were off, flying in tight formation, doing a loop of the field and a fly-past, before straightening up and heading north, towards Stoke. Dave called his dad, let it ring three times, then hung up.

I asked him what he did for a living. Wedgwood, he said, he'd been there for over thirty years. 'I do a bit of everything, casting, foot-levelling, labouring, kiln work. People think Wedgwood's shut, but it's still going. Used to be over five thousand people working there, but now it's down to 130.'

Dave's wife worked at Duchess China in Longton. Before retiring, his mum and dad had worked in the pottery industry their whole lives too: his mum a gilder, hand-painting the gold lines on cups; his dad working in the slip house, making the clays.

He talked about Wedgwood's recent history, how the firm had been bought by an American luxury homeware business, owned in turn by a US-based private equity firm, who'd then sold it on to a Finnish company in 2015.

'We're passed around like a parcel,' Dave said. There had just been more redundancies.

Did he think the new owners could turn around the fortunes of the company?

'No chance,' he said. They had spoken to the workers on the shop floor, he told me, and asked if they had any ideas. 'I'm like, hang on, these people are probably on £50k–£60k a year. No word of what we'd get out of it. We used to have profit-sharing. We used to get stuff at Christmas. Now nothing. Not a bonus. Not a turkey. They used to send the grandkids to a pantomime at Christmas, hold parties for the families, through the welfare. All gone. The only bonus we get these days is to keep our jobs.'

He checked his watch again. It had been ten minutes since the hens had flown. But still no call from his dad. Dave called, let it ring more than three times so his dad would pick up.

'Not back yet?' he asked. 'We'll give it a few more minutes, then.'

Dave turned back to me. 'There is a union at work,' he said. 'But they've got no clout now. We had a vote over strike action because they wanted to reduce our hours. And people were too scared to vote for it, scared they'd lose their jobs. I said to them, "You're going to lose your jobs anyway." Everyone regrets it now, because sure enough they are getting rid of people.'

He told me about the devastation all this has caused on the estates in Stoke-on-Trent. 'Me dad always used to go down the working men's club a few nights a week. But it shut down and so he just sits at home.'

I asked Dave how he planned to vote in the referendum. He normally didn't vote, he said. Stoke was such a strong Labour city that there was no point. But he would be voting on the 23rd, and he would be voting out along with, he reckoned, about 90 per cent of the people he knew.

'We've sold everything off,' he said. 'We've got to start making things again. Become a great manufacturing country again, like we used to be. We're good at making things. The working class of this country have been sold out.'

His daughter, he said, was all for staying in the EU.

'She says we're going to have nothing,' Dave said. 'I told her that we've not really got much left now. How much worse could it be if we left the EU? We did all right on our own before and we can become strong again.'

Dave's phone rang. Three times. Then went silent.

'Right, then,' he said. 'Time these birds were on their way home.'

He released them and, like the hens before them, the cocks flew in a big loop before heading off north, towards their 'promise'.

'Right, then, Mike, I'd best be off,' Dave said. 'Nice to meet you.'

He jumped in his car and pulled out into the road, heading back to Stoke.

'Good luck with the race,' I shouted after him.

I entered the outskirts of Stafford. Just outside the main gates of the town's prison, I fell into step with a man. By now, spending my days outdoors, just walking, living without walls, I was used to talking to anybody and everybody, actively seeking out conversations, as if that regular communion was as essential as eating and drinking. In the world; of the world. I'm not sure what shifts – whether it is just in the self, or in the self with others – but the world becomes a much more benign place; people respond; nobody feels like a stranger, at least not in the same way that they do in the city, where my life is an endless process of moving from one enclosed place to another. Is it the walls?

I turned to the man and said hello. He said hello back. He looked at my pack and asked where I was going, and I told him I had just walked from Stoke-on-Trent and that I was staying in Stafford that night. That's a long way to walk, he said. And I told him that now, to me, it didn't seem that far, that racing pigeons could do it in ten minutes – which, free of context, was probably an odd thing to say.

We walked on together, and he asked me why I was on the road, so I told him about the People's March for Jobs and my father. He said he remembered the march, that he'd been in his mid-twenties at the time. 'My name's Ron,' he said. 'If it's OK, I'd very much like to buy you a drink.'

We found the pub I was staying in that night. Ron went

to the bar and ordered a couple of pints of lager, and then we found a table in the corner and sat down. I took off my boots and wiggled my toes.

Ron had been born in a village just outside Stafford. His dad, who had been forty-eight when Ron came along, was a lover of wildlife, and taught him about birds and trees and animals. When Ron was nine, his dad had fallen ill and they'd had to move to Stafford for his care. Ron found himself moved from a tiny school with fifteen pupils into one with 350.

'To be honest with you,' Ron said, taking a sip of his beer, 'I don't think I ever quite recovered from it.'

When his parents died, Ron had kept their council house. He'd met his current wife fourteen years ago. He'd never had kids.

'I have always read deeply about environmental things, even all those years ago,' he told me, 'and I made a conscious decision not to have children.' He'd done various jobs in his life, and was currently working as a school caretaker.

His great passion these days was wild bees – bumblebees and solitary bees. I had read about the declining numbers in the UK and asked Ron about it. There were two huge problems, he said: habitat loss and the use of pesticides called neonicotinoids, which had been devastating our bee populations. The European Union had imposed a moratorium on the use of those neonicotinoids on flowering crops that are attractive to bees. Ron was alarmed about what would happen if we voted to leave the EU.

'Whatever government was in power in this country, without those EU controls I think they'd quash the moratorium. There's so much money in pesticides,' he said. 'To me that is really worrying. Bees are responsible for pollinating one in every three mouthfuls of food that we eat globally. We can't afford to lose them. We've got two species here that are teetering on the verge of extinction and another seven that are called Biodiversity Action Plan species. They have to be in big trouble to get that little title. We've got eighteen species of social bumblebees and nine of them are in big trouble. The great yellow bumblebee and shrill carder bumblebee are teetering on the brink.'

Ron gave talks on bees locally, and spoke about them to the kids at the school where he was a caretaker.

'I keep chipping away – that's all we can do really, isn't it, and console yourself with the idea that every little bit might add up to a whole in the future. Us conservation people, it's like Dunkirk. We're just holding out for as long as we can in the hope that somebody will come to the rescue.'

It reminded me of what Danny Flynn said, back in Stoke, about people waiting to be rescued.

Ron told me that he was basically quite a contented soul. But he was worried about the future. 'Not so much for me at my age, but for the children growing up.'

Those people on TV, he said, they spend millions telling us that we need all this stuff. 'And people go for it. We've been fed this lie. I was banging on to a friend about organic food and he said, "Nah, can't afford it, it's too expensive." And I said to him, "You've just spent sixty quid on a Manchester City football shirt." And his wife says to him, "He's got you there."

'I don't think we value food at all. Those shirts cost a few quid to make and then you've got to look at where they come from, and the conditions people are working in that make these things. No one seems to be seeing the bigger picture in anything. "I want it, so I'll have it." We've been bullied into this, in my opinion.'

I'd nearly finished my third pint and could feel my eyes growing heavy, my legs stiffening up. But I wanted to ask Ron what he felt could be done about it all, how we could start repairing the damage.

'We must start with the idea of rebuilding communities, but from the ground up, not from the top down,' he said. 'When communities are strong, they will fight for their rights. We are much stronger when we work together.'

Ron thought that any new housing should have a community garden, which would not only benefit the pollinating insects but also bring people together, to look after it all.

'People start talking, share a common passion of looking after their world. Before you know it, you've got a community. The way we live now, in isolation from each other, is not doing us any good at all. We are social animals, like bees, best when we work together for the greater good. That gives us purpose. But we've become disconnected from the natural world. It's been proven that if somebody is in a hospital bed, if they can see trees or flowers out of the window, they recover quicker than people who can't. That's a medical fact!'

I said farewell to Ron and made my way up to my room. I lay on the bed fully dressed and closed my eyes. In my half sleep, I heard people outside my window, sitting on tables outside the pub, talking loudly, excitedly. When I opened my eyes, the light was still streaming through the net curtains, but the world outside was still, the people gone, replaced by the dawn chorus of birdsong. I kicked off my boots, rolled over and went back to sleep.

II

A DIFFERENT PATH
(STAFFORD TO CANNOCK)

I had breakfast in a little room at the rear of the pub. As I was eating, I caught sight of myself in the mirror that ran the length of the wall. I was fifty-two, with receding grey hair, jowls, and bags under my eyes. At Pete's funeral, many of his friends told me how much I was now looking just like him. I really hated that, but it was true.

Pete photographed well. Better than me. In the box of his things that I'd looked through before going on the walk, I had found many photo albums. They were all from his life after he had left us. I recognised a few people in the pictures, but not many. In almost every photograph, there was Pete, looking handsome – though as the years went by you could see drink and age taking their toll – with a succession of young women, perhaps half his age, around whose shoulders Pete's arm stretched. Judging by the plants and the architecture and the light, most of the pictures had been taken on foreign holidays.

While Pete was gallivanting around the Med with younger women, my mum was dying. I hated him for what he had done: to my mum, to me, to our family. I don't think I stopped hating him until the day he died, hollowed out by cancer, like my mum before him.

When I first got together with my ex-wife, I took her to meet Pete for the first time. I was in my early thirties, and Pete his late fifties. She was a model, six feet tall, bright and smart. By then, Pete was living in his flat in the run-down council block in south London, sleeping on the mattress laid out on top of two old doors. The Communist Party had collapsed a few years before, and Pete was back on the tools. He seemed a bit lost; his drinking had spiralled, the flat was a mess, dirty clothes on the floor, empty whisky bottles everywhere. I remember standing there, surrounded by filth, with my arm around my goddess of a girlfriend, looking at Pete. I felt safe from his mess, that somehow I had escaped from 'our' story.

A couple of years after that visit, I got the call saying that Pete had fallen into a drunken sleep with a pan left on the cooker and nearly died from inhaling smoke. I went to see him in hospital. By then my short marriage was falling apart, and so was I, my own drinking getting out of control. I stood there watching Pete sleeping, with tubes coming out of him, a breathing mask fixed to his face. I reached out and touched his upturned hand, and his calloused fingers lightly, delicately gripped mine.

I turned to the pub mirror: the jowls, the bags under the eyes, the toll the years were taking. There was Pete staring back at me. 'When one stays wound-identified one will hate the face in the mirror for its similarity to those responsible for the wounding,' wrote James Hollis in *The Middle Passage*, his seminal text on finding meaning in midlife, 'and feel self-hate for one's failure to break free of the past.'

I smiled at myself.

I walked along Gaolgate Street and then onto the footpath beside the River Sow, running through the centre of Stafford, tendrils of green algae whip-cracking in the fast flow.

At Milford I got off the towpath and turned south, past the gatehouse of Shugborough Hall, the ancestral home of the

Earls of Lichfield until, following the death of the fourth earl in 1960, it had been handed to the National Trust in lieu of death duties.

Shugborough was right on the edge of one of the Midlands' greatest assets, Cannock Chase – at twenty-six square miles, mainland Britain's smallest designated Area of Outstanding Natural Beauty. I was soon walking through its wildness, following my compass and my OS map, traipsing through the bracken and the gorse that smelled like Hawaiian Tropic, sending pheasants scurrying. In the birch woodlands and coniferous forests I lost my bearings, wandering up and down the folds and crevices of the land, which were short and steep and a shock to my legs and lungs after my relatively flat journey up to that point.

I felt as if I was moving towards to the edges of my territory, for Cannock Chase had been the place we went to on school nature trips. The geography teacher would want to talk to us about the underlying Triassic Bunter formations, the endemic Cannock Chase berry, the Iron Age hill forts and the rare and endangered birds that inhabited the heathlands, such as the migrant nightjars. But all we wanted to ask her about were the Beasts of Cannock – the werewolves and the pumas and the giant black dogs and the UFOs and the ghost of the little girl with coal-black pits for eye sockets and even Bigfoot. For all of them had been reported as roaming the Chase over the years, ever since the nineteenth century. It was that kind of place.

And adders. Cannock Chase was famous for its adders. So even if we couldn't see an alien or Bigfoot, we might get to see Britain's only venomous snake. Now that was the kind of thing that could make or break a school field trip.

I emerged from woodland and met a man out walking with a Jack Russell. I asked the dog's name as I gave it a stroke, and the man told me he – the dog – was called Ben. As usual, I didn't ask the man's name.

'Have you seen any adders?' the man asked me.

I had not, I told him.

He dug in his pocket and pulled out a phone.

'You've got to be careful round here,' he said, scrolling through pictures on the phone's screen. 'Look!' And he held up a photograph of a beautiful pale brown snake, coiled on a rock, with a dark brown zigzag pattern running down its back.

'Female,' he said. 'Saw her this morning. They like to come out of the woodlands on sunny days like this, for the warmth and the light. They can kill a dog.'

He looked over to where Ben was snuffling through some bracken.

I told him I'd be careful and walked away. What I would have given to see an adder on Cannock Chase. What a thrill to imagine such a creature living in Britain in 2016. That we still had such wildlife. Surviving. I think I'd even have preferred seeing an adder to Bigfoot.

I came across a giant piece of granite sitting lonely in a clearing surrounded by trees. It was the Katyn Memorial, in honour of '25,000 Polish prisoners of war and professional classes who were murdered on Stalin's orders' in 1940, many of them killed in the Katyn Forest in western Russia.

On top of the rock was a white eagle, from Poland's coat of arms. Fresh flowers lay on the plinth. The memorial, originally built and dedicated in 1979 by the Polish community in the West Midlands, had been well looked after and renovated over the years. In the current version of the inscription, below the line remembering the dead had been etched into the marble plaque: 'Finally admitted by the USSR in 1990 after 50 years of shameful denial of the truth.'

Preserved below the memorial were phials of soil from the Katyn Forest. What a lonely death those people must have suffered, deep in a remote wood, miles from home. And how apt that Poles in Britain had chosen this lonely spot in a wood, miles from 'home', to remember them.

A few hundred yards further on, I came to the Commonwealth War Cemetery, rows of brilliant white headstones marking the graves of British and New Zealand troops who died in both world wars, the headstones, in precise lines, sitting on an immaculately kept lawn within a frame of equally immaculate and fiercely clipped privet hedges.

At the cemetery's centre was a simple white stone cross, and either side of that a neat set of three silver birch trees. The perfect symmetry and order was in stark contrast to the wildness of the Chase surrounding it, and I wondered if the dominion over nature, the restoration of order over it, and the almost pathological neatness seen in war cemeteries everywhere, played an important part in our recovery after the chaos of conflict.

A few hundred yards from the Commonwealth cemetery was a German military cemetery with nearly five thousand graves, the final resting place of Germans and Austrians who died while serving in the military or held as internees during the two world wars. The dead lay beneath gentle slopes on either side of the cemetery, separated by a little valley. On the far side of the graveyard, a couple stood silently before a headstone, and then knelt and placed some flowers on the ground. The man put his arms around the shoulders of the woman and pulled her towards him.

The last few miles into Cannock were tough. After I'd walked across the Chase, deeply embedded in its wildness, the road symphony seemed more invasive than ever, and the things that might ordinarily wash over me – the loud music coming from cars, the squealing of brakes, the constant hiss of tyres on tar-mac – jangled and irritated me, as if my nervous system had been instantly placed back on high alert.

That anxiety got worse as I walked into Cannock town centre, where, forced now into following a prescribed route, as metal railings funnelled me towards crossings, I had to wait, impotent, as the cars thundered past, until a little green man flashed up, and that infernal beeping commenced, my brain now linked to my environment only through harsh noises and bright cues.

I walked across the bus station, up some steps and into a cafe. The woman behind the counter asked me what I would like, speaking in a Black Country accent. I realised that, having started the day in a town where they spoke with a Stafford-shire accent, somewhere along my route through the forests and heathland I had crossed a line to a place where the accent was completely different.

As I was now in the Black Country – or, perhaps, almost, because no two Black Country men or women will ever agree on where it starts or ends – there was only one thing to order.

'Can I have a hot pork bap, please?' I said.

'Stuffing and crackling, bab?' the woman asked. I had also moved from the land of shugs and ducks to the land of babs.

'Oh, yes, please,' I said.

While I was waiting for my pork bap, I phoned my sister, Sue, at her home in Wednesbury, about ten miles south. I was going to be staying with her for the next few nights, as the People's March route had meandered around the West Midlands, before heading towards London. My brother-in-law, Phil, picked up the phone.

'Where am ya?' he asked.

'I've made it to the Black Country,' I told him. 'I'm in Cannock.'

'That's not the Black Country!' he said. 'Yam a fool!'

Sue came on the line and said she'd be along to pick me up. I collected my pork roll, took it outside, and sat on the steps of the bus station, where I unwrapped it and squeezed the gooey mess of pork, gravy, stuffing and crackling between the two halves of the bap, so that it oozed out of the sides and dribbled down my fingers. I then took a big bite. A hot pork bap with gravy and stuffing and crackling would be my last meal on death row, no question.

In front of me, at the foot of the steps, a dozen young lads had gathered, all wearing hoodies and tracksuit bottoms and brilliant-white trainers. They must have been in their late teens, and again I felt that recently acquired sense of being a little intimidated, vulnerable, in the presence of a group of young men.

One of the older youths was louder than the others, and walked with a great swagger, as if his testicles were monstrously swollen. He dug his hand in his pocket and pulled out some little white pills. The group crowded around him, looking at his upturned hand.

'Yam been to prison?' one of the younger men asked him.

'Yeah,' he said. 'Fucking breeze.' Some of the youngsters looked at him with something like awe, while a couple of the others giggled and pushed each other. I thought about all of those young men lying under the earth just a few miles up the road. But if there was something to be gleaned from the thought, I didn't know what it was.

Sue took me back to her house, just up the road from the roaring M6. She made some tea and then we sat chatting around her kitchen table for a while, catching up. I loved staying with my sister. She was two years older than me, and had lived in the same house for nearly thirty years. In that same time, I had lived in over thirty different places, most of them 120 miles down the road, in London.

Sue's life revolved around her family. Her two children lived a few miles away, and she saw them, and her grandchildren, daily. I'd never had children. She had nursed her mother-in-law through dementia until her death in Sue's front room. Way before that, in the eighties, Sue had nursed our mother through her final cancer in that same room, where she had also died.

The stories of Sue's life were all there, in that house, in its floorboards, in its brickwork. They were there in the street where she lived, where she knew everybody, and they were there in Wednesbury's high street, along which a walk with Sue was like a gathering of friends, to the bus station at the end, where she worked as a supervisor, helping passengers to find the right buses and dealing with the daily dramas of lost purses, lost children, cancelled buses, and, occasionally, disruptive people, usually drunk, whom she always treated with tenderness and compassion.

I'd sometimes watched her at the bus station while she worked. And it was always with wonder that I watched her navigate her life. For the most effective maps were not the paper ones we bought but the ones we made ourselves, carried within us. Sue followed her map's lines and trails every day. There was the park where she first held hands in the rain, aged eighteen, with the man who was to become her husband; just opposite her house was where her daughter passed her driving test; there, outside the butcher's in the high street, she'd seen her son with his first girlfriend and felt the incipient pangs of loss; there, in the front room, our mother had taken her last breath, and Sue had been there, holding her hand. Sue had been the first on the scene after the phone call from the police to say that Pete had been found dead, on the boat, nearby. She'd helped carry his body out of the boat. By the time I'd arrived, from London, the body was gone.

My map might have been much bigger. But it was too diffuse to be of much use to me, really. It was like a life of abstraction, of ideas not events, a world that existed in the mind, not so much in the heart.

I had often tried to work out why Sue had stayed and I'd left. Up until I was around eighteen, all I'd ever wanted to do was live in Birmingham, the place where my map was. I had my name down on the waiting list to become a train driver. I would call the depot every week to see whether my name had inched anywhere nearer the top of the list. It never had. My backup plan was to work in a sports shop.

I'd been expelled from school when I was seventeen. Like Danny Flynn, I was a bit of a dick. Mum persuaded me to go to sixth form and get some A-levels, and then to go to a local college and get a degree, a journey she had made herself.

In the second term of my first year, I broke into the student union bar and stole a lot of beer. It had closed for the afternoon and I was still thirsty. I was often very thirsty in those days. I also took the cigarette machine off the wall and took it back to my room in the halls of residence. It didn't take the college security guards very long to find the culprit. As I say, a bit of a dick. I was thrown out of college. They only allowed me back onto my course after months of Mum's persistent petitioning. I owe her so much.

By the time I finally, miraculously, graduated in 1986, I knew that I would never be a train driver, or be happy with a job in a shop. I would be leaving my home town. Something fundamental had shifted in the early 1980s: the inner-city riots of 1981, the mass unemployment in industrial towns, the sense of decay, the beginnings of the assault on the working class, the destruction of a culture. Suddenly, everyone seemed to be talking about making money. The music in the charts was full of it. The yuppie had arrived. Thatcher attacked the whole idea of society – a sentimental idea, outdated, a brake on progress. We must all stand on our own two feet! You couldn't expect anybody to look after you but yourself! Aspiration and ambition were the only show in town . . .

Back in 1981, Iain Picton, the national chairman of the Young Conservatives, had suggested that the riots were a natural reaction to mass unemployment and the despair it was creating. The then Employment Secretary, Norman Tebbit, responded with his now infamous quote: 'I grew up in the thirties with an unemployed father. He didn't riot. He got on his bike and looked for work, and he kept looking till he found it.'

Tebbit, the son of working-class parents, who'd grown up in Ponders End, Middlesex, had been a new kind of Tory, in many ways a poster boy for the Thatcher project. He'd spoken with a recognisably working-class accent, in stark contrast to the patrician Tory voices we'd been used to, leading Harold Macmillan to comment: 'Heard a chap on the radio this morning talking with a Cockney accent. They tell me he is one of Her Majesty's ministers.'

Tebbit later claimed that the meaning of his 'on yer bike' quote had been taken out of context and that he was simply saying that rioting could never be justified by unemployment. But for many, myself included, it was a totemic statement, one that said the world was changing, and that staying still and fighting against those changes was as futile as protesting against the sun coming up.

If I look back to 1981, and also think about those questions from some of the original marchers about why I hadn't joined them, it seems to me that maybe, even back then, I thought I could see the futility in the fight, could see the writing on the wall. It shames me to think like that now, to think that when others were fighting, I was hitching my wagon to Thatcher's vision. But there it is.

In the period after I left college and started working in advertising, I would return to Birmingham for visits, wearing my cashmere overcoat bought in Milan, pretentiously clutching my Filofax. I'd assumed that Sue would be proud of me. But she just seemed embarrassed and angry. At the time, I'd put it down to grief for our mum, and jealousy, because I had escaped, and she hadn't. I don't think like that any more. I think she was angry because her map, with its contours of belonging and connection, which had had to be severely redrawn when Pete walked out on us, had been completely ripped up by mum's death. My leaving had been another stab in her heart.

I think she saw it as a betrayal, a rejection of the values and culture that had formed us. She was angry that I'd run away from the mess and the pain of our mother's final years and months. And she was angry with her brother, visiting from London, speaking with an affected new accent, who now so obviously looked down his nose at this place, her home, her map.

Did she also see me as like our dad? After all, we had both left for London – Pete in 1983 to take up his job with the Communist Party of Great Britain; me in 1986 to make my fortune. Left our mum, left her.

12

THE GREAT EDUCATION TRICK
(CANNOCK TO WOLVERHAMPTON)

Sue dropped me off at Cannock bus station the next morning for that day's fourteen-mile walk to Wolverhampton. After saying goodbye, I walked through Cannock's pedestrianised shopping area. For the first time since leaving Liverpool I was walking without a rucksack, sitting as it was at Sue's house, and I felt as if I was floating, my feet not really sure how to behave, as if they'd been freed from gravity.

The sun was shining, the blossom swirling around in the strong breeze like snow. I passed a war memorial, in front of which a man played an accordion. I dropped a pound on the rug he'd laid out in front of him and, when he'd finished his tune, he thanked me with what sounded like an Eastern European accent. I asked him where he was from. Albania, he replied. Coming back to the area I'd grown up in was making me realise why asking that question was now so important to me.

On the outskirts of Cannock, I passed an Asda superstore. Opposite it was a lovely park, with neat trees and flower beds and clipped hedges, indistinguishable from municipal parks up and down the land. But there did seem to be one difference. On one of the brick pillars at the entrance to the park was a sign that read: 'This park is the property of Asda Stores Limited and is provided as an amenity for the people of Cannock.'

Private parks! Was nothing sacred any more? It seemed not.

I thought about those maps that we carry inside us, that help us navigate our world, that tell us where we belong, that mark out the connections, our common paths. And I thought how those maps might look to us when huge swathes of them were stamped 'private'.

But so inured have we become to the selling-off of state assets to the private sector over the past three decades or so that it has almost become part of natural law, despite the surveys that regularly confirm overwhelming support for more state control of key industries. A YouGov poll in 2013 found that a large majority of respondents believed the state should be able to control energy prices (74 per cent) and public transport fares (72 per cent). That same survey found 67 per cent believed the Royal Mail sell-off was wrong, with only 22 per cent supporting it. Even Tory voters (by 48 per cent to 43 per cent) opposed it, and the figures among Ukip voters were an extraordinary 67 per cent against and just 25 per cent in favour – indicating that Ukip's message on immigration was only a part of the party's attraction to its core demographic, those feeling increasingly left behind and marginalised.

When it came to the question of renationalising the railways and the energy companies, the same poll found 66 per cent and 68 per cent in favour respectively. I guess most people might arrive at such conclusions after struggling to name a single privatised industry that had provided an improved service and better value for money for its users, the two things that advocates of privatisation always claim it delivers. Yet the sell-offs just keep coming. Now they've got our public spaces in their sights.

In October 2010, during the first year of the Conservative-Liberal Democrat coalition government, Caroline Spelman, then Environment Secretary, had announced plans to sell off about half of the 1.85 million acres of woodland overseen by the Forestry

Commission, a government quango. The sell-offs, she said, were necessary to reduce the country's deficit. The Department for Environment, Food and Rural Affairs had been hit hard by the spending review, set to lose around 30 per cent of its £2.9 billion budget by 2015.

Allan MacKenzie, secretary of the Forestry Commission Trade Unions, told the *Sunday Telegraph*: 'Once we've sold it, it never comes back. Once it is sold, restrictions would be placed on the land which means the public don't get the same access ... The current system means a vast amount of people can enjoy forests and feel ownership of them. It is an integral part of society.'

In the end, in February 2011, after ferocious opposition, a humiliated Spelman announced in the House of Commons that the government was abandoning the plan, admitting that 'we got this one wrong'.

It would be comforting to think the government had learned its lesson from the forests episode and the outrage it generated. And perhaps it had. Because the privatisation of our country's 27,000 parks wasn't happening as a consequence of a stark Commons announcement, and therefore likely to attract co-ordinated opposition – it was being surreptitiously carried out through the drip-drip impoverishment of our local authorities, via year-on-year budget cuts from Whitehall, which left them having to make unenviable choices between offering services such as social care, which they had a statutory obligation to provide, or parks, which they did not.

In 2016 the Heritage Lottery Fund published its second UK Public Parks report, showing the changing face of funding for our parks and green spaces. Parks had received £850 million in lottery funding, which had helped to regenerate and maintain many of our communal spaces, with the help of the 5,900 friends groups in the UK, community organisations that supported their local parks through volunteering and fundraising. Friends groups themselves generated about £50 million a year to keep our parks going. And it could be argued that revenue from the National Lottery was yet another tax on poorer people in the UK, seeing as it was predominantly them who played it.

Yet despite the input of lottery money, half of local authorities had sold off parks and green spaces or transferred the management of them to others in the three years up to 2016, with the figure expected to rise to 59 per cent by 2019. In short, we were in the midst of the largest sell-off of common space since the enclosures of the eighteenth century.

The same report found that 50 per cent of local authorities had transferred outdoor sports facilities to community groups, and that 22.5 per cent of funding for parks now came from external sources, a figure that was also expected to rise considerably in the coming years.

Already we were seeing the future of our 'public' parks. In 2015, in south-west London, the private company Go Ape had started renting space in Battersea Park from Wandsworth Council and was charging parents between £20 and £35 for their children to be able to use their adventure playground.

In Bexley, south-east London, there was a ferocious campaign against plans to sell off four green municipal spaces across the borough to housing developers as the council sought to find £56 million in savings by 2020.

A survey by We Own It, a group that campaigns for public ownership of public services, found that over 70 per cent of respondents thought the privatisation of our parks was unacceptable.

But what difference does it make if the bench we sit on while we eat our sandwiches, or the grass we walk across while exercising our dogs, is owned and run by Asda, and not Cannock Chase Council?

A look at what's happening to former public spaces in many of our cities is salutary. In Liverpool, it is now possible to walk from Lime Street station almost to the banks of the River Mersey without setting foot on public land. Even more extraordinary, all of that land is now owned by one company, the Duke of Westminster's Grosvenor Estate. Liverpool One, described as a shopping, residential and leisure development, incorporates thirty-four streets previously owned by the Liverpool municipal authority, effectively putting a huge chunk of a UK city centre into private hands.

What was happening in Liverpool was also happening in, among other places, Birmingham (Brindleyplace), Bristol (Cabot Circus), Portsmouth (Gunwharf Quays), Exeter (Princesshay), and in London's Canary Wharf and King's Cross (Granary Square).

This privatisation of public spaces begs many questions. Whose rules are people using these spaces expected to follow? Those laid out by civic legislation, formulated by democratically elected bodies? Or arbitrary rules drawn up by the new owners and enforced by armies of private security personnel?

In February 2016, Anna Minton, university lecturer and author of *Ground Control*, which records the privatisation of public spaces in Britain, told the *Observer* about one of her students who was at Canary Wharf doing a project. 'There's an art installation tucked away somewhere and he was there taking notes,' she said, 'but was taken to a control centre to prove who he was.'

A year earlier, Nico Goodden, a photographer, was stopped taking pictures in Granary Square after being told by a private security guard that he needed a permit. The year before that, Drew Gardner, another photographer, was told to put his camera away by a private security guard while taking pictures of London's St Pancras station.

The Intu group, which owns shopping centres throughout the UK, has a code of conduct that includes 'please make sure any clothing with a hood attached is worn down', 'no swearing [or] shouting' and 'no running'.

'It's about whether we have a city that looks to people first and foremost as consumers, is welcoming only to a certain class of ABC1 shopper, or is a diverse, open and inclusive city that offers a wealth of experience for all sorts of people, young and old,' Anna Minton had said.

These sentiments were echoed in the same *Observer* article by the sociologist Paul Jones, from the University of Liverpool. 'It's a question of what are cities for? Who gets the right to these spaces?' he told the paper. 'Who has the right to be where, when and how?'

Minton raised a further key point about the increasing privatisation of urban outdoor spaces, so often heavily securitised with CCTV and guards: that it restricts the possibility of public protest.

'The right to assembly is a key political right,' she said. 'It's at the heart of democratic representation from the nineteenth century onwards and now it's being threatened.'

We had a taste of how corporations might threaten the right to protest back in 2011, when the Occupy movement, demanding curbs against the growing powers of multinationals, was barred from entering Paternoster Square, the location of the London Stock Exchange, by a court order obtained by the owners of the land, the multinational Mitsubishi Estate Company. Oh, the irony.

This threat to democracy and accountability was likely to get worse, Paul Jones had suggested, as these private companies became more powerful, weaving themselves into the tapestry of public life. He told the *Observer* that the proposals for Liverpool Waters – a vast sixty-acre plot, listed as a World Heritage Site, where the city's council had recently approved one of the biggest planning applications in the UK – would see the management company, Peel Holdings, 'deliver public services such as schools and training in areas of the city that are extremely deprived. The local authority can't afford to do it.'

At a protest against the privatisation of public space in February 2016, the comedian and activist Mark Thomas attacked the government's introduction of Public Spaces Protection Orders, which allow councils to make activities such as sleeping rough illegal in an attempt to drive homeless people from our towns and city centres. As poverty and homelessness grow in twenty-first-century Britain, in no small part due to government cuts, and as we sell off our public spaces, where were these people, increasingly excluded from the common areas, supposed to go?

The migration of public life into the hands of the private sector and the impoverishment of local authorities may not be entirely unrelated to the fact that, according to analysis by the Equality Trust, the hundred richest families in Britain had seen their combined wealth increase by at least £55 billion between 2010 and 2016. Gerald Grosvenor, the sixth Duke of Westminster, whose company now owns half of Liverpool, was estimated at the time of his death in 2016 to be worth £9.35 billion (a sum, incidentally, that his estate avoided paying inheritance tax on because the bulk was placed in family trusts).

By contrast, the Equality Trust found, median household income in Britain had increased by just £4 a week since 2010, and median wealth by £8,600.

'Extreme inequality is ravaging society,' said the organisation's executive director, Wanda Wyporska, when the analysis was published. 'Where inequality is high, we see increased rates of violence, mental and physical ill health and lack of trust . . . If politicians are serious about building a genuinely shared society, then they urgently need to address this dangerous concentration of power and wealth and tackle our extreme inequality.'

I wasn't holding my breath. The only wonder is why we were not all taking to the streets with flaming torches. But then again, we probably wouldn't be allowed to.

As I looked at the Cannock park, with its 'Owned by Asda' plaque on the entrance, I thought about Pete. When I was a little boy, he used to drag me around building sites, selling copies of Robert Tressell's *The Ragged-Trousered Philanthropists* from the boot of his car to labourers and brickies. 'This, Mick, is the most important book ever written,' he would say to me, adding that even though it had been published in 1914, every word of it was true today and would be true in the future, too.

He would read out sections of his own well-thumbed copy to me, though I was too young to understand what it all meant. His favourite bit was a speech by the rebel and hero Owen:

'Poverty is . . . caused by Private Monopoly. That is the present system. They have monopolised everything that it is possible to monopolise; they have got the whole earth, the minerals in the earth and the streams that water the earth. The only reason they have not monopolised the daylight and the air is that it is not possible to do it. If it were possible to construct huge gasometers and to draw together and compress within them the whole of the atmosphere, it would have been done long ago, and we should have been compelled to work for them in order to get money to buy air to breathe.'

The suburbs of Wolverhampton replaced the fields and hedgerows, and I passed the derelict twelve-acre site of the former

Springfield Brewery, now reduced to crumbling red-brick walls, broken windows and rusting ironwork. Brewing at the site had ceased in the early 1990s, and vandalism and arson attacks had left it in its sorry state. In 2014 the University of Wolverhampton had announced that it was taking over the site, and aimed to turn it into a £60 million campus.

If the privatisation of so many of our public services has been one of the biggest changes in Britain in the past thirty-odd years, then the growth of higher education has been another. But, like the privatisations, it's sometimes difficult to tell exactly what the net gain to the nation has been, apart from an awful lot of young people with an awful lot of debt.

In the 1950s, just 3.4 per cent of the population went to university. Between 1960 and 1970, the number of graduates more than doubled. And 1980 was perhaps the high-water mark for equality of access to degree-level study, when student grants were increased from £380 to £1,430. By the time I went to West Midlands College of Higher Education in 1983, approximately 10 per cent of the population was taking a degree and the numbers were rising. Coming from my poor background, the grant system had been a godsend.

Margaret Thatcher had been ideologically concerned about the growth of higher education, and although it continued to expand after she came to power in 1979, funding did not – the amount spent per student fell by 47 per cent during the years until the Tories lost the 1997 election.

In 1981, against a backdrop of cuts, universities were given just one month to slash their budgets by an average of 18 per cent. Already this story has a very familiar feel to it: funding cuts leading to an impoverished, malfunctioning sector, leading to privatisation.

In 1984 the Education Secretary, Keith Joseph, first mooted

plans that would force parents to contribute to tuition fees, but in the face of protest they were abandoned. In 1989 the Tories froze grants for all but the poorest and introduced student loans. The commercialisation of higher education had begun.

In 1992 the Further and Higher Education Act was passed, allowing all polytechnics and Scottish central institutions to become universities and award their own degrees. Overnight, the number of universities almost doubled, from forty-seven to eighty-five. At the turn of the century a second wave of institutions gained university status, and by 2016 a further forty-nine had been created, taking the nation's total to 130 universities.

The thorny issue of how to fund this expanding sector was becoming politically toxic. In 1997 New Labour was elected on a manifesto that included a pledge that 'the costs of student maintenance should be repaid by graduates on an income-related basis'. That same year, the Dearing report recommended that students should pay roughly 25 per cent of the cost of tuition but that government grants should remain in place. In 1998 New Labour's Education Secretary, David Blunkett, announced that tuition fees of up to £1,000 would be paid by every student in each year of study, and that the student grant of £1,710 was to be abolished and replaced by student loans.

At the Labour Party conference in 1999, Tony Blair declared that the 'class war is over', but that the 'struggle for true equality has only just begun'. A big part of that struggle, Blair said, would involve getting more people from poorer backgrounds into university. New Labour lifted the cap on student numbers. 'Today,' Blair said, 'I set a target of 50 per cent of young adults going into higher education in the next century.'

In 2001 Labour was re-elected with a manifesto pledge that it would not introduce 'top-up fees'. But just two years later the government published a white paper setting out proposals to allow universities to set their own tuition fees, up to a cap of £3,000 a year. The fees were to be repaid once graduates earned above £15,000. Blair faced a backbench rebellion on the motion, but scraped through, winning by just five votes. Iain Duncan Smith, then Conservative leader, pledged that all university fees would be abolished under any future Tory government and condemned the fees as 'a tax on learning'.

By 2005 almost all universities had set their fees at the maximum level of £3,000 per year. In 2006, despite the fees, universities said that they still needed £1.3 billion in extra funding to accommodate all of the extra students. That same year, the new Conservative leader, David Cameron, reneged on Duncan Smith's 2003 pledge and said that tuition fees were unavoidable.

In 2010 the Browne report on higher education funding recommended that the cap on fees should be removed entirely, with graduates paying off their loans once they earned above £21,000. In the run-up to the 2010 general election, the Liberal Democrat leader Nick Clegg famously pledged to oppose any increase in tuition fees. Two years later, in Clegg and Cameron's Tory-Lib Dem coalition government, the cap on fees almost trebled to £9,000. Almost all universities instantly started charging students the maximum amount. Tony Blair's magic 50 per cent number was finally achieved in 2011–12.

In 2014–15 the government increased the cap on university places in England by 30,000 students, and from 2015–16 removed the cap altogether. That year saw 532,300 people enter higher education in the UK, the numbers swollen by students from overseas – who could be charged fees of up to £35,000 a year – and an 11 per cent rise in those from the EU. The number of graduates in 2015 represented a 2,000 per cent increase from 1960, when 22,500 full-time students obtained first degrees in the UK. In 2015 universities received nearly £9 billion in undergraduate tuition fee income, the highest level on record.

Higher education has been a great success story, not least for university vice-chancellors, who in 2015 commanded an average salary of £272,432 – 6.7 times the average pay of their staff. The highest single earner that year was Professor Andrew Hamilton at the University of Oxford, who received £462,000.

It has been an extraordinary shift in the space of a few decades, moving higher education from the margins of public life in Britain to centre stage, and has made getting a degree as vital to the life chances of young people today as, say, getting decent O-levels was to my generation's. A 2010 study by the UCL Institute of Education, which tracked children born between 2000 and 2002, found that an extraordinary 97 per cent of 'millennium mothers' wanted their offspring to go to university.

As part of his 1999 speech, Tony Blair had said, 'In today's world, there is no such thing as too clever. The more you know, the further you'll go.'

But how true was that? A 2015 report from the Chartered Institute of Personnel and Development (CIPD) found that six out of ten university graduates were in non-graduate jobs, warning that over-qualification had reached saturation point, and was leading to employers asking for degrees when recruiting for low-skilled work in call centres, bars and coffee shops.

The report compared the situation in Britain with that of Germany, with its strong history of vocational training, where about 10 per cent of graduates were in non-graduate positions. 'The assumption that we will transition to a more productive, higher-value, higher-skilled economy just by increasing the conveyor belt of graduates is proven to be flawed,' said the CIPD's chief executive, Peter Cheese.

According to the 2014 Labour Force Survey, 11.5 per cent of childminders are graduates, as are one in six call-centre staff and about a quarter of cabin crew and theme park attendants – all jobs that didn't require a degree. Other careers that now routinely demand a degree include policing, nursing, hotel management and estate agency.

Perhaps just as pertinently, the non-graduate schoolmates of all these graduates taking up traditionally non-graduate jobs were finding themselves increasingly locked out of the labour market for all but the most menial and low-paying jobs.

The mantra supporting the expansion of higher education has always been that graduates can expect their investment in education to be repaid handsomely over the course of a working life. In the first decade of this century, Whitehall bandied about the figure that graduates could expect to earn £400,000 more over their working lifetime than non-graduates. After the 2008 financial crash, that figure was revised downwards to £100,000 – close to parity with non-graduate lifetime earnings after you take into account the debt from studying, and amounting to just £2,500 a year extra over a forty-year career.

And what of the much-vaunted claims that higher education breaks down class barriers and is a key driver of upward social mobility? Up to a point. But the career prospects of a graduate emerging from the London School of Economics with a first-class degree, and moving into a City job paying six figures, are going to be very different from someone doing business studies at one of the newer universities in the north-east, say, who decides that they want to stay and work in the same area.

A 2016 survey by a team of researchers from Cambridge, Harvard, the UCL Institute of Education and the Institute for Fiscal Studies found that students from the richest families did far better than everyone else in the graduate job market – and earned far more than even those who'd done the same course at the same university at the same time.

This all begins to make Tony Blair's claims that 'the more you know, the further you'll go' look at best naive, and at worst like a monumental con. Keith Mullin in Liverpool, now a lecturer himself, had seen the indebtedness his students face on graduation. Although he believed passionately that education was a key driver in increasing the life chances of poorer people, it could only really work if it was free to access.

'They leave college with so much debt that their aspirations are curtailed. They are far too busy just trying to survive,' he'd told me. 'How do you control a disaffected generation who are a little bit casual about money? You get them into debt. Then their whole priorities change. The privatisation of education is a complete betrayal of a generation and generations to come.'

I'd asked Keith why he thought recent governments had been so obsessed with getting half of our young people into higher education. He thought it represented the perfect solution for a post-industrial society that had fewer and fewer of the jobs that young working-class kids would have traditionally taken up.

'On the one hand, you've got all these kids in huge debt,' he'd said. 'On the other, at a stroke you get to remove millions of young people aged eighteen to twenty-one from the unemployment figures. And when they leave college, they enter a system where we reward the few over the majority, and we do that so that the majority keeps striving to be part of the few. Fighting each other. It's a warped system that we run. Warped, but you've got to admire the genius in it.'

The Cambridge economist Ha-Joon Chang, in his book *23 Things They Don't Tell You About Capitalism*, likened the scramble for degrees to people standing up at a theatre or a football match to get a better view. As each row stood up, those behind them had to stand up too. In the end, no one could see the play or the match any better, and everyone was a lot more uncomfortable.

On the road into Wolverhampton, I crossed over the canal, and stood on the bridge as a narrowboat passed underneath. Back in 2005, my sister and her husband must have passed under this very bridge on their new boat as they brought it back from the manufacturer in Liverpool.

Sue had remortgaged her house to help buy the boat, which was to be lived on by Pete, then homeless and workless after the building jobs he'd reverted to in London had either dried up or begun to be too much for a hard-drinking, hard-smoking man now in his mid-sixties.

Sue had found a permanent mooring for Pete in Smethwick, a mile or so from where he'd grown up. A deal had been struck: Pete would live on the boat, but for a few weeks of the year he would hand it over to Sue and Phil for their holidays cruising the canals. Pete would look after their house while they were away.

That plan lasted as long as it took Pete to move on board and turn the pristine white paintwork yellow with his chain-smoking, burn holes in the upholstery, and leave mountains of filthy dishes permanently piled up in the sink and rotting food in the fridge and the cupboards.

We never seemed to learn, Sue or I, that this was what Pete did to acts of kindness, especially from us. Every time we made ourselves vulnerable to him, tried to forge some kind of intimate, trusting relationship with him, he recoiled, sabotaged it.

Sue was heartbroken by Pete's behaviour, to the extent that she could no longer bring herself to visit him on the boat. In Pete's papers, I'd found a copy of a long letter he'd written to Sue, in response to one from her raising the possibility of them selling the boat and reducing her financial burden if Pete wouldn't look after it properly.

Pete started his reply by stating how important the boat was to him and the big contribution he made to the community, delivering coal and diesel to the other boats, going around keeping the common spaces tidy, and cooking a three-course meal daily for his neighbour, who had cancer.

'I give more to the moorers than they give me,' he wrote. 'However, when in need they are all there for me.' He had underlined the word 'all'.

He went on to tell Sue how much he'd appreciated her help with the mooring fees over the years, but then came the recoil, the attack, to offset the terror of vulnerability. 'I guess more than you appreciate the sacrifice Norma and myself made in the sixties giving you a decent childhood,' he wrote.

Pete then reverted to the back foot, telling Sue again how important the community was to him, how happy and secure he felt there. 'A move to a sink council estate, I would find devastating, the loss of security and friends unbearable to contemplate, such a move, to start all over again, would be too much for me,' he wrote. 'At the age of 72, I need no hassle. I trust you will respect my position. Pete.'

Attached to that carbon-copy letter by a paperclip in Pete's box was Sue's reply. It was painful to think of him filing them together.

'Dad. We all make sacrifices as parents but never tell our children,' she wrote. 'We have the choice to have children so we do whatever is within our powers to make them happy. Trying to make me feel guilty about my childhood is very unproductive . . . You are nasty and hurtful when you have been drinking, but you won't ever see that. You will end up a very sad and lonely man if you keep alienating people. Don't you ever wonder why Mike doesn't keep in touch?

'You chose not to have family roots. Perhaps that's why I choose to live my life surrounded by close family. You have always criticised me for my choice, telling me I am suppressed and under-achieving. Why couldn't you have just been happy for me? You have pushed people away all of your life. I don't understand why you do that and don't suppose I ever will. No matter how much you have hurt me over the years, I will always be here for you because you are my dad and that is what love is. Sue x'

The last sentence had brought tears to my eyes. Sue had not given up. Could not give up. I don't think children can ever truly stop trying. Indeed, what was my walk if not that?

I thought about Pete's upbringing. By all accounts a shy, sensitive boy, with alcoholic parents, living in poverty and chaos, one of six children largely left to fend for themselves, leaving school at fifteen, illiterate. It was my mum who had taught him to read. 'If we'd have been growing up today,' Pete always liked to tell us, 'all of the kids would have been taken into care.'

I could understand why he might have told himself early on that lasting bonds were too unreliable, and that the only way to survive life was to treat love with suspicion and contempt. In that interpretation, trashing the boat would have been entirely consistent; it would have kept him safe.

I wasn't sure that Sue was right in saying that Pete made a choice not to have close family ties, though. I don't think he felt like he had a choice.

13

THE SHIRT OFF OUR BACKS
(WOLVERHAMPTON TO WALSALL TO
WEST BROMWICH)

I walked around the streets of Wolverhampton. It was a handsome old city in the sunshine, with many fine municipal buildings and the imposing old Chubb factory near the centre. The company's name ran around the top of the building in white glazed brick, a reminder of when Wolverhampton was the country's main lock-making centre, supplying the locks for, among other things, the first postboxes and the security cage for the Koh-i-Noor diamond at the 1851 Great Exhibition. The factory is now an arts venue and media centre.

Beyond it, I could see the roofline of Molineux, Wolverhampton Wanderers' ground. You didn't have to look hard to see the connections between the city and its football club. On Princess Street stood the Billy Wright pub, named after Wolves' legendary centre-half, who'd spent his entire playing career at the club and who'd also captained England a record ninety times. In nearby Queen Street was a lovely old sports shop run by Ron Flowers, another Wolves legend who was a member of England's 1966 World Cup-winning squad. At the front of the shop was a tribute to Ron, still going strong at eighty-one, with a glass case containing his England cap and one of the shirts that he wore while playing for his country.

I saw a billboard in Market Street for the *Express & Star*, the Black Country daily paper, which read 'Controversy over Wolves shirt sponsor rumbles on'.

For many years, the club's iconic gold and black shirts had been sponsored by Goodyear, one of the city's major factories, at its peak employing seven thousand workers making tyres for cars, trucks, tractors and even Formula One racing teams. In June 2015, Goodyear had announced that it would close its factory by the end of 2016. Workers were offered the opportunity to transfer to Goodyear's factory in Mexico. Nobody had taken them up on it.

Wolves fans were furious when the club announced that the new shirt sponsor for 2016–17 was to be The Money Shop, a payday loan company.

It wasn't the first time a club's supporters had reacted in that way. Back in 2013, Newcastle United fans had protested against their club's sponsorship by the payday loan firm Wonga, which went ahead regardless.

Determined to stop the same thing happening in Wolverhampton, two of the city's MPs and a host of councillors joined in the protest, and thousands of supporters signed a petition handed to the club's chief executive, Jez Moxey, which stated: 'We strongly feel that The Money Shop's business practices, whilst legal, do not fit with the ethics of the football club, the supporters and the area it represents.'

In a blog post for the Wolves Fancast, a website and weekly podcast for supporters, David Handley wrote, 'In a city which is increasingly dishevelled, rocked by low public funding and shops being closed throughout, should a well-run, family orientated football club really be partnering with a business which profits mainly on the despair of others?'

He added a more pragmatic note: 'The truth of the matter is that football has no morals. It is a soulless corporate business now. Talk of it being the people's game is just a marketing tool. The people don't really matter unless they have a billion dollars . . . the owner of Dollar Financial, the company behind The Money Shop, is worth over $6 billion. Would anyone complain if he came in and bankrolled us to the Premier League?'

In the face of the storm, Jez Moxey announced a range of charitable initiatives, including a new project delivered by the Wolves Community Trust to teach young people how to be responsible with money. That reminded me of the Drinkaware logo in the small print of alcohol adverts.

Like booze shops, payday loan companies are now ubiquitous on our high streets. It seems strange to think that just over a decade ago the industry barely existed. Marketed initially as one-off loans for unexpected expenses or luxuries, payday loans were soon being used to fund everyday things such as groceries and utility bills. It was after the financial crash of 2008 that the sector exploded, as banks and building societies tightened their borrowing criteria and shrank their presence on the high street, with the payday loan companies moving in to meet the demand.

In 2014 the Competition Commission found that 80 per cent of payday loans were taken out online, but borrowers using high street firms were significantly more likely to be social tenants, in part-time work or unemployed, lone parents, unqualified or on low incomes. In the same year, a debt charity reported that one client's £200 payday loan debt had grown to £1,851 in just three months.

Research by the Bureau of Investigative Journalism, also in 2014, compared the distribution of payday loan shops with government data on poverty and found that they were clustered in areas of deprivation. Glasgow, with forty stores, was the UK's payday loan shop capital. Nearby West Dunbartonshire and Inverclyde also featured in the UK's top ten for payday loan shops per head of population. A recent report by West Dunbartonshire Council found that 26 per cent of children in the local authority were growing up in poverty and that one in four residents derived some or all of their income from welfare support, compared to a UK average of nearly one in seven. Lewisham, one of London's poorest boroughs, had the country's highest per-capita density of payday loan shops, with nearly eight per 100,000 residents. In contrast, wealthy areas such as Kensington and Richmond had less than one loan shop per 100,000 residents.

The industry hit a peak in 2012, when twelve million payday loans worth nearly £4 billion were taken out. This Wild West of lending to some of the country's poorest and most vulnerable people, backed up by lavish TV commercials, had gone on more or less unchecked by successive governments in thrall to 'light-touch regulation' and the belief that the market could look after itself.

But in 2014 the Financial Conduct Authority (FCA), the City regulator, belatedly intervened to shake up the industry. In June of that year, Wonga was ordered to pay more than £2.6 million in compensation after sending threatening letters to its customers from fake law firms. It was later forced to write off £220 million worth of loans to 375,000 borrowers which it admitted should never have been given to them.

QuickQuid and Pounds to Pockets – let nobody accuse these firms of subtlety in their branding – wrote off more than 2,500 loans to customers and refunded about 1,500 people following the FCA action.

Wolves' new shirt sponsor, The Money Shop, Britain's second biggest payday lender after Wonga, had been ordered by the FCA in October 2015 to refund £15.4 million to 147,000 customers after it was found to be lending more to borrowers than they could afford to repay. The Money Shop's parent company, Dollar Financial – part of the US-based DFC Global Corp, ultimately owned by private equity giant Lone Star – had been charging customers interest rates as high as 2,962 per cent. After the ruling, The Money Shop had cut its interest rates to a mere 743 per cent.

At the time, Guy Anker, managing editor of MoneySavingExpert.com, said, 'The payday lending industry has been a parasite on this country; it lived in a void of regulation for too long. Thankfully we have started to see much greater scrutiny of the ways these dangerous businesses in this dangerous industry operate. And now their horrible practices are starting to catch up with them.'

Indeed they were. Since the regulatory assault on payday lending had begun in earnest in 2014 – which included the introduction of a cap on interest rates in January 2015 and stamped down on firms raiding bank accounts to grab money on payday – more than 1,400 companies had been forced out of the industry. The Money Shop had seen its chain of high street outlets more than halve, from 562 to just 230, but was still charging an annualised interest rate of 709 per cent on a £250 loan repaid over four months.

Company statements loaded with contrition abounded. After the FCA ruling, The Money Shop's chief executive, Stuart Howard, said, 'I accept the findings of the review and apologise to anyone who may have suffered difficulties as a result.'

Russell Hamblin-Boone, of the Consumer Finance Association, which represented around 75 per cent of payday lending firms, said that the industry had been transformed. 'It is unrecognisable today from a few years ago,' he told the *Guardian* in 2016.

But there are plenty of people who believe that, far from reining in the business, the regulatory changes were simply making these companies alter their business models while still targeting their core market. The same *Guardian* article quoted Carl Packman, who had researched payday lenders for the poverty charity Toynbee Hall. 'It's not really the case of the rise and fall of the payday lenders,' he said. 'It's the rise, a hiccup, and probably another rise to come. They are shifting to slightly longer two- or three-month loans, which are still extortionately priced. The fact that they have been able to pay these fines shows they are not just scraping by.'

Jez Moxey, Wolves' CEO, remained bullish about the sponsorship deal with The Money Shop. 'It's a highly regulated business,' he'd said in a club statement. 'It's a service that if it wasn't available, the alternatives to the people who need it are quite stark. I don't think we could have associated with a more reputable firm.'

Opposite me, on the other side of Market Street, next to a payday loan shop, was a pub, outside which a group of Wolves fans were drinking in the afternoon sunshine. I went in, ordered a pint, and went outside to where the fans were standing, many in their Wolves shirts, bearing the name of Silverbug, an IT consultancy, the previous season's sponsors.

Wolves had finished fourteenth in the Championship, a bitterly disappointing result for a club desperate to get back into the Premier League. I asked one of the men whether he had signed the petition against the new sponsors. He had.

'For our club to associate with vermin like this just shows how low we've sunk,' he said. Some of the other men agreed. They talked about their club being stolen from them, how it had no dignity. They talked about the new shirt being 'the shirt of shame', and how horrified they would be that the rest of the country would see it and somehow associate the city with payday loans.

'It's about our identity as a city,' one said. 'We've lost most of the jobs. Our football club is one of the few things we've got left that we might be proud of. Fuck knows we're struggling enough as it is.'

One of the men even said that he hoped the club didn't get promoted in the next three years – the term of the sponsorship deal – because he didn't want The Money Shop to get that sort of exposure.

Standing close to the main group was another man, perhaps in his fifties, drinking on his own. He'd been listening to the conversation, but hadn't said anything.

I asked what he thought. He looked away for a moment, then turned back and spoke softly. He told me how he'd supported Wolves his whole life, as had his dad and grandad before him. His dad had died recently, he said, and the club was the place they used to go together, first when he was a young boy, and later as two adult men together. The club had been one of the strongest ties that held them together.

'My dad would have been furious about the new sponsor,' he said. His face took on a granite expression, and he swallowed hard. I thought for a moment that he was about to cry.

'My dad hated those parasites. I know he'd have stopped going because of it if he was alive now. So it's stopped being my club. And it's stopped being my dad's club. And it hurts, because I can't go any more and it feels like I've lost my dad all over again.'

*

The next morning, the newspapers were running through their routines. The *Sunday Express* was giving its readers a rest from the immigrant scaremongering and reverting to its other staple: our health. 'New statins safety alert' screamed its banner headline. The *Mail on Sunday* led with 'Farage: I'll back Boris as our PM', while the *Sunday Telegraph* went with 'Boris: How EU wants a superstate, as Hitler did'.

As I headed out of Wolverhampton to walk the seven miles to Walsall, I thought about the Wolves fan at the pub, and his bond with his dad, and remembered finding a photograph in Pete's box of me and him playing football together on holiday on the Isle of Wight. I am in my little West Brom replica kit, probably three years old, as we kick the ball to each other. I remember kicking the ball, clumsily, so that it never went straight to him, and then saying, 'Sorry, dad,' and Pete saying, 'No need to apologise, son.' Every time I kicked it, it wouldn't go to him, and I'd say sorry, until, eventually, Pete said, angrily, 'Stop bloody apologising,' and I started to cry, because I wanted so much to be good at kicking the ball to him. My crying only made it worse, because Pete just picked up the ball and walked off to where my mother and my sister were sitting and I was left standing there, feeling like my world had ended.

As I walked, my mind went back to a dinner party I'd gone to in an expensive part of west London a few years previously, before Pete had died. I was sitting opposite a banker, a man I'd never met before, a corpulent fellow with ruddy cheeks and red braces and a laugh that spoke of expensive schooling and privilege. We'd all had a fair few drinks and, perhaps thinking he was batting on a friendly wicket, he started talking about people on benefits and how the poor were largely to blame for their own circumstances. Before I knew what had happened, I was out of my seat, fists clenched, threatening him. He looked shocked, as did the hostess, unused to such behaviour. But it was something the fat man in braces said to me afterwards, when it had all calmed down, that stayed with me. He asked me why I seemed to take it all so personally. 'It's as if you're trying to prove something to somebody,' he said.

I walked along streets lined with boarded-up factories, and then into Walsall, through the new shopping centre at the north of the town, and into Park Street, the old shopping street, where so many of the units were displaying 'to let' signs. At the end of an alleyway I emerged into the bus station, where Sue was waiting to greet me.

*

The next day I walked out of Walsall, along Bradford Street, where there were more payday loan shops, bookies and pawnbrokers than anywhere I'd been on the walk. They were clustered together, symbiotically, just as you find with parasitism in nature.

Devotees of the lightly regulated free market often used the Darwinian language of evolution to explain its global spread. It was just nature working efficiently, the survival of the fittest, a system that best reflected man's innate drives of self-interest and ruthlessness. In 1989, after the fall of the Berlin Wall, Francis Fukuyama had famously declared 'the end of history'.

This was what the end of history looked like: impoverished high streets full of organisms that had grown to feed off the misery, right next to each other, painted with the same sort of bright colours that tropical flowers might use to attract a hummingbird.

I went into a branch of Cash Generator, a national chain with 223 pawnshops. It was busy that day. In the locked glass cases were laptops and mobile phones, tablets and stereos, Xboxes and remote-controlled cars. At the counter, a man emptied out a laundry bag of DVDs, the shop briefly full of the sound of them clattering onto the counter. The shop guy started sorting through them, making two piles, while the man whose DVDs they were just stood there, silently, watching with dull eyes.

I went up to another counter, sealed off from the shop by a thick glass screen, with a gap of a few inches at the bottom, behind which was a till and a young Asian man, sitting on a high stool. I asked him how they knew whether any of this stuff being brought in was nicked or not.

'We check the serial numbers. But who knows theirs? I don't. We are careful as we can be, but . . . We get the list of stuff that's been stolen from the police. It says things like "Black Toshiba laptop". How can we tell?'

I asked him what it was like working in the shop. He scribbled down a phone number on a scrap of paper. 'That's head office's number, mate,' he said. 'I'm not allowed to talk about stuff like that.'

A hundred metres further up the road, I went into the Jerome K. Jerome museum, commemorating one of Walsall's most famous sons, the author of *Three Men in a Boat*, one of my favourite books, never out of print since it was first published in 1889.

The museum was sited in the house where Jerome was born in 1859. It had opened in 1984, with a grant from the Department of the Environment and Walsall Council, while I was at college in the town, the crumbling and derelict Grade II listed building restored to its former glory amid much civic fanfare and pride. I remember the stories about it in the local paper.

In the entrance hall there were a few panels about Jerome's life, but when I tried the inner door, it was locked. Through the glass I could see a young woman sitting behind a desk. She came to the door. I asked if the museum was closed. It shut down ages ago, she said. The building was now a solicitor's office. She didn't know when it had closed. 'I'm quite new,' she said. 'We get people from all over the world knock on the door and they're always really disappointed.'

In fact the museum had closed down in 2007, after the Tory-run council had withdrawn its grant. Jeremy Nicholas, the president of the Jerome K. Jerome society, had told the *Daily Telegraph*, 'It's like he's been airbrushed from history. Walsall has got deprived areas where literacy is a real problem, but do they fight that by pointing out a local hero to children needing someone to look up to? No.'

I walked under the M6. Standing on the pavement by the side of the road was my sister, taking one of her rare days off work to walk with me for the rest of the day's short hop to West Bromwich, six miles away. On 16 May 1981 she had met the People's March for Jobs on that exact spot as it passed through Wednesbury. She was nineteen years old, newly married, and had cooked up a load of bacon sandwiches to bring to the marchers.

As we walked, Sue said she could recall the march as if it were yesterday, the sight of it coming over the crest of the hill, the banners flying, the chanting, the heavy sound of boots on the road, the carnival atmosphere, her handing out the bacon sandwiches, the sound of all these regional accents, Scouse and Manc and Yorkshire, and how it was still unusual back then, in Wednesbury, to hear any accent other than a Black Country one.

'Of course, it was a joyous thing, all these people standing up and fighting for something, prepared to walk three hundred miles for their jobs and communities,' she said. 'But it was very sad that they'd had to do this thing. I had the sense, even then, with everything else going on in the country, with all the jobs disappearing, that the writing was on the wall.'

Every time a bus went past, Sue waved, and the driver would wave back and toot his horn. Before long I was waving too. I wondered whether anybody watching this middle-aged pair walking along the street hand in hand waving at all the buses might think we were bonkers.

I asked Sue whether she could remember the time I turned up at her house, not long after mum had died, wearing my ridiculous cashmere overcoat with its ridiculous shoulder pads. She nodded.

'I hated you then,' she said.

'I'm sorry,' I said.

'I know,' Sue said. 'I know you are.'

14

LITTLE LOCAL DIFFICULTIES
(BACK TO WALSALL)

The People's March for Jobs had taken a rest day in West Bromwich on 17 May 1981. But instead of spending my day off there, I went back to Walsall to have a better look around. I'd been shocked the day before at the way the town had changed in the thirty years since I'd lived there, how shabby and poor and desolate it now seemed.

I'd arranged to meet the leader of the Labour group on the council, Sean Coughlan, in the afternoon, and spent the morning wandering around.

I started off at St Matthew's Hall, originally Walsall's first library when it was built in 1830, an amazing building with columns built in Greek Doric style. Now it was a giant Wetherspoons pub.

From here, I walked along Bridge Street, a thriving shopping street three decades ago, but now full of boarded-up units. In the window of a temp agency, I scanned the board advertising for cleaners and care assistants and forklift truck drivers. Most cards carried the figure £7.20, the minimum wage for those aged 25 and over.

I walked into The Crossing at St Paul's, a church whose ground floor was now converted into a shopping centre, filled with independent little outlets selling jewellery and gift cards, ladies' clothes and Christian books. From a florist in the corner wafted the sweet scent of gardenias.

The church's columns and vaulted ceiling had been preserved and incorporated into the new design, split by the three new floors built around the edge of the church, so that looking up I could see the full height of the building, to the glass roof lantern, which flooded the space with light and from which was suspended a giant cross made of green glass.

Upstairs, I knocked on a door with a sign saying 'church office'. A young woman opened it. I told her that I used to live in the town and that I was retracing a 1981 march.

'That was the year I was born,' she said.

The church, she told me, had been facing closure and demolition in the 1990s. A plan had been hatched to save it, which involved converting some of the space to retail and conference rooms. It had reopened in its current form in 1995, with the chapel on the top floor. 'We can now keep the church open seven days a week,' she said. 'Our rental income helps keep our friendship groups for people with mental health issues going. We issue food vouchers for people whose money has been stopped.'

She told me about the relationship the church had with the Glebe Centre, a homeless shelter up the road. 'There's been a massive increase in homelessness in the past few years. More women these days as well,' she said. 'There are twenty-one food banks in Walsall now. That's doubled in the last ten years.'

She said that if I wanted to know anything more, I should talk to Andrew, a volunteer, who was working in the next room.

Andrew, now in his mid-fifties, had been born in Walsall. His mum had worked in the leather trade in the town, making belts and saddles, the industry that made Walsall rich and gave Walsall FC their nickname, the Saddlers.

His dad had worked down the pits and then in a steelworks, but after he was made redundant the family moved to Telford, a new town in Shropshire. When Andrew left school, he did a youth training scheme and a few factory jobs, before starting in care work, first with elderly people, then adults with learning difficulties. 'I had a short run with teenagers and children who'd been abused,' he said. 'That wasn't fun, but it had to be done.'

About ten years ago, after his dad died, Andrew moved back to Walsall. 'It felt more like home than Telford ever did,' he said. 'But there's been a big decline here this past decade.'

He told me about his daily duties as a volunteer in the church, about how since the cut in budgets for day centres, libraries and other organisations looking after vulnerable people, the church was now at the forefront. He thought the sell-off of council housing had been one of the biggest catastrophes for poorer people.

'The bedroom tax has been a disaster,' he said. 'We have people coming in for the food bank. They've had to pay their bills out of money they'd usually use for food. I hear terrible tales of hardship. People are embarrassed to come here, but they've got nowhere else to go. We try and reassure them that they're not the first and they won't be the last.'

In March 2016, a study by the Office for National Statistics showed that Walsall was Britain's fourth most deprived town. Neighbouring Sutton Coldfield had come fourth in the same report's list of least deprived areas. A district survey in November 2015 showed that in Blakenall Heath, an especially deprived area of Walsall, the number of children in poverty had reached 42 per cent, and borough-wide the survey found that 16,000 kids were living in poverty, with 9 per cent of children always or often hungry.

The then deputy mayor of Walsall, Kath Phillips, also a magistrate, told the *Express & Star*: 'We need to look seriously at what we are doing. I see poverty week in, week out at court . . . we are fining people who are stealing food.'

According to statistics published by the Trussell Trust, which runs 420 food banks across the UK, in 2008 – the year of the financial crisis – it had given out roughly 26,000 three-day emergency food supplies. In 2016 it provided 1,182,954 – a near 4,500 per cent increase in eight years. The Trust largely blamed the rolling out of Universal Credit, and found that in the areas where it had been implemented, food bank referral rates were rising at more than double the national average.

Chancellor George Osborne's decision to introduce a mighty £3 billion reduction in work allowances – the amount Universal Credit recipients can earn before their benefits start to be taken away – had led the Institute for Fiscal Studies to warn that this, added to cuts in child tax credits and a freeze in benefit rates, would mean that nearly three million working households with children would be on average £2,500 a year worse off.

It could only get much worse. Planned benefit cuts were set to reduce government spending by about £15 billion a year in the long run, with the poorest working-age households facing losses of between 4 per cent and 10 per cent, according to the IFS.

These Tory reforms to the benefits system were taking a terrible toll on the nation's mental health, according to analysis published in 2015 by the *Journal of Epidemiology and Community Health*. It found that between 2010 and 2013 the Work Capability Assessment – the tougher 'fit for work' test now being used to assess eligibility for disability benefit – was associated with 590 extra suicides, 279,000 extra cases of self-reported mental health problems and the prescribing of an additional 725,000 antidepressant items.

'The pattern of increase in mental health problems closely matches the increase in [use] of the Work Capability Assessment,' the report's principal author, Benjamin Barr, told the *Guardian*. Barr, from the University of Liverpool, said that areas of England where the highest proportion of people had gone through the new fit-for-work tests, such as Knowsley, Liverpool and Blackpool, had experienced a much larger increase in suicides, mental ill health and antidepressant prescriptions.

Andrew, at The Crossing at St Paul's, was witnessing the effects of all this daily. The worst thing was seeing the children whose parents had had their benefits stopped because they'd missed an appointment and been sanctioned. It had been happening a lot more recently, he said. 'At the end of the day, I just hand it all over to God. I've always said, "God's will is my will."'

'What might God make of all this?' I asked.

Andrew paused. 'He probably wouldn't like it.'

I walked back along Bradford Street, heading to the Glebe Centre, the YMCA-run homeless shelter that Andrew had said was doing great work with Walsall's most vulnerable people.

Homelessness, along with food bank use, had seen an enormous increase since the coalition government came to power in 2010, and the number of rough sleepers had doubled between then and 2016. Sixty-two per cent of homelessness professionals who responded to a survey conducted by the charity St Mungo's said that they'd noticed an increase in the number of people with mental health problems sleeping rough in their area. A report by St Mungo's noted that many specialist homelessness mental health teams had shrunk or been closed as a result of the funding cuts which began after the 2008 financial crisis, and which had seen local authority funding for services helping vulnerable people avoid homelessness slashed by 45 per cent between 2010 and 2015.

The charities Crisis and Shelter say the official statistics hugely under-represent the homelessness problem in the UK, as they exclude those who are homeless but not approaching local authorities for assistance or who do not meet the statutory criteria.

According to a House of Commons briefing paper in December 2015, local authorities had a statutory duty to secure accommodation for 'unintentionally homeless households' who fall into a 'priority need' category, but there was no duty to secure accommodation for all homeless people. 'For example,' the paper stated, 'there is no statutory duty to secure housing for homeless single people and couples without children who are not deemed to be vulnerable for some reason.'

Most of the people I saw at the Glebe Centre, housed in a building owned by the United Reformed Church, would not fit the government's definition of vulnerable, but they seemed pretty abject all the same. Mostly men, ranging from late teens to late sixties, probably about thirty or forty in number, they sat around noiselessly, staring into the distance, bundled up on tatty armchairs. A couple of men played pool and eyed me warily. Most had the puffy facial features and glassy eyes of heavy drinkers.

One man was crashed out on a sofa, snoring, buried under a sleeping bag, while above him, on a TV screwed to the wall, Katie Price, on *Loose Women*, was discussing online abuse directed at her disabled son. The stench of feet and sweat was overpowering, but after a few minutes I stopped noticing it.

On the walls, the signs were in English and Polish. I knocked on the office door and entered. It was a big space, with desks overflowing with paperwork and black bin bags everywhere, bursting out with clothing. In the corner was the centre's manager. The church had told her I would be popping in, but she was too busy to spend much time with me.

'There are only two of us running this place,' she said. 'I've no time.' She hammered furiously on the keyboard of the computer in front of her and only looked up when the door opened and more bags were brought in.

She wearily answered my questions without looking up or

208

stopping typing. There was no statutory provision for the homeless in Walsall, she said. The Glebe ran only as a day centre for most of the year, providing meals for 50p or sometimes for free. They ran mostly on donations from the public and some funding as a charity. Walsall Council gave them some money, for now.

'A lot of what we do depends on the kindness of strangers,' she told me. 'The church plays a huge role in terms of donations of money, food, clothing. All the churches do it for no reward. We'd be lost without them.'

From November, she said, if it was freezing for two consecutive nights, the council allowed them to open as a night shelter. 'Where do people sleep?' I asked. Jane looked up momentarily, as if it was a stupid question.

'On the sofas or on the floor,' she said.

She talked about the huge increase in homelessness in the past few years, how they were seeing more women now. 'There's been a massive rise in the numbers coming to our centre,' she said. They now saw a lot more people who had fallen through the cracks, who perhaps wouldn't have needed their services a few years ago. 'They can be a bit arrogant: "Why me? I don't deserve it," and all that,' she said.

I left the centre, grateful for the fresh air. On the other side of the road was a group of twelve almshouses, in Queen Anne style, with finials and terracotta ridge tiles, arranged around a three-sided courtyard. I walked over to have a look. At the centre of a gable, a panel read: 'These almshouses were erected and endowed by Henry Boys A.D.1886.'

Boys had been a Walsall brick manufacturer, and had built the almshouses for twenty-four impoverished Walsallians 'aged over sixty, sober and industrious', to live 'free from rent, taxes and water works charges', according to a local newspaper of the time. In 1885 there had been a terrible recession in the Black

Country and, coupled with an extremely severe winter, this had caused great suffering among the poor. The houses were Boys' contribution to the alleviation of that suffering.

I thought back to the People's History Museum, about the hard-fought struggles of working people in the twentieth century to gain statutory protections and human rights. Even a few years ago, the idea of people having to rely on philanthropy and the altruism of others to survive would have felt as anachronistic as the sentiments behind those almshouses. Not now. It felt as if we were coming full circle.

Outside the Glebe Centre, two men were sitting on a low wall, smoking. I went over and said hello. One of the men got up and walked away, but the other sat there, smiling up at me, sucking hard on his roll-up. Had he been using the Glebe? 'Yes,' he replied. Why? 'At the moment I am homeless,' he said, with an Eastern European accent. 'Here you can get good meal for free, sometimes 50p.'

He had been in the building trade, in casual work, but three weeks ago the work had dried up and he'd been thrown out of his digs. I asked him where his accent was from. Poland, he said. He looked to be in his forties and, like most of the men in the Glebe, he had a drinker's face. How long had he been in the UK? Four-and-a-half years. Why had he come to Walsall?

'Because it sounds like Warsaw,' he said. 'That is my home town.'

He came to Walsall just because it sounded like his home town? Yes, he replied, and laughed.

I asked him what he thought about the EU referendum.

'I think that to leave is very important for England,' he said. 'England is island. Before, England is imperium. Like Russia. Now, so many people coming here, too much. Taking benefits. Too much money for immigrants.'

He rolled another cigarette, lit it and then stared ahead. His friend was still standing about thirty yards away from us, leaning against a wall.

'In Poland I lost my family,' the other man said, eventually. 'My wife gone. Divorced. Two children, gone. Now I have new girlfriend. She in Poland. She won't come here. So next year, I go back home. Forever. So I can eat good food. Good everything.' And he laughed at the thought of it all.

I walked back into Walsall, past the Cenotaph, commemorating the town's dead in two world wars, and through the Saddlers Shopping Centre – like the football club, named in honour of the town's former leather-working industry. That industry, now mostly migrated to East Asia, had once employed up to ten thousand people locally.

I stood on the spot where, in 1981, the Walsall North MP David Winnick had addressed the People's March for Jobs after walking with them for six miles. A week later, he told the House of Commons that there hadn't been a single hostile remark from the thousands of onlookers.

'I believe that when the public saw the marchers, they remembered the devastation that has come to the West Midlands and the Black Country areas in the last eighteen to twenty months. They know and understand that the marchers are the conscience of the nation . . . They represent the best in our country.'

Winnick demanded to know why Margaret Thatcher was 'so high and mighty that she will not receive the marchers . . . It is her policies that are largely responsible for the unemployment from which we are now suffering . . . Why does she not defend them to the victims of monetarism?'

Thatcher was not in the Commons that day. Instead, Peter Morrison, the Under-Secretary of State for Employment, replied. He spoke about the march giving false hope to the unemployed. 'Dramatic action is seductive, especially in hard times . . . but the efforts of the union representatives who organised the march would be better spent in trying to reach serious agreement with employers to make industry more competitive,' he told the House. 'That is a less glamorous, more difficult and demanding approach, but it is more constructive.'

Morrison then attacked the Eurosceptic Winnick, by saying how much money from the European Regional Development Fund had poured into deprived areas of the Midlands and north-west since 1979. 'The Common Market has substantial advantages because of the funds that are available,' he said. 'I can assure the honourable gentleman that if we were not a member millions of jobs would go, thanks to the lack of trade that would result from our withdrawal.'

I walked into Gallery Square. In front of me was The New Art Gallery Walsall, a starkly modernist, five-storey building clad in pale terracotta. It had been opened in 2000 by the Queen, built with £21 million of public funding – an expression of intent from Walsall, a bold statement about regeneration and the importance of art for a blighted community struggling to rediscover its confidence.

It had won several architectural awards, despite the essayist Theodore Dalrymple describing it as resembling a 'fascist foreign ministry'. In its first year it attracted 237,000 visitors.

Standing there, in the centre of Walsall in 2016, with everything I'd heard and seen about how the town was suffering, it looked like a grotesque folly, as maybe the great medieval cathedrals of France – in Chartres, Amiens or Reims – had looked to the impoverished citizenry living in their Gothic shadows. Maybe that's why the gallery was under threat of closure, the council struggling to justify keeping it open.

I walked through the cavernous reception area, clad in

concrete and thick Douglas fir, and then up a wide, sweeping staircase, to a gallery filled with Turners and Monets and Renoirs and Whistlers. Under some of the artworks were little handwritten notes from visitors, invited to say what the pieces had meant for them. Next to the oil painting *Le Canal*, by Stanislas Lépine, somebody had written: 'This painting inspired me to live when my chances were slim.'

I had listened to a radio programme recently, where a writer had been called on to justify spending on art in an age of austerity. Against him in the studio was a hard-nosed businessman, who barked at him, 'You can't eat art!'

But, just like Kim Laycock in Liverpool, I remembered growing up in a household full of books and paintings and books about paintings; my parents were among the many in that postwar working-class generation who had found great inspiration in art and literature, a world that had opened up. One of my mum's favourite quotes was from Pablo Picasso. 'Art washes from the soul the dust of everyday life,' she would say to me. I remembered going to a funeral of a miner when I was six or seven years old. As I walked into the crematorium, with beautiful music coming from the speakers, the man walking next to me, a gruff old retired pitman, turned and said, in a thick Glaswegian accent, 'Ach, Beethoven. Don't you just love it?'

No, you couldn't eat art. Neither could you measure the worth of it in monetary terms, as local authorities are now being forced to. Like friendship, like philosophy, art was not strictly necessary, C. S. Lewis wrote in *The Four Loves*. 'It has no survival value; rather it is one of those things that gives value to survival.'

On one wall of the Walsall gallery hung a vast drawing by Adam Dant called *The Fight Between Temperance and Liquor*. It was a modern reimagining of Pieter Bruegel's 1559 painting

The Battle Between Carnival and Lent. Dant's version had transposed Bruegel onto contemporary Walsall, with bacchanalian and boisterous scenes around the town centre's famous landmarks. It was a clever, chilling piece.

Outside I met up with Sean Coughlan, who ten days earlier had seen his Labour group emerge from the local elections as the biggest party in the council, but with too few seats to gain overall control. There was to be a full vote on 25 May as to whether Sean would lead the council. Labour had been in charge in Walsall for a total of sixteen months in the past sixteen years, he told me, citing the pockets of poverty alongside wealthier areas in the borough as the reason.

As we walked, Sean told me how he remembered the People's March for Jobs hitting Walsall, listening to David Winnick's speech. Sean was in his mid-twenties then. 'There was a momentum to it,' he said. 'You felt you were working class, part of something bigger. But I also felt, even back then, a real element of fear – that things were only going to get worse. It felt like the last throw of the dice.'

Sean was a local man, born and bred, from Willenhall, 'a very proud Black Country lad', one of five kids raised in an Irish Catholic family with 'a rabid Thatcherite father'.

He learned his politics as a coal miner in the seventies and eighties, and during the strike in 1984 he and his brother, a police sergeant, had found themselves on opposite sides of the picket line. 'An interesting time for our family!' he said, raising an eyebrow.

After the mines closed down, Sean went to work in the steel industry. Six years later the plant was taken over by an American company, which had then mothballed it. Sean was at a loose end, but he had also been working as a councillor during that time.

In 2000, aged forty-four, he decided to take a degree in politics and sociology at a local university. 'Having that piece of paper was nice,' Sean said. 'But it was the whole process of learning and engaging with different people that set me up really.'

Newly graduated, Sean got a job as a council officer in Dudley, charged with strengthening the community's engagement with the council, but in 2011 he was made redundant again. 'And I will blame the Tories, again,' Sean said, 'because it was a Tory administration that decided to get rid of the whole team.'

We went into a coffee shop in the high street, ordered and sat down. Sean had been looking at the figures coming out of Whitehall, about funding for the council for the next five years. 'We've been tasked with setting a budget for 2020 where there'll be no revenue support grant,' he said. 'Our funding will be based solely on business rates. We'll lose £60 million a year in that process alone. I honestly believe we'll be able to do not much more than adult statutory services in social care and children's services. That's it.'

People, he said, were increasingly falling through the net and the council just couldn't cope with their needs. 'We're moving in the same direction as America, where people will die on the streets for lack of access to healthcare. We have more people sleeping rough than we've ever dealt with. Numbers have gone up dramatically in the last six years, especially people with mental health issues. They're angry, but they take it out on the support services.'

I asked Sean what he thought was behind the divisions that were becoming increasingly apparent both in the UK and in the US. 'I think we're recreating a cold war mentality, but based on ethnic and religious lines,' he said. 'We seem to be becoming more and more polarised, with a very right-wing Christian view of the world and this very Islamic view of the world. And everyone in between is being played off against one another. It's like we're going through a modern-day middle ages.'

We finished our coffees and headed back outside, and walked along a street full of figures huddled in doorways. 'When people see alcoholics and drug addicts sitting out here in the street,' Sean said, 'they sometimes say to me, "Well, at least they're not burdens on the taxpayer." And I say, "Well, they should be bloody burdens. We should be doing our bit to support these people."'

Where did he think that loss of compassion had come from? 'I would say the obvious, that there was a red line drawn in the 1980s with Thatcherism,' he said. 'Suddenly, it was all about "you're an individual, forget about your brother and your sister, the person across the road. It's all about you, what is good for you, what you want. You'll create your own benefits from your own endeavours." Well, for every one that succeeds in that system, there are ten losers. It's that perception where people are willing others to fail, because as long as they're surviving, they've accepted there will be victims in life.'

I thought back to my chat with Danny in Stoke, about the tacit acceptance that there had to be winners and losers in this system, and that those of us who had been beneficiaries of it, and had done nothing to challenge it, could not be entirely absolved of blame.

'We had big industries that employed people that weren't academically gifted, that were good with their hands, who actually made things that could be sold,' said Sean. 'All that disappeared in a decade. And that left many people thinking that maybe Thatcher was right, that they had to forget about everybody else, and stop going down the working men's club, because that's working class and now I own my own home, so I can't be working class.'

Sean remembered the selling-off of council houses under right-to-buy, and thought that it was a huge part of the changed narrative in the UK.

'The main thing underlying it was the idea that council homes were wrong,' he said. 'And people started to believe that. And it wasn't just about selling off the houses, it was about restricting councils from spending money on the houses that stayed under council ownership.

'So council homes did go into disrepair, and you could see the house that was lived in by an ex-council tenant, because they were investing in their home, so it was looked after. And next door would be a council house, and through lack of money it would look run-down. So there was a physical reality to the selling-off process that people could see, as well as the ideological process.'

Sean talked about the perilous state local politics was in, how central government cuts were emasculating councils and what they could do for people.

'Not so long ago,' he said, 'if people had a problem, their default was to give the council a ring. The council was a friend that could help and protect you. That's almost gone. Now we're the hated enemy. We get our budgets cut year after year and have to carry out those cuts on local services. But Westminster doesn't get blamed, we do. "Ah, what's the point in voting," they tell me out on the street, "politicians are only in it for themselves." That really scares me.'

We entered the town hall and walked down a long corridor, from whose walls hung the portraits of Walsall's council leaders stretching back over the years, all in ceremonial garb, redolent of civic pride, speaking of an era now gone.

We walked into Sean's office, and waiting for us was Mark Lavender. Mark had first met Sean when they worked together at Dudley Metropolitan Borough Council.

'Mark decided to leave Dudley and come and work for us,' said Sean. 'Which was great for Walsall.'

'And great for Dudley as well!' laughed Mark.

Mark, in his mid-fifties, was responsible for regeneration in the Walsall area. All of the big cost-cutting programmes fell under him. He talked about some of the run-down estates he served – he himself was raised on the Priory Estate in Dudley, one of the area's poorest. People living on those estates now felt that they had nothing more to lose. They sit and watch TV all day, he said, 'seeing their benefits reduced, their opportunities disappearing, and then they see that many in the world are getting richer and richer. If you're going to encourage people to grasp opportunity, to aspire, to do well in education, then you've got to give them a reason to do that, some goal.'

Mark described the air of resignation he encountered in these estates. 'There's a cracking Black Country expression that goes, "Why aim for second best when third best will do?" I think we're in danger now of going for fourth best.'

He thought people were now expecting things to get much worse all the time, so that when things got only slightly worse, they felt grateful. His comments reminded me of Danny Flynn's in Stoke-on-Trent, when he said that many poorer Stokies had slipped into a culture and a mindset where they'd lost the fight, where things not getting any worse was a result, the best you could hope for. It sounded like the symptoms of depression.

'These communities almost used to be their own self-help groups,' Mark said. 'They only went outside that group for help and support if they needed it. We've lost that. We've become an insular society and yet we are, by our natures, a species born and bred to support each other. Part of the government strategy for healthcare and other things is to get that back into the communities again. So we've created broken communities, and a society and government that doesn't care or offer any real support, yet the government is saying that the only way we can survive, particularly in the disadvantaged areas, is by going back to that. But a community was mostly born as part of your working environment. There's none of that any more. So where are the catalysts to create those community groups going to come from?'

Mark was in no doubt that the biggest factor in the problem facing Walsall – and other towns like it – was the loss of its industries. When the town had those jobs, he said, most people could join a factory, go on apprenticeships. 'Those apprenticeships were seen as really achieving,' Mark said. 'You could move up the ranks, have a decent standard of living, self-respect, and be a happy and worthwhile member of the community. Worthwhile work that is respected is the biggest single determinant of a person's future. If you haven't helped somebody, or your job doesn't add value to the world, it eats away at the fabric of you as a human being.'

He talked about the lack of structures now for kids who didn't want to go to university, or who weren't degree material. The government, in driving through all these cuts, hadn't thought it through at all, he said. 'We can hardly support these kids any more,' he told me. 'There's no guidance, no careers advice outside schools, and even inside schools it's limited. The more people you have that generate wealth, the more people you can support. But now the number of wealth-generators is being swamped by the number of takers, because people are living longer and are becoming disenfranchised at an earlier age. That's a recipe for bankruptcy.'

Mark recalled conversations he'd had with his son as a teenager, about what he wanted to do after his GCSEs. He asked him whether he'd considered working in manufacturing, going into industry, getting an apprenticeship. 'He told me, "I'm not doing that. That's crap. Money's crap. Be dirty and horrible." Young people have these perceptions of what it's like to work in manufacturing which are so far from the truth.'

Sean chipped in, saying how he often saw comments on social media attacking refuse collectors or street cleaners. 'They write things like, "They're idiots, stupid, morons. Not even clever enough to collect my bin properly." It's becoming an everyday way to talk about your fellow human beings and we're seeing a lot of that kind of language in this EU campaign and in the US election. It's becoming very normal, this anger.'

Mark nodded. He talked about the firefighters and ambulance staff and A&E workers who regularly came under physical attack when trying to do their jobs. In the month I was walking, figures released by the NHS Business Services Authority revealed that violence against NHS staff had rocketed 25 per cent over the past five years, with on average 186 assaults against doctors, nurses and paramedics every single day. NHS leaders put the surge down to funding pressures on the service, with waiting times increasing and already hard-pressed staff overwhelmed. 'A lot of people feel it is acceptable to behave that way now,' said Mark, 'The boundaries of acceptable behaviour and tolerance have shifted so much.'

He had a theory as to why this might have happened. 'When people are under threat, when their lives feel precarious, they do one of two things,' he told me. 'They either roll over and give up, and I see a lot of that, or they fight back. I think that some of the anger that's coming out, some of the increase in mental illness that we're seeing, comes from people who are really at the edge of what they perceive to be the abyss for them and their family. They are fighting back, through anger, in the only way they think is available to them.'

If all of the cuts to local authority funding were coming from Westminster, why did Sean and Mark think it was largely local authorities being blamed by voters? Why wasn't there more anger against the government? Mark rolled his eyes and sighed deeply.

'Local authorities are being asked to deliver services within a budget which means that they can't deliver them,' he said. 'So every local authority has to make drastic cuts to services. The government has pulled off a magical bit of spin, whereby nobody's blaming them. Surely there has to come a time when the local authorities get together and say to the voters, "Look guys, it's not us doing this to you, it's somebody down in London. Unless you lot get together and tell them to stop it, or vote for someone else, it's not going to change."'

I walked out of Walsall, heading for my sister's. It had been shocking hearing Sean and Mark describe the transformation of local authorities from being seen by citizens as largely benevolent and facilitative, to being seen as callous and indifferent and gleefully slashing services. But this transformation, like so much of what's been going on in Britain over the past thirty-odd years, has been no accident. It has been part of a bigger agenda, driven from Whitehall, that has turned our country into one of the most centralised in the western world.

It was, of course, Thatcher's administration that first started the assault on local government, with its self-contradictory twin belief in the universal good of the free market and the desirability of a strong central state.

The ultimate logic of Thatcher's plan, as the political scientist Andrew Gamble pointed out in his 1988 book *The Free Economy and the Strong State*, was that government policy would lead to the eventual abolition of local government. Between 1979 and 1990, the Tories systematically set about their task. They did this by, among other things: reducing council funding; introducing caps on their rates of spending and taxation (ultimately introducing the poll tax); centralising the collection of business rates and redistributing the revenue raised through a formula concocted in Whitehall; deregulating local bus services; forcing councils to put services out to tender; taking polytechnics and colleges out of local authority control; and creating 'urban development corporations', exempt from local government regulations and taxes.

Right-to-buy legislation saw councils forced to sell off their social housing stock, reducing a vital revenue stream; they were also barred from spending most of the proceeds of these sales on building new homes. The Education Reform Act of 1988 offered schools the chance to opt out of local authority oversight. New Labour, when it got into power, left most of the new restrictions on local authorities in place.

Since 2010, the Tory leadership had continued this attack. They extended right-to-buy and introduced the free-schools programme and the forced academisation of primary schools, so that local authorities would ultimately have no role at all in the education system. Democracy and accountability had been replaced with the faith that the market alone was God.

In an essay for the *London Review of Books*, Tom Crewe listed services formerly provided by the state that were now partly or fully run by private concerns. They included the parole service, schools, roads, prisons, GP surgeries, hospital services, the Royal Mail, tax credits, care homes, welfare assessments, refugee and detention centres, deportations, the provision of court interpreters, government payrolls, broadband roll-out, IT programmes and government security, and of course the privatised rail, gas, electricity and water networks.

Currently mooted for future privatisation were the student loan book, the Land Registry, child protection services and the law courts. Most of those services that had already been outsourced were handled by just four firms – Atos, Serco, Capita and G4S – who between them received around £4 billion a year from taxpayers and who paid very healthy dividends to their shareholders. When the Tories unexpectedly won the 2015 general election, Serco's share price rose by 5.95 per cent, Capita's by 6.72 per cent and G4S's by 7.35 per cent.

'The establishment of a neoliberal consensus in Britain has been . . . an anti-municipal project,' wrote Crewe. 'Austerity is Thatcherism's logical end-point, effecting simultaneously the destruction of local government as a potentially rivalrous state-within-a-state, and the marketisation of nearly every aspect of public policy . . . People can no longer expect the services they pay for to be run in their interest, rather than the interest of shareholders; and they can't assume that the companies that operate these services are in any way transparent or accountable to them.'

All of this had ensured, among other things, that wealthier Britons were taxed much less and poorer citizens much more, having to pay a much higher price for services that they could once have accessed for much less. In 1981, the year of the People's March, for example, rent for a council property cost less than 7 per cent of the average income. In 2015, for a private tenancy, that figure stood at 52 per cent of average income, and in London 72 per cent, a far higher proportion than anywhere else in Europe.

Was it any wonder that Sean and Mark, and councils up and down the country, were approaching despair? They probably knew that the writing was on the wall, that at this moment they were effectively just hatchet men, delivering central government cuts. The time was approaching when the entire operation would be outsourced to the private sector and local government would be no more.

That morning the newspaper headlines had once again been full of talking points from the Leave campaigns, about taking back control, accountability, investment in communities, how Brussels was the enemy. The further I walked through England in the spring of 2016, the more it seemed that our real enemies were a lot closer to home.

I ducked through the backstreets of one of Walsall's leafier suburbs, and was soon outside my old college, formerly West Midlands College of Higher Education, and now the Walsall campus of Wolverhampton University. When I tell people I took a degree in leisure and recreational management, there is always a slightly confused look, before a response along the lines of, 'Were you supposed to be a manager of a leisure centre, or something like that?' And I say, no, that's not it at all.

In the 1970s, with increasing automation, the idea was gaining ground that most of our jobs would soon be done by robots. We'd still have the same wealth as a country, and indeed as a planet, but we wouldn't have to go to work, or at least many of us wouldn't. The idea had been around since at least the 1930s, when John Maynard Keynes had predicted that technology would have advanced sufficiently by the end of the century that everyone in Britain and the US would be working a fifteen-hour week.

So there was growing concern about what all these people would do with their leisure time, seeing as how leisure would transition from being something residual to a core part of the daily human experience.

It was big, pressing stuff, and it was upon us. Without some kind of paradigm shift we might end up without enough decent jobs to go around, and whole areas of advanced countries might outsource their manufacturing and heavy industry to low-wage economies. And then where would we be?

As it happened, mine was the penultimate intake. In 1984 Margaret Thatcher's National Advisory Board recommended our course for closure, among many others. It seemed that those in charge were happy to make no preparation for this brave new world of leisure – instead they would just stand by as industries were destroyed, communities hollowed out and trade unions emasculated, and look upon an expanding welfare bill as a price worth paying for the freedom of the market.

So what happened to Keynes's utopia? Well, according to the anthropology professor David Graeber, in his witty and brilliant essay 'Why Capitalism Creates Pointless Jobs', as the numbers employed in traditional industry collapsed, the numbers of professional, managerial, clerical, sales and service workers soared. Rather than letting citizens enjoy a massive reduction in working hours, whole new industries such as financial services and telemarketing had been created, and there had been a vast expansion of sectors such as corporate law, academic and health administration, human resources, advertising and public relations.

Graeber calls these 'bullshit jobs'.

'It's as if someone were out there making up pointless jobs just for the sake of keeping us all working,' he wrote. Further, Graeber claimed, many people employed in bullshit jobs secretly felt that their jobs were pointless, adding little of value to the human experience.

'There is a whole class of salaried professionals that, should you meet them at parties and admit that you do something that might be considered interesting . . . will want to avoid even discussing their line of work entirely,' he wrote. 'Give them a few drinks, and they will launch into tirades about how pointless and stupid their job really is.'

Graeber wrote about the profound psychological violence at play here. How could you ever speak about the dignity of labour when you felt that your job should not even exist?

The genius of the system, Graeber thinks, is that it has managed to channel the festering rage and resentment of people doing mostly pointless jobs towards the people actually doing jobs that have undeniable social value. Witness the fact that the more obviously a person's work benefits other people and society – nurses, firefighters, teachers, cleaners, care workers – the less that person is likely to get paid for it, relentlessly squeezed and exploited, and the more likely they are to get denounced by the right-wing press and government if they dare to ask for more.

Add to this the fact that striking tube drivers, teachers or firefighters can paralyse cities and countries, and it's clear just how vital their jobs are to society. Consider, in contrast, what would happen if all of the advertising or PR executives went on strike. Would we even notice? Some might even say it could temporarily make the world a better place.

'If someone had designed a work regime perfectly suited to maintaining the power of finance capital,' Graeber concluded, 'it's hard to see how they could have done a better job.'

And yet with the unceasing advances in robotics and artificial intelligence, and the profits to be made doing away with workers, the issue of how we are going to organise ourselves in a post-work world isn't going to go away.

The Institute for Public Policy Research estimates that more than ten million jobs in the UK – including many of Graeber's 'bullshit jobs' – are at risk from automation over the next two decades, with the potential for automation lowest in London and the south-east (39 per cent of jobs) and highest in the north-east and Northern Ireland (48 per cent), with the West Midlands not far behind (47 per cent).

But for now, the road to salvation through work – witness the Tory saw of deserving 'hard-working families' against the undeserving 'skivers' – remains the only political show in town.

15

BRICKS AND MORTAR
(WEST BROMWICH TO BIRMINGHAM)

My niece came to wave me off next morning, meeting me on West Bromwich high street. She was working as an NHS dementia nurse nearby and was frazzled from overwork and diminishing resources. But as always she had a broad-beam smile, and as she said good luck and turned to go back to work, I felt a surge of pride in my family.

Alone again, I looked at the council building where in 1981 the men and women of the People's March had been billeted on camp beds overnight. Then I looked across the road for the public toilets. Pete had built them, and every time we drove through West Bromwich when I was a kid he would point them out. 'I built that,' he would say, and as it slid past the window I would think my dad was as important as Isambard Kingdom Brunel or Thomas Telford or any of the great engineers we were reading about at school.

But the toilets were gone. There was now a giant supermarket there. It should not have been a big surprise. Public toilets have been rapidly disappearing from our high streets, with over 1,700 facilities closing in the past decade, as local authorities have been forced to spend their slashed budgets elsewhere.

In response to those figures, the BBC asked Raymond Martin, a spokesman for the British Toilet Association – and isn't it an utter delight that there is such a thing? – to comment. He replied that providing public toilets was about health, wellbeing, equality and social inclusion – and also about 'public decency and public dignity'.

Bravo, Mr Martin from the British Toilet Association. Let's hear it for a citizen's right to pee!

That Pete's toilets had been demolished made me feel sad on many levels. I went into the supermarket and used theirs in defiance of the 'for the use of customers only' notice on the door. A small victory.

A little further along the street was West Bromwich's register office, housed in a beautiful 1830s white stuccoed building, with a hipped slate roof, set behind a landscaped garden. In October 2011, I had gone there to register Pete's death. The registrar's manner had been calm and kind, as I suppose she was trained to be, and mine jaunty and casual, because I wasn't remotely upset. Far from it. I felt lighter than I had done for years. I sat there joking with the registrar, asking about her suntan – she'd just been to Tenerife – and how long she'd been doing the job, whether it was satisfying, how she dealt with the terribly upset people she must get sitting in these chairs.

But I was thinking at the time: this couldn't be right. I felt nothing but relief, happy even. How could that be an appropriate response to the death of the man who brought you into the world?

I walked past the Hawthorns, West Bromwich Albion's ground, where I had spent an inordinate amount of time in my youth both as a spectator and as a worker, walking around the pitch with a big plastic tray selling Wagon Wheels and cartons of Kia-Ora to fans. What a thrill! That was my team. And there I was, in the 1978–79 season, walking past the players warming up – probably the best side West Brom ever had. Derek Statham, Brendon Batson, Tony 'Bomber' Brown, Cyrille Regis, Laurie Cunningham, Bryan Robson . . . what a line-up.

That season we finished third in the top division, and for a while had looked as if we might win it. We also reached the quarter-finals of the UEFA Cup, where we drew with Red Star Belgrade in the home leg and went out on aggregate. I even sold their centre-forward – a colossus of a man who spoke in some mysterious tongue – a Blue Riband, which he unwrapped and ate while playing keepy-uppy in the warm-up.

Rarely had West Bromwich felt so exotic. Of that 1978–79 squad of seventeen players, fifteen were born in England, Scotland or Ireland. Big Cyrille was born in French Guiana, and came to the UK with his parents when he was five. Brendon Batson's family brought him here from the West Indies when he was nine.

Turning off the Birmingham Road, I headed down Middlemore Road and into Rolfe Street. After a few hundred yards, opposite the Old Corner Hous pub (the E had fallen off – or maybe been removed in a nod to the Black Country accent), I came to the entrance of the Engine Arm, a dead-end stretch of canal that once served big factories but now provided residential moorings for narrowboats.

I stood outside the gate, high and topped with sharp spikes. Once I would have texted Pete to say that I was outside, and watched him clamber out of his boat, the *Throstle* – one of West Brom's nicknames is the Throstles – and lumber and roll towards me, in his tracksuit bottoms and big jumper and a solid overcoat. He'd arrive at the gate and unlock the big, clunky padlock, saying, 'All right, Mick?'

We'd have a hug. Pete had started smelling differently, as if he wasn't washing enough. Then we'd walk down to the boat and sit at the table, an overflowing ashtray between us. He'd ask if I'd eaten. My heart would sink, because no matter what you answered, Pete would say he'd prepared something and extract an enormous plate from the fridge. And although the type of food on the plate would change, the amount wouldn't. A typical Pete Carter lunch might consist of layers and layers of tuna, mini pork pies, pickled onions, boiled potatoes, mashed potatoes, celery, leftover lamb, carrots, coleslaw, Heinz Sandwich Spread, sweetcorn, olives, tinned anchovies, avocados and much more. 'Eat it all up,' he'd say, and sit there watching me eat. He never once joined me, always saying that he'd eaten earlier. I'd get about halfway through and rub my belly and say that I was stuffed. It was only after he died and I found his false teeth, in one of the drawers on the boat, that I even knew he wore them. I later found out that they hadn't fitted very well, so he'd always taken them out to eat, and was embarrassed. I wish he'd told me. I'd have loved to have sat there with him as he gummed a pork pie.

But then I would have loved to know about his lung cancer as well. He never told anybody about that either, until it was well advanced and he was so weak that he could no longer get on the bus to his chemotherapy and had to ask Sue for help. He hated that. Hated being pushed around in a wheelchair, hated the vulnerability of needing help. He had been a bull of a man. It can't have been easy for him.

When Pete was very ill, I went up to see him on the boat. I sat down opposite him at the table. He was rasping and skeletal, wearing a large oxygen mask, like John Hurt in *Alien*, with the monster clutching his face, keeping him alive. He hadn't cooked anything, thankfully, but he had got some red wine in for me, and poured me a glass. He didn't have one himself. Pete rarely drank in front of me. Only when he was alone would the whisky come out, and I only knew that because if I ever called him in the evening, his voice was always slurred, his focus gone.

Our telephone conversations would go one of two ways. He would either get sentimental, morose and self-pitying, and talk about his failures as a father, how his own upbringing was to blame; or he would go on the attack, denouncing Sue and me, her for a lack of ambition, or her nagging over the state of the boat, me for my emotional fragility, my inability to tolerate closeness in relationships, my tendency to run away, to never commit to anything. 'You're always running, Mick,' he would say, 'and that's my fault as well.' He always seemed to enjoy that analysis, just as an author might enjoy the dysfunction of the characters in their book after they'd dreamed them up and sent them off into the world on the page.

On that last visit, I asked Pete how the treatment was going, and what the oncologists were saying. Pete said they were very happy with his progress. He asked how I was doing, and I said, you know, OK, and then we sat there in silence. I finished my wine and he poured me another. As I was raising the glass to my lips, Pete said, 'You should be careful. Alcohol does terrible things to your liver.'

I'm still not sure what happened when he said that, what tectonic plates in me shifted, but the next thing I know I was jabbing my finger across the table at him, telling him what an arsehole he was; how dare he pretend to care about my health? Where the fuck had he been when I needed him? Where the fuck had his care been then? When he'd failed to turn up time after time, at school plays, sports matches. When he'd let us down so often. When he'd fucked off and left us. He'd probably caused mum's cancer, I said. I reeled off grievance after grievance, the anger and the hurt he had caused, to me, my mum, Sue – the abandonments, the cruel words, the lack of support, the selfishness.

I reminded him about the time I went travelling, just after mum had died, and the letters he had sent to me, full of love, when I was at a safe distance on the other side of the world. How I'd come home after a year and walked into his office, dreaming about the reunion, about starting again, and how he'd looked up from his desk as if I was a stranger, said that he was busy right now, and asked if I could come back in a few hours. Of all the disappointments I suffered with my dad, I think that was probably the worst.

Pete looked shocked, scared even. I had finally connected! I carried on and on. He was on the ropes, shrunken and hollowed out, taking blow after blow. I felt possessed. I couldn't stop.

'But Mick,' Pete said, weakly. 'It was all about the struggle. I sacrificed everything for the struggle. That was more important than anything else. You don't understand.'

I looked at him. Took a deep breath. I could feel the tears running down my cheeks.

'The struggle, the fucking struggle, it's all we ever heard,' I said. 'Look around you. It's all fucked. All that struggle. Your life's work. For what? Was it worth it?'

I climbed out of the boat, into the car, and sped away from the Engine Arm, up past the Hawthorns and onto the motorway. At Warwick Services, I parked up and sat for about an hour, crying in pain, like a wounded animal. A week later I got a letter from Pete telling me he was proud of me and that he was sorry, but I couldn't bring myself to call him, not then. A few days after that I got the phone call saying that Pete was dead.

I turned away from the gate, trudged back out onto the main road and headed towards Birmingham, through Handsworth, scene of riots in 1981. I'd been caught up in them, along with my best friend Jimmy. One sultry evening, we were standing on a street in Sparkhill, a long way from the burning and the destruction, when an unmarked van pulled up and a bloke with a shaven head leaned out of the driver's window and told us in no uncertain terms to get off the streets.

I was seventeen and cocksure, so I told him in no uncertain terms to go fuck himself. The rear doors of the van burst open and a dozen or so uniformed coppers leapt out, ran towards us and started pummelling us, with boots and batons. It was a shocking thing to experience as a young man – the first time that I had even seen, let alone been at the sharp end of, the state violence that would often find expression throughout the 1980s.

By some kind of miracle, my mum was driving past when this was happening; she saw the group of coppers and heard my voice, screaming at them. She pulled over, walked towards the melee and said to the coppers, 'That's my son, officers.' They told her to take me home before they took me in, to which she replied, 'Of course, sorry if he's been any bother,' and I shouted, 'I'm not fucking sorry.' She dragged me off to the car, where I sat all bloody and battered and swollen, with Jimmy in the back seat, and told her that I hadn't done anything.

'I know,' she said. 'I know.'

It began to rain and the sky felt so heavy that it was a struggle to lift up my feet. The walk past Pete's old mooring had added to my heaviness too, I was sure.

I stopped by some railings outside the New Bingley Hall conference centre. They were very familiar to me, from photographs I had found in Pete's box. In those pictures, from 2010, Pete was standing at those very railings, then aged seventy-two, holding a one-man demonstration.

Pete's letters preceding that demonstration had been increasingly heartbreaking to read. Centro, the organisation for whom he carried out those bus surveys, had sent him for computer training. Pete had written to them afterwards, pulling out of it. 'I can cope with the work I was initially taken on to do,' he'd written, a man who had never used a computer in his life. 'But I know my limitations and your excellent presentation only reinforced my lack of confidence in adjusting to the additional work. It was pointless for me to carry on.'

He acknowledged that he'd get less work as a result. 'However,' he wrote, 'I remain available, and at all times, for work I know I can do efficiently. Sorry if I've caused you problems. Sincerely, Pete Carter.'

The work must have been curtailed, for in February 2010 there was a letter from Pete to his bank applying for a £2,000 overdraft. In the same week, he'd sent a letter applying for a full-time job as a bus station supervisor. Full-time job! He was in his seventies! By March, Centro were planning to forcibly retire Pete. His letters to them got increasing bullish, challenging their actions, morally and legally. In letters to Sue, Pete had been less bullish, talking about his fears of impending poverty, his miserly state pension barely covering his living costs.

And so, in the summer of 2010, Pete staged a one-man picket line at Centro's AGM at New Bingley Hall, wearing one of my old suits, haranguing the directors as they arrived, giving out leaflets, and holding a placard reading 'Centro is an ageist organisation: Watch this space'. The fire had still not left him. The struggle had indeed been everything. It was, as one of the speakers at his funeral a year later said, 'Carter's Last Stand' – a funeral, incidentally, where at the conclusion of the eulogies, as the curtain slowly drew around Pete's coffin, the packed crematorium had risen as one and applauded and cheered. I had never seen that at a funeral before.

Pete lost that fight with Centro. But he lived to see the default retirement age in the UK finally abolished. That happened on 1 October 2011, ten days before he died.

I walked past the old Jewellery Quarter. My maternal grandparents had both worked there, making delicate little chains for necklaces. Now it had been redeveloped, the former factories now all expensive apartments, the grotty old pubs I remembered from my youth now independent coffee shops or bars selling artisan beers.

I walked into the city centre, along streets still so familiar to me after all those years, with buildings and shops that seemed barely to have changed, and then along streets which were recognisable only from the name, the new glass and steel high-rises like an army that had invaded during my long absence.

I walked along Corporation Street and Colmore Row, through the churchyard of St Philip's Cathedral, and stood in front of the new Library of Birmingham, an extraordinary building of gold, silver and clear glass, made up of a stack of four different-sized rectangles like a giant birthday cake, the whole building filigreed with thousands of intersecting metal rings, as a nod to the Jewellery Quarter's role in Birmingham's history.

Work started on the construction of the library in January 2010, before austerity had arrived. It opened in September 2013, at a cost of £189 million, a flagship project for the city's redevelopment, the largest regional library in Europe, the continent's largest public cultural space. The schoolgirl Malala Yousafzai, who had survived an assassination attempt by the Taliban in her native Pakistan for daring to go to school, and who now lived in Birmingham, conducted the opening ceremony. 'Let us not forget,' she told the crowd, to cheers, 'that even one book, one pen, one child and one teacher can change the world.'

A little over a year later, in December 2014, the Labour-led Birmingham City Council, facing £113 million of cuts imposed by central government, announced that it planned to reduce the library's opening hours from seventy-three a week to just forty, and that nearly one hundred of the library's staff were to be made redundant.

When the plans were confirmed in February 2015, Sir Albert

Bore, leader of the council, who'd been at Pete's funeral, pointed out that by 2018 the council would have to make savings of £821 million per year from the budget it had had in 2010. It had so far achieved £462 million of that. 'The government cuts that are being handed down to us mean we now really have reached the end of local government as we know it,' he said, his words carrying strong echoes of Sean's in Walsall. 'We'll work closely with our communities and partners, but things will undoubtedly need to be significantly reshaped in the years ahead.'

I walked into Victoria Square, a public space as magnificent as any in the world. The municipal buildings there spoke of a different time, a time when the local authority was the beating pulse of the city, its provider, protector – when the people of industrial Birmingham, as the city of a thousand trades, had helped make Britain the richest nation on earth.

I paused to look at the old post office, a fine example of Victorian architecture, in the French Renaissance style, across the square from the spectacular Town Hall and Council House. In Pete's box, I'd found a photograph of him from 1976, then aged thirty-eight, standing in front of that post office, grinning broadly. He looked like a rock god, with a deep suntan from working outdoors in that sweltering summer, with his thick, curly, windswept black hair. His denim shirt was unbuttoned all the way down to the waist, his lithe, muscled torso showing. He was at the very height of his powers.

In that photograph, he was standing next to Jack Mundey, a builders' union leader from Australia, who had been successful in his country implementing 'green bans' on building projects that were deemed harmful to the environment. It was one of the earliest examples of trade unions working in coalition with the green movement.

Pete had been inspired by Mundey's work, and when the old

post office was scheduled for demolition in 1973, to be replaced with modern, ugly high-rise office blocks, he led a campaign to save it, forming an unlikely alliance between UCATT and the Victorian Society, headed by the poet laureate Sir John Betjeman and the architectural scholar Nikolaus Pevsner. After five years of campaigning, the post office building was reprieved and fully restored.

Forty years later, I was standing on the exact same spot where my dad had been in that photograph. In the spring sunshine, the post office still looked magnificent, although its days as a post office were long gone. Pete's toilets in West Bromwich might have been demolished, but his post office was still standing. For the first time in a long while, I felt so much pride in my dad that I thought my heart would burst.

I thought back to that last visit to Pete's boat, and I couldn't tally that image of him, with his ruined lungs and the oxygen mask clamped on his face, with the photograph of him and Jack Mundey, chests puffed out, standing there in the Birmingham sunshine, the momentum of history on their side.

It was no wonder, really, that Pete had believed then that the victories would keep coming. That year, 1976, with social mobility at its height, the UK reached 'peak equality'; that year, according to a 2013 economic study, the country was better off than it has ever been before or since, as evaluated by 'genuine progress indicator' per capita – a measure that, unlike gross domestic product, takes into account a country's wellbeing.

Towards the end of his life, Pete would say to me that he was glad he'd lived through the times he had, that he genuinely believed when he woke up every morning that the tide of history was on the side of ordinary people. It was like your football team, he'd say, after a lifetime of slogging it out in the lower divisions, suddenly winning the league, the FA Cup and the European

Cup, with every sign that the success could be sustained.

The year after that photograph of Pete was taken, standing in front of the post office, he left my mum, and before long he had moved in with a high-ranking official of Friends of the Earth, taking his holidays not in a caravan in Wales, but in a villa in Tuscany or on an island in Greece that I couldn't find on a map, let alone pronounce.

He now lived in a very middle-class household in an affluent area of Birmingham, with the new woman's very middle-class children. When Sue and I visited, we'd get served nut rissoles – we had no idea such things existed! – and be taken out into the large garden to see the vegetable plot, fertilised with the family's urine. Urine! The dirty sods.

Sue and I would get the bus home, talking about what we'd seen, giggling, taking the mickey out of Pete and his new life, wondering what to make of it all, with his new-found vegetarianism and weird new clothes. I think he even gave up smoking for a while.

I guess such a move made some sense for Pete. In that era of upward social mobility, he had certainly scored a hit on the 'genuine progress indicator' measure, taking the new alliance between the working class and the middle-class green movement to a logical personal conclusion.

Sue and I would return home, sit with our broken mother.

'How was your dad?' she would ask.

And we would tell her what we'd done and seen, and she would smile thinly at us, as we told her that Pete had become a stranger, a total wanker, really.

Mum would tell us off for talking about him like that. But somewhere in our young heads we were battling for her, this woman, our mother, in the fight of her life. And somewhere inside her body there were cells mutating – cells whose devastating effects would, a few years later, have Sue and I telling ourselves that story, the one in which Pete killed our mother; our script, locked down, inviolable, as fixed as tram tracks.

I walked away from the old post office, along pedestrianised New Street, lined with smart coffee shops, people sitting outside them in the sunshine, the city centre so much more glamorous and confident than how I remembered it growing up.

Nearby was a shop, an Adidas superstore. I stood there for a while, staring at it, remembering. Back in 1981, I'd taken a Saturday job in a different sports shop that stood on the site, now long gone. It was a dusty, old-fashioned sports shop, selling ping-pong balls and shuttlecocks and squash rackets and ref- erees' whistles, staffed by people, mostly middle-aged, who'd worked there a long time. One day, sometime in 1983, we were told that the store was to close for a month for refurbishment. It had been bought by an American chain.

After the refit, I walked back into a place unrecognisable. There were now giant screens everywhere, blasting out pop vid- eos. The racks were filled with tracksuits bearing Italian names I'd never heard of, costing the equivalent of the average monthly wage. I couldn't understand who was going to be buying this stuff.

The middle-aged staff never returned, only the younger ones on temporary contracts. The old manager had gone too. The new one had a military background and handed us little books, in which we were to write down all of our sales so that our 'per- formances' could be assessed. I asked him if we were now to be on commission. His eyes narrowed. 'No,' he said, 'your reward will be to keep your job.'

The cleaners had gone, too. So we were expected to hoover and polish after the store had closed for the day. The lunch hour was cut to forty-five minutes. But probably the greatest innovation was the company's new store card, offering instant credit. There were rewards on offer to anybody persuading customers to take these out, in the shape of discount vouchers to be used in the store.

Predictably, things got very competitive on the shop floor as we all tried to nab customers as they came through the door, then hassled them to buy things. Even more predictably, the very expensive tracksuits in the shop became objects of the greatest desire for precisely the sort of young men who had no chance of ever being able to afford one, or qualify for a store card. You could see the lust in their eyes as they looked at them, stroked them. Thefts became more commonplace, the newly installed alarms at the entrance shrieking regularly, blending in with the loud music. A few of us were assaulted as we tried to apprehend thieves, often working in huge gangs. But I could understand why these young men were willing to go to such desperate measures. It seemed an entirely rational response to try to steal an object of desire that this new world was spending so much money on telling you that you needed, but had no chance of ever getting.

Danny Flynn had talked about the time heroin came whistling through Stoke. It was around 1984. That was the same year thugs were on the rampage in my sports shop. Something huge was happening in the country. I reckon that was the year the future arrived, when we stopped selling ping-pong balls.

The forty-five-minute lunch break soon came down to thirty minutes. In Pete's box, I'd found a letter I sent him at the time, with his new London address at the top, in which I talked about failing my exams and then about working at the shop. 'Yesterday, I got the sack as my militant mouth went into overdrive after they'd told us we could only have a thirty-minute break all day,' I wrote. 'I hit the roof and shouted at the manager on the shop floor. I was later summoned to his office where he fired me . . . Lots and lots of love, Mick. PS Mum sends her love.'

The letter reeks of a desperation to please my dad. I too could fight for a cause. Maybe that would bring him back. Mum sent her love? Or was that me trying to knit our family back together? He'd never answered that letter, but he'd kept it. All those years later, it was there for me to find.

A little later, in a quiet Birmingham suburb, I knocked on the front door of a house. A woman answered and invited me in. This was Tara, another of the originals from the 1981 People's March for Jobs.

'Would you like a cup of tea?' she asked. Her voice was still, soft, calming. She returned from the kitchen with two mugs and handed one to me. It was her mug from the People's March.

'That's very precious to me,' she said.

It had her name on it, and her marcher's number. I told her that most of the people I'd met who'd been on the march still had their mugs, even thirty-five years later.

'I'm not surprised,' Tara said.

She reached up to some shelves, and brought down a book and a large manila envelope. The book was *Black Boy* by Richard Wright. Tara said she'd stolen it from her school's library. 'It was the only book they had by a black writer,' she told me. She'd been one of only three non-white children among five hundred pupils, her father a Bengali Sikh who'd come to the UK as a sixteen-year-old, her mother a white Scot.

The school curriculum was British economic and social history, religious education taught using only the Bible, and English literature. *Black Boy* was the first book about non-white culture that she'd ever seen, and by a non-white author to boot. She'd clung on to it ever since.

She opened the envelope and spread its contents on the carpet at my feet. They were photographs, mostly portraits, taken in Montana, where Tara had gone in 2013 for eight months to study photography. The portraits were stunning, eyes burning into the lens with ferocious intensity. Tara liked photographing people, she said, liked to tell their stories. 'I go up to strangers in the streets, ask if I can take their picture,' she said. 'Then we chat. They tell me their stories. All we really have is our stories.'

If Tara had her time all over again, she told me, she might have become a photographer. 'Nobody ever suggested that to me when I was at school. It never entered my head. It was just that you had to leave school and find a job. I dunno,' she said. 'I'm fifty-one now. It's probably too late.'

Tara's father had arrived from India in the late 1940s and settled in Scotland, where he'd met Tara's mother. They had married in 1957. It was tough being a mixed-race couple back then in Scotland, Tara said, but her parents had never liked talking about it. 'It's a shame,' she said, 'because I would have loved to have known about it.'

The family moved to Leicester, where Tara was born and went to school. Being half Indian was difficult. Most white British people viewed her as 'foreign, or Indian or a Paki or whatever'. Asian people frowned on her because she was mixed-race. First-generation Indian immigrants still held very traditional, conservative views. There were specific ideas about marrying within the religion, and within your caste. 'I was about fourteen before I met anybody else mixed-race,' Tara said. 'I was reading the other day about how many mixed-race relationships there are now.'

Her face broke into a soft smile.

Tara had left school at sixteen, with seven O-levels, a bit of a rebel. Her father had been disappointed in her for walking away from education. She'd done a youth training scheme at £25 a week in a full-time job, working for the Red Cross, doing placements in hospitals and playgroups. She'd decided that nursing was for her, but back in 1981, with unemployment rocketing, there was a two-year waiting list. Tara found herself on the dole.

Tara's sister, Morag, three years older, had heard about a march of unemployed people walking from Liverpool to London and decided to join it. 'She was part of a political group, always on demos and stuff,' Tara said. 'But my interest was always more about race issues. The National Front was pretty active in Leicester back then, and I'd turn out to oppose them.'

Aged sixteen, she decided to join her sister on the People's March, to protest against the rising tide of unemployment in which she had been caught. 'But just as much as anything, I went for the adventure,' she said, smiling.

She remembered that the march was mostly men, that she didn't see much of her sister. That she would just talk to anybody and everybody. She recalled the long miles, the blisters, the painful feet, the towns where they stayed, how welcoming everybody was, sleeping on the floors of town halls and community centres. She had felt the communal pull of the march, not only among the participants but also in the people who came out every day to clap and cheer. 'Normal, everyday people would pat us on the back, reach out to shake our hands, as if we were doing something on behalf of the whole country,' Tara said. To this day, her mum kept a picture of the sisters on the march taken by their local Leicester newspaper. 'She's very proud of that,' Tara said.

Tara returned from the march a changed young woman. She hated Leicester. Was worn down by the racism she felt. 'The city always had an edge to it,' she said. She moved, aged seventeen, to Birmingham and immediately felt at home. 'It's a lovely place. It felt safe and comfortable. Still does. For a "feeling" person like me, that's very important.'

She drifted for a couple of years, then in 1984 trained as a nurse. She worked in general nursing for two years and then started specialising in mental health. 'A couple of years later I finally went to university and trained to be a social worker,' she told me. 'I've been trying to get out ever since!'

She laughed. 'No, no, I've loved it. But I've got to the point now where I'm thinking about doing something I really want to do. That's why I'm getting my photographs out, thinking about that again.' They were really fantastic, I told her, and they were. Thank you, she said, but she sounded as if she didn't believe me.

Tara talked about the Community Care Act of 1990, after which most big psychiatric hospitals were closed down. 'I'm not sure where all that money they saved went,' she said. After the hospital closures there were still day centres and community ventures, but most of those had gone now as well. 'There is nothing now for people that I see in the community,' she told me. 'The line is that they don't need specialist services, that they should do mainstream things or go to college. But in reality not everyone wants to do that, or has the ability. They're left with nothing.'

The biggest shift she had seen was the state placing the burden of looking after vulnerable people on their families and on unpaid carers. As services were cut, it was families that took up the slack. 'A lot of my clients don't have families or carers,' she told me. 'So they are heartbreakingly isolated, living in poor accommodation in the private sector, in squalor. They often end up with depression from the physical, emotional and financial impact on their lives. GPs don't have the time or resources to really help, to sit down and ask "What's happened?" or "Has anything changed?" They just give out antidepressants.'

Tara told me that she'd worked with a lot of people who had attempted suicide, some of whom had eventually been successful. The numbers were rising. She was interested in photographing them. When you just looked at statistics, all you saw were numbers, she said, and people would just turn the page. But photographing these people made them human, could have much more of an impact in telling the story of this epidemic. 'I'd like to focus on what it was that helped them. Rather than why they ended up in that dark place.'

Tara thought a modern-day march across the country to protest against these cuts would not be successful. Society had changed in the last thirty-five years. It often felt now as if it was every man for himself. When people failed now, Tara said, the line was that they were somehow to blame for their own downfall. 'I've even heard mental health professionals talk like that,' Tara said, 'that benefits are a disincentive to work and where's the motivation for them to recover. If some of my colleagues are saying that, then . . .'

The EU referendum debate, she said, seemed to be stirring up racist views. 'Not just the usual thugs, but respectable people too. All this stuff about making Britain great again.'

She went off, came back with a couple of photographs. They were pictures of some Sikh men. 'They were on an English Defence League march in Brum,' Tara said. 'Sikhs! I was gobsmacked. I went up to them, said, "What are you doing?" One said to me, "All Muslims are paedophiles." There'd been a grooming story about Muslim men in the press. I said to him, "Look, I work in children's services, and in Brum the two highest rates for sexual abuse are Shard End and Northfields, both majority white areas." I told him that sexual abuse occurs in all classes and races, but he wasn't having any of it.'

Tara looked away, at the stunning portraits on her floor, of people grappling with mental illness. Then she looked at me. 'I was always such an optimistic person, Mike,' she said. 'But I'm struggling a bit now.'

Tara went off to make some more tea. While she was away, I thought about what she had been saying, about society getting more selfish, less compassionate. In her 2007 book *The Shock Doctrine: The Rise of Disaster Capitalism*, Naomi Klein put forward a theory about how this might have happened. Klein wrote about the neoliberal right, how in the sixties and seventies they'd railed against what they saw as the historical anomaly of the post-war settlement, with its redistributive agenda. Their ambition was to create free markets even less regulated than those that existed before the Great Depression, and so reverse the Keynesian 'New Deal' programmes that had supported economies from the bottom up.

Early experiments had taken place in Chile, in 1973, and later in Argentina. These had taken the form of three waves of shock: first, a brutal US-supported coup and the overthrow of a democratically elected government; next, the application of the economic ideas of Milton Friedman and his Chicago School (essentially privatisation, deregulation and deep cuts to social spending); and finally, for the dissenters, torture and repression. In Chile, eighty thousand people were imprisoned, over three thousand were disappeared or executed, and two hundred thousand fled the country; in Argentina, thirty thousand were disappeared.

In advanced western nations such as the US and the UK, Klein said, where such violence against sections of the population would in all probability fail, neoliberal economics were ushered in gradually, though the ballot box, in the form of Ronald Reagan in 1980, and Margaret Thatcher in 1979, both evangelical free-marketeers. In 1999 Thatcher visited General Pinochet, Chile's torturer-in-chief, while he was under house arrest in London, as Spain sought his extradition for crimes against Spanish citizens. Thatcher had called him a friend and thanked him for having 'brought democracy to Chile'.

Just as in countries subjugated by the military, in the US and the UK there soon followed privatisations, deregulations and savage cuts to public services. But they had the good sense to ostensibly invite us to the party, at first through buying shares in the utilities we already owned, or buying the houses that our taxes had already paid for. Politicians told us that 'there is no alternative', that what we were seeing was simply economic Darwinism. Every government since Margaret Thatcher's in 1979 had essentially used the same incantatory mantra.

This thinking has infiltrated so many aspects of our society. In 2014 students at Manchester University joined forces with students from nineteen other countries to protest about the dominance of narrow free-market economic theories being taught on their courses, accusing academics of acting as cheerleaders for the market models that helped push the global financial system into the 2008 crisis.

Neoliberalism has reached nearly every economy in the world, with the pattern always the same: witness what happened to the 'tiger economies' in the 1997 Asian financial crisis, and Russia's fire sale of state assets – and the immiseration of so many of its citizens – after the fall of communism.

Klein argued that in the 2003 invasion and occupation of Iraq, where the tactics used were neatly described as 'shock and awe', we saw an attempt at the most comprehensive implementation of the shock doctrine yet. We would march in and privatise and deregulate (and, in Iraq, without troublesome regulation, also torture). The private sector would then move in and clean up. That hadn't quite panned out. But still, the global cheerleaders for neoliberalism, the economic institutions such as the World

Bank and the International Monetary Fund, tell us that a rising tide lifts all boats. I wondered if they had spent much time in Stoke recently, or Cannock or Walsall, where the tide went out many years ago and has never come back.

Towards the end of her book, Klein talks about the common landscape of countries that had transitioned to a neoliberal, deregulated economy. They were all about winners and losers. Small groups do very well, she wrote, sucking up more and more of the wealth, while large sections of the population become fragmented, left with decaying public infrastructure, declining incomes and either rising unemployment or, as in the UK, increasingly precarious work, with a gradual and systematic erosion of workers' rights. At the core of the neoliberal worldview was the vital need to keep convincing us that there is no alternative, that any dissent is dangerous and subversive, must be crushed, a message enthusiastically channelled through our right-wing media.

Klein thought that the 'shock' started to wear off after around thirty years, that people began to wake up to the giant theft that had been perpetrated against them. I thought about Tara's words, how she was tired of it all, how she used to be such an optimistic person, but was struggling now. Was it any wonder? I felt the same way too.

Tara came back with a top-up of tea in the People's March mug and handed it to me. Thank you, I said. Then she looked at the photographs spread across the carpet, those stunning portraits of the marginalised and the broken.

'Do you really think they're good?' she asked again.

'I do,' I said. 'I really do.'

16

FATHERS' DAYS
(BIRMINGHAM TO NUNEATON)

The next morning I was cursing Pete, but for once it had nothing to do with my unresolved narcissistic wounds and long-held grudges against him as a parent. No, it was because the next leg to Nuneaton was twenty-five miles, by far the longest stretch of the walk so far. And who had organised the original march? Twenty-five miles with a heavy pack, at an average of three miles an hour, with a break for lunch, meant I was looking at ten hours, minimum.

The sky was brilliant blue again, with not a cloud to disturb it. The forecast was for temperatures in the low twenties. I remembered Chris Jones, one of the original marchers, telling me that by Birmingham he'd been as fit as a butcher's dog. But he'd been a young man then. I was fifty-two years old, and my arthritic left big toe had been throbbing continually since Macclesfield. I dug into my pack, found the ibuprofen and popped a couple. Then I put one foot in front of the other.

My life at that moment was so simple, so pared back. Everything had to be carried, so everything had to be justified: the minimum of clothing, all selected for utility, not fashion; clothes for dry weather, clothes for wet weather and layers to help regulate my body temperature; two pairs of shoes, one for rain, one for dry; four pairs of socks, to be washed every few days, ditto underwear. I had a hat for the sun and my hood for the rain; my toiletries were minimal – toothpaste and tooth-brush, essentially; I had my OS maps, but I'd removed the cardboard covers to save weight. When I walked off the edge of a map, I would just leave it in a pub and hope that somebody else might find it useful.

I'd left Liverpool with much more, and I had started dis-carding things immediately, because it was miraculous how that question of necessity shifted when your body had to bear the burden. I guess that is one of the purposes of a long trip: the opportunity for divestment, and not just of the material variety.

I walked past St Andrew's, Birmingham City's ground, and out of the city, through Bordesley Green and Lea Hall and Kitt's Green, with shops flying the Romanian flag, their woodwork painted blue, yellow and red, and employment agencies with little cards in the windows written in English and Romanian, most paying the minimum wage. Then through an area with Pakistani supermarkets and Islamic cultural centres, flying the dark green flag of Pakistan, with its star and crescent, the wood-work of these buildings all painted green, these parades of shops free of nail bars and beauty salons and tattoo parlours.

Soon I crossed over the M6, and the urban sprawl of Birming-ham stopped abruptly, replaced by fields, as if the motorway was a deep river or canyon which the city could not cross. A tension lifted. A sign said sixteen miles to Nuneaton.

My phone beeped. It was an email from Tara. I sat down on a plastic bench in a bus shelter and removed my shoes and my socks and wiggled my toes, which were alabaster-white and wrinkled, like tiny nematodes from the lightless depths of the ocean.

I opened the email. After I'd left her, Tara had been thinking about my walk and my dad, and she had started thinking about her own father.

He'd been a draughtsman for thirty years, Tara wrote. His

drawings, which she'd dug out, had been meticulously tied up in a bundle with string. Interspersed with the drawings had been an old CV and employment references ranging from the 1950s to the 1980s, which charted his moves around the UK after he'd arrived from India in 1948, after partition. His notes showed that he'd leave home early in the morning to get the bus to work, some distance away. He'd get home late in the evening and do overtime on a Saturday to try to make a decent living.

After our conversation, Tara wrote, she wanted to tell me a little about her father. It felt important to her. She'd read glowing references commending his high standards, his timekeeping, his skill and his industrious nature. 'They stated that he was a first-class employee,' Tara wrote. 'But a second-class citizen it seems, because in spite of his good character and his capability, he was never promoted.'

Yet he had worked without complaint, Tara wrote, because his priority had been to support his family. Her father had lived in Britain for over fifty years and had only returned to India twice. The first time was when his mother had died. 'The only other occasion followed my mother leaving him after thirty-five years of marriage, due to finding boredom in an empty nest.'

He had died suddenly at the age of seventy-four. Shortly afterwards, Tara had gone to India to see her father's brothers. The brothers had referred to her dad as 'the noblest soul in the family'. They had told her stories of his life that she had never heard. She learned that her father and his mother were so close that when he left for England she had been inconsolable and had grieved for many years. He had never seen her again.

In India, an uncle told Tara that her father's dream had been to become a doctor, but that the fees to study medicine had been too high. So his father had chosen engineering for him instead. 'In the seconds those syllables left my uncle's lips,' Tara wrote,

'I felt myself crumble inside. My father, the man who worked tirelessly for us, who never complained about a job he must have loathed.'

How could he have survived, Tara asked, 'being bound to a desk, meticulously drawing lines and curves of turbines and of engines with skill and precision but with no hope of progression. He should have been using forceps and scalpels, not set squares and slide rules.'

A bus pulled up and the door opened. 'Sorry, mate,' I said, 'I'm not waiting.' The driver looked displeased. With a swish of air brakes, he was off, the passengers on the bottom deck all craning at me, looking through narrow eyes.

I went back to the email. 'In that momentary revelation,' Tara wrote, 'I felt the sudden crushing realisation that when, at sixteen, I had foolishly and indignantly announced I was leaving school with a handful of O-levels and with no job or prospect of one, that my father was not disappointed in me, he was disappointed for me. Disappointed that I might not achieve a more successful and more fulfilled life than his own had been.'

The year that she'd left school, Tara wrote, had been the only time that her relationship with her dad had been strained. 'There I was at sixteen, outraged by an education that I felt had failed me, and by a society that I felt no part of.' Later on in life, she wrote, with 'new-found empathy and awareness', she had tried to put herself in her father's shoes. 'I could not begin to comprehend what he must have endured,' she wrote. 'Arriving in England in 1948, a kind, gentle, sensitive young man, struggling to seek acceptance in the motherland of hostility, where discrimination was so great that legislation was required to address it, though that was not until seventeen years after his arrival.'

It was not until adulthood that Tara had started to regret her decision to leave school 'with the ignorance and impatience of youth'. At the age of thirty she had finally gone to university, and later returned to gain a master's. The awards ceremony had been a grand affair, she wrote, held at the Symphony Hall, a place her father had frequently gone to for the classical concerts he had loved.

Walking out onto the stage, Tara had thought about how proud her father would have been of her. But he wasn't there that day. 'His name was Ajit, which means invincible, and I thought that he was,' Tara wrote. 'But he had died suddenly the week before.'

She still had all of her father's drawings, she wrote, with the ink gradually fading now from blue to grey, the handwriting so neat that it looked typewritten. She still had all of his fine ink pens and mechanical pencils. 'I keep them all in his old brown leather briefcase under the desk in my office,' she wrote. 'It's a reminder of what he endured and the sacrifices he made, to give me that which he was denied: the freedom to choose and to follow my own path. Best wishes and good luck on the rest of your journey, Tara.'

I closed the email and put my phone in my pocket. I sat there for a while, thinking about what Tara had written, about her father's journey through life; and her own journey, from headstrong, angry, rebellious teenager, to coming to really see her dad, accept that he'd done his best, following the path laid out before him. She had told herself the story of her father; and in so doing had been able to tell herself the story of her. That's all we could ever do. It was perhaps our most vital task.

I passed a sign saying 'Welcome to Warwickshire'. At Blyth Bridge, the pavement ran out; I dug out my OS map and saw that there was a public footpath just there. Not only was the thought of getting away from the busy B4114 delightful, but whereas the road curved and meandered, the footpath looked as if it went exactly in the direction I needed to go: my desire path.

Soon I was walking along the edge of a field of young wheat, bluebells scattered in clumps, where the noise and hiss of the traffic had been replaced by the frantic alarm calls of the skylarks nesting in the crop, occasionally hurling themselves into the air if I got too close, and of chaffinches, with their lovely, exotic descending trill. To me, the chaffinch's song always sounded slightly incongruous in England, as if it really belonged in a tropical rainforest. Around my feet were vermilion flashes, as peacock butterflies danced like tiny kites.

Ahead of me, the hedgerow rustled and a muntjac appeared, about the size of a Labrador, stopping me in my tracks. I held my breath. A *Daily Mail* story had once 'named and shamed' the deer as one of many foreign invaders wreaking havoc on our land. Along with Chinese mitten crabs, the Russian zebra mussel and the South American creeping water primrose, it was 'taking over Britain' apparently. Bloody foreigners.

We tend to be selective about which 'alien' invaders we would like to eradicate and which ones we embrace. The snowdrop, for example, arrived in Britain from Brittany in the sixteenth century, and we generally like them. The horse chestnut tree, with its conkers, beloved by British children, came from the Balkans. Buddleia, brought from China by botanists a century ago, is known as 'the butterfly bush' because its nectar is loved by our butterflies.

'It is sometimes hard to remember that most of the 2,300 or so alien species in England are benign,' wrote Fred Pearce in his 2015 book *The New Wild*, 'and generally add colour and variety to the landscape.' Nearly every species that turned up, Pearce argued, improved biodiversity in the long run. In fact, biodiversity in the UK was probably greater now than it had ever been.

In that same book, Pearce related the Cambridge geographer Stephen Trudgill's view that our strong sense of which plants belong where is unhistorical. Before we took up farming, eight thousand years ago, wrote Pearce, 'there was no golden age of stable, rich ecosystems full of native species'. The land had gone through huge changes after the ice age, and nearly all of the animal and plant life now in Britain had arrived in the last ten thousand years. 'Everything is visiting. Nothing is native,' wrote Pearce.

Flora and fauna had been travelling around the world since the beginning of time. Long before Victorian botanists brought back their cuttings and animals, seeds and insects were dispersed on the wind, or carried around the world by birds in their feathers or their digestive systems; animals had journeyed across oceans on driftwood, or walked across ice bridges. Nature, of which we are only part, was protean, unsentimental, concerned only with perpetuation.

The only species on the planet concerned with nativism was us humans, among whom the whole question of what belonged where had acquired an emotional, narrative element. In the UK, it harked back to a fantasy 'Merrie England' when everything was wonderful, said James Dickson, a botanist at Glasgow University – a time that never existed, but one that many seemingly believed we needed to get back to.

The muntjac sniffed the air, turned and saw me. It paused for the briefest of moments, before crashing back through the hedge and into the adjacent field of oilseed rape (a crop probably introduced to the UK by the Romans), where I could follow its progress only via the disturbed wake in the yellow sea.

I was battered by the time I approached Nuneaton, my skin burned from the sun, the soles of my feet feeling like they had been bashed with a tenderising mallet. I had reached a level of exhaustion where I felt on the verge of bursting into tears. The rain from the west had been chasing me all day and eventually caught up just as I entered the ribbon development of Nuneaton's long approach, which took an age to walk through.

By the time I was nearing my B&B, I was soaked to the bone. The place I had booked was one of the cheapest in town, and as I walked up the street it was on, it began to dawn on me why. In a row of otherwise unremarkable terraced houses, it stood out like one of those homes that got completely made over for Christmas.

It was festooned with Italian and Union Jack flags, with a dozen or so hanging baskets that poured out geraniums in the hues of Italy's tricolour. The front wall was plastered with signs, also in the Italian flag's colours: 'the place to be seen, for parties', 'family anniversaries or that quite [sic] meal', 'party centre', 'disco, dance, live music'.

A free-standing sign on the pavement read 'Home of Stars in Your Eyes'. In the window of the restaurant was the programme of events for the month: tribute acts of Abba, UB40, Rod Stewart, Lady Gaga, Kylie and Adele. Gordon Davis was Elvis. There were Ladies' Nights with strippers, evenings of drag cabaret, and karaoke nights.

I could see that the rooms were right above the restaurant. I scanned down the list to find out what was going to be on that night, praying it wasn't AC/DC. By some miracle, there was nothing on at all.

I looked again in the window. There was a display of photographs and press cuttings with the same man in all of them, who I assumed was the owner. They seemed to start in the 1980s, judging by the fashions and the hairstyles, and there he was, back in the day, with a thick head of hair, with the Nuneaton Carnival Queen and her maids of honour, with the local football team and a trophy, with the mayor in his ceremonial chains. I imagined him determined to bring La Dolce Vita to Nuneaton back then, fresh off the plane, perhaps.

As the pictures moved down through the years, the owner's hair started to thin and then disappear, and the pictures of beauty queens were replaced with ones of him surrounded by hen-night parties, or drag acts, or strippers. But there he was, in every picture, smiling at the camera.

I knocked on the door and waited. Eventually, a young man let me in. I would never meet the owner. He was away. All I had was my story of him.

I walked up a narrow staircase, my movement triggering fairy lights that lined the stairs, as bright as the sun, in red, white and green. The bottom half of the windows in my room were covered in opaque plastic panels of red, white and green too, and when I turned on the fluorescent lights by the windows, they were also in the colours of the Italian flag.

I sat on the bed and reread Tara's email. It struck me that her description of her dad as a gentle, sensitive young man seeking acceptance, belonging, could also easily apply to Pete. I took out my tablet and compiled an email to Tara:

'I've been thinking about my own father's journey through life. It was quite something. After leaving school and home at fifteen, illiterate, he'd drifted for a while, labouring, sleeping rough and singing in nightclubs. One story had it that he sang in a nightclub in King's Heath, and slept there in a cupboard under the stairs.

'Pete once alluded to me rather cryptically that he'd belonged to a far-right gang in his teens. After his death, I found a blog that claimed Pete had once been linked to "gangs of aggressive youths, trying to keep dance halls as white as possible", citing a "highly reliable source" who said that Pete had admitted to him that he was once affiliated to a far-right movement. The National Front had been mentioned, but given the likely dates in the 1950s, the organisation was probably Oswald Mosley's Union Movement. The source claimed Pete had told him he had "overcome a deeply difficult mistake".

'By the early 1960s, he had trained as a bricklayer, and on the sites had encountered men who were members of the Communist Party. He joined the Young Communist League. At a YCL meeting, he met a beautiful young woman called Norma Patrick and her husband. The couple took Pete into their home, where they lived with their young son, Andrew. Pete got into Norma's bed. Norma divorced. Andrew's father fought for custody of him and won. Norma and Pete set up home. Pete would always claim that it was Norma who radicalised him. She'd certainly taught him to read and write, a Henry Higgins to Pete's Eliza Doolittle.

'Recently, I had a visit from my half-brother's father. Now long remarried and in his eighties, he sat in my flat, next to his wife, and started telling me about Norma leaving him, nearly sixty years ago. His eyes became moist and his voice faltered. Imagine! Sixty years! "I don't think your dad was very bright," he said to me. How long these wounds stay with us. My half-brother blames Pete. As do Sue and I. Norma is always saintly, beyond reproach. I think that Pete became a convenient scapegoat in our family. And the funny thing is, he seemed to accept that, as if he thought he was no good all along.

'Pete enthusiastically embraced his new political world. Perhaps he had finally found the acceptance and belonging he had always sought. In 1962, aged twenty-four, he became the Midlands YCL district secretary. A year later, he became the full-time YCL national organiser, and Pete and Norma and my sister, Sue, who had been born in 1962, moved to London so that Pete could fulfil his new role. I came along in 1964.

'In London, we lived with James Klugmann, then in his fifties, a Communist Party intellectual and alleged KGB agent, given the codename Mayor by Moscow, who was thought to have been involved in recruiting the Cambridge spies. Needless to say, James's house was heavily bugged by MI5. With Pete and Norma often away on party business, James was something of a surrogate father to Sue and me. Pete loved James, too. I suspect that he was like the father Pete felt he'd never had. When "Uncle" James died in 1977, it was the only time I ever saw my father cry. It was in the car on the way back from James's funeral that Pete told Norma, with me and Sue in the back seat, that he was leaving us. I wonder now whether, for Pete, love had once again proven itself dangerously unreliable.

'In 1969, Pete left his role at the YCL and our family moved back to Birmingham. Pete returned to bricklaying and got a role as branch secretary of the Amalgamated Union of Building Trade Workers. In the 1970s came my father's great campaigns for building workers' rights. In the words of one of his obituarists, he had been "a brilliant organiser".

'In 1981, Pete helped organise the People's March for Jobs, which is where your story, Tara, overlaps with mine. The year after, he moved back to London to become the industrial organiser of the Communist Party of Great Britain. In that decade, Pete was part of the Eurocommunist wing of the party and was involved in the bitter struggle that eventually tore the CP apart. To the Stalinist old guard of the party, Pete's fierce opposition to the Soviet invasion of Czechoslovakia in 1968 made him a hate figure for the next quarter of a century. He enthusiastically embraced the modernising of the labour movement and linked up with new social movements such as Greenpeace and CND. Those Stalinists wouldn't have been surprised by Pete's stance during the miners' strike of 1984–85, when he'd been critical of the tactics of the NUM leadership – tactics that some noted Pete had himself enthusiastically endorsed and used in the 1970s.

'According to one writer, "Every criticism that was being levelled at trade unionists by the media, the Tories and the government was uncritically retold by Carter . . . His pamphlet 'Trade Unions – The New Reality' considered the Conservatives' anti-trade-union legislation and the campaign for free trade unionism against the backcloth [of] what he saw as a generational realigning of the hard left and the soft left. For him, Communists needed to stand shoulder to shoulder with Neil Kinnock, not Arthur Scargill."

'During the miners' strike, Pete held a meeting with Scargill and Mick McGahey, the Scottish miners' leader, to discuss how to reunite the miners after the strike. According to that same writer, "Given Carter's total hostility to Scargill, the meeting ended up as a complete row." Pete later prepared a pamphlet on the strike, the tone of which "was so hostile and combative, even to his political friends, that [it] never saw the light of day".

'By the late 1980s, under Mikhail Gorbachev, the Soviet Union was unravelling, too, and Pete embraced glasnost enthusiastically. To some on the old left, my dad was a class traitor, a man from the Black Country who'd risen to prominence as a passionate orator and labour organiser, fighting for the rights of the working class, but who abandoned his roots and sold out to the modernising, middle-class intellectuals of the left.

'I'm not sure my dad ever recovered from the political devastation wrought by the 1980s. In 1991, the CPGB broke up. The world was turning its back on socialism and the newly emancipated former Soviet countries were enthusiastically embracing the free market. Britain had had over a decade of Thatcherism. The old left, whose strength had come from heavy industry and organised labour, was becoming an irrelevance.

'I guess that Pete was too, in some ways. Whereas many of his Eurocommunist colleagues went on to jobs as newspaper columnists, or founded think tanks, or were embraced by the rapidly reforming Labour Party, there was no role for old class warriors like Pete. Then in his early fifties, and growing increasingly disillusioned with politics, Pete turned back to laying bricks – and to the Scotch. "Too principled to be attracted to New Labour," wrote Pete's obituarist in the *Guardian*, "he found himself beached by Blairism."

'Tara, I met a man earlier on this walk, in Stoke, who told me there was a sense, when Blair was elected, that things might finally start to change for the better for working-class people. That hope hadn't lasted long. Clause IV was abandoned the year after he became leader. Then followed the light-touch regulation of the City, the intense relaxation about people becoming filthy rich, the courting of plutocrats, Blair even becoming godfather to Rupert Murdoch's daughter, Grace. PFI was embraced, the outsourcing and selling off of state assets continued, the country's sold-off council-housing stock wasn't replenished and Tory anti-union laws were retained. New Labour kept corporate taxation low and VAT (disproportionately hitting the poor) high.

'Blair supported the US-led invasion of Iraq in 2003. In 2004, New Labour opened the UK's borders to people from the former communist countries that had just joined the EU, the only big European economy to do so. More than a million migrants arrived over the next four years, and led to huge pressures on wages and services in some of the UK's poorest areas. No wonder Margaret Thatcher, when asked what her greatest achievement had been, had replied "Tony Blair and New Labour".

'So, Tara, I wonder if Pete, even in his wildest dreams, ever imagined that the modernisation of the left would have led to where we find ourselves today. Maybe the anger I feel towards him is partly driven by a feeling that he was wrong about the world, that what he told me when I was a boy, when he was sole custodian of the truth, was false. Worse, that he sold out, forgot his roots. Like father, like son, huh? Pete the scapegoat. I said as much to him the very last time I saw him alive. It was without doubt the worst thing I have ever said to anybody, and there isn't a day goes past when I don't wish I could take it back. These are preposterous burdens to place on a father, but then the burdens children place on their parents usually are. Best wishes, Mike.'

I put down the tablet. Then I lay on the bed and turned on the TV that was screwed to the wall, flicking through the channels, every one of which was a snowstorm apart from one, which was showing an episode of *The Jeremy Kyle Show*, which I watched in my half-sleep, as a succession of broken people, faces contorted into rage, screamed in pain.

*

I woke up after a good ten hours' sleep, and had to stretch and bend to untangle the knots in my back and thighs after the previous day's long walk from Birmingham.

I hobbled out of the B&B and walked into Nuneaton under a grey sky. My oldest friend, Jimmy, whom I'd met on our first day at secondary school, was coming on the train to Nuneaton to walk with me to Coventry. It was only a short walking day – eight miles or so – so we'd arranged to meet at lunchtime. While I was waiting, I planned to have a look around the town.

I went past the Ropewalk Shopping Centre, named after Nuneaton's once-thriving rope-making industry. In the multi-storey car park next door, by the entrance, there was a little garage full of mobility scooters, which people could hire for the day after parking their cars. I walked into the town centre, along one entire street of charity shops, and then another of pound shops, and then another of closed-down shops festooned with 'to let' signs. In many of the doorways lay the homeless or the drunk, clutching cans of strong lager or cider.

Of all the benighted places I'd seen on my walk so far, Nuneaton seemed the most abject, but I couldn't quite put my finger on why exactly. People looked sallow and grey and worn out, fixing me with hard stares, with so many on walking frames or sticks, or driving mobility scooters, and by no means were they all elderly: so many of the men and women scooting along were hugely obese. Of all the changes I'd seen in my lifetime, our expanding girth was one of the most visible.

I walked past the statue of George Eliot – the pen name of Mary Ann Evans – in Newdegate Square, where she sat gazing down on the shoppers hurrying past. She was born in 1819 at South Farm on the Arbury Estate near Nuneaton, which was fictionalised as the town of Milby in her early works.

Nuneaton seems very proud of her. The hospital is named after her, as is a pub not far from the statue. The town's library has one of the most extensive George Eliot collections in the country.

My phone rang. It was a Birmingham number I didn't recognise. Maybe it was from a friend of one of my relatives who lived there, or a hospital, telling me some grave news. I sat on a bench and pressed the little green button to pick up the call.

'Is that Michael?' a woman's voice said at the other end. She sounded quite young. Maybe she was a nurse, or a police officer. I braced myself. Being called Michael was always bad news.

'Yes,' I said.

'Our records show you have recently been involved in a car accident that wasn't your fault,' said the woman.

I was relieved for a second, then relief turned to something else: not quite anger, but close to it.

I'd started to get these phone calls after a friend's car was written off in an accident while her son was driving. I'd been on the policy as a named driver, and it was likely that the insurance company had sold on the details to solicitors.

I tried to be gentle with the young woman on the phone. If nothing else, I could become one of the people that day who didn't tell her to fuck off. Maybe we could have a brief conversation, might even be able to make some human connection. I could say something like, 'I bet your job is tough, eh, having to cold-call people', and she might say, 'Yes, yes it is. But I can work from home so the commute's not bad!' and I would laugh, and through that connection we might make both of our days a little more bearable.

'The thing is,' I said, 'I don't even have a car, but . . . hello. Hello?' She'd hung up.

At home, the only calls I ever got on my landline these days were from people trying to sell me something, despite the fact that I had a block on cold calls. I didn't answer my landline any more. It just sat there ringing, in the corner, predatorily. And I just sat there listening to it ring, feeling that even in my own home there was no escape.

At the other end of the bench was an older man, with a woolly hat pulled down over his ears.

'Bloody cold callers,' I said to him.

'They're always calling me,' he said. 'I tell 'em to fuck off.'

He looked at my backpack. 'Passing through?' he asked.

'I am,' I said, 'walking to London.'

'Bloody London,' he said, 'whatever they want, they get. Wembley. They put tenders out, but you knew the national stadium would stay there. Heathrow. They'll get the third runway.

Won't come to Birmingham or Manchester. Parliament. That could come out of London.'

'Crossrail,' I said.

'Aye, Crossrail,' he replied, and tutted.

He liked his railways, he said, especially steam trains.

I told him that so did I; that I had recently been on the Bluebell Railway in Sussex.

'I was disappointed by the Bluebell,' he said, but didn't explain why. He reeled off a list of other heritage lines he'd visited.

He'd recently retired after working as a foreman in a warehouse. He was loving retirement. 'I garden, play golf, a lot of walking, and of course the steam railways,' he said.

Was he planning to vote in the referendum? I'd grown quite bold in asking that question. Nobody had been remotely reticent about answering it.

He said he would vote out. 'But it's not about foreigners or immigration,' he said. 'We need these people coming into the country. Most people seem to get on well. They bring a lot of experience. There's one or two that won't contribute, but then we get that with the natives.'

For him, the EU vote was about taking back control, making Britain great again. He reeled off a list of big factories that had closed down in Nuneaton, just like I would reel off the great West Brom side of the late seventies, and said the town was really suffering.

'We need decent jobs that pay decent money. If I was a young man now, I would have to leave to find good work. Most of our young have to leave. I love this town. It would have broken my heart to have to leave it.'

How would leaving the EU help that, I asked him. I said that many people were forecasting economic catastrophe if we lost access to the single market; that many of those EU migrants that he said we needed might be forced to leave.

He sat there and thought for a moment. 'You know what some people round here are saying?' he said. 'They don't care if the economy collapses. Why should they? Nobody in London gives a shit about us. If the economy goes down the toilet, at least those bastards will finally know what it feels like to be us.'

I went into the George Eliot pub. It was busy despite it still being morning. I ordered a coffee. While I was waiting, I looked at the newspapers laid out for customers to read. On the front of the *Daily Express* was a picture of a smiling Labour MP, Pat Glass, above the headline 'Outrageous! Pro-EU MP brands voter "racist" over migrant concerns'.

The *Daily Mail* was splashing with the huge headline 'Migrants spark housing crisis'. I went out into the beer garden and sat down reading the *Mail*. Its lead story was based around an EU report that warned about the shortage of housing in Britain and recommended that the UK government should 'take further steps to boost housing supply'.

The *Mail* had reported this – using figures about expected UK population growth in the next decade or so – as 'Britain has been ordered by Brussels to build more houses – to cope with all the EU immigrants'.

Chris Grayling, the leading Brexit campaigner and Leader of the House of Commons, was quoted as saying that building enough houses to cope with 'migration on this scale' would 'change the nature and character of many parts of this country'.

The story also quoted Liam Fox, another leading Tory Brexiter, who said that ordinary people were aware of EU migration 'in their daily lives by the lack of school places, the difficulty seeing a GP and competition for housing. Of course those who fund the Remain campaign – Goldman Sachs, the big banks, the big corporates, the oil companies – don't really care because they don't use those services.' Fox hadn't mentioned anything about his government's funding cuts to all of those services.

One of my favourite finds in Pete's box was a 1983 press cutting from the *Mail* with the headline 'Red Pete in plot to black nuclear firms'. Until I found that cutting, I had no idea that the *Mail* called my dad Red Pete. The story concerned the building of the nuclear weapons installations at Greenham Common in Berkshire, the RAF base where the US was to house its cruise missiles. 'Left-wing' unions and councils, the story said, were being encouraged to boycott firms doing construction work on the site. The 'key figure in the Communist campaign,' the story went on, 'is Peter Carter, a Midlands organiser of the left-wing construction union, UCATT.'

Mr Carter, the *Mail* continued, 'nicknamed "Red Pete"' (yeah, by you), was to lead a demonstration at Greenham Common on Good Friday. 'And last night he warned he would be back with a mass picket later next month to "persuade" construction men not to work on silos for Cruise missiles at the American air base.' I loved the menace attached to the inverted commas around the word 'persuade'. Then there was a quote from Pete. 'Having nuclear installations like this is equivalent to building Hitler's gas chambers,' he'd said. 'We shall fight to stop projects like Greenham going ahead.'

Using the prefix 'Red' for those whom newspapers see as dangerous subversives is of course nothing new. But it perhaps found its nadir when the *Daily Mail* savaged 'Red' Ed Miliband on 28 September 2013, as Geoffrey Levy wrote a piece about the then Labour leader's late father, Ralph Miliband. The headline screamed: 'The man who hated Britain: Red Ed's pledge to bring back socialism is a homage to the Marxist father he idolised.'

A few days earlier, Ed Miliband had said in a speech at the Labour conference that his party, if elected in 2015, would tackle profiteering energy firms. It would introduce a tougher regulator and freeze prices for twenty months, to reflect the fall in oil prices that these private companies were not passing on to British consumers, already paying some of the highest energy prices in the world.

The *Daily Mail* (owned by the billionaire Lord Rothermere), which came out for the Tories as usual in 2010, unleashed hell on Ed Miliband, as did the *Metro*, also owned by Rothermere, aided and abetted by the *Sun* and the *Times* (with a billionaire owner who lives in the US, and who also backed the Tories in 2010), and the *Telegraph* (with billionaire owners who live on the private island of Brecqhou and supported the Tories in 2010), and the *Express* and the *Daily Star* (then owned by a billionaire who made much of his fortune from pornography, and backed the Tories in 2010).

These publications and their Sunday sister titles, in 2013, accounted for 67.2 per cent of newspaper readers (print and online) in the UK. On this measure, 52.2 per cent of our 'free press' is owned by two billionaires, and 77.8 per cent by six billionaires. 'Total liberty for wolves is death to the lambs,' as Isaiah Berlin put it.

I thought what Ed Miliband was saying seemed perfectly reasonable. After all, since the Tories had privatised the utility companies in the late 1980s and early 1990s, prices had risen steeply. Besides, in November 2013, just over a month after the pledge by 'Red Ed' to turn Britain into a Marxist wasteland, a YouGov poll found that 68 per cent of the British public thought the energy companies should be nationalised, with only 21 per cent saying they should remain in private hands. Even among Tory voters, 52 per cent believed energy firms should be nationalised.

Quite why 'Red Ed' had invoked the full rage of billionaire newspaper owners, when all he was doing was reflecting the wishes of the vast majority of the country, would have to remain a mystery. Anyway, in May the following year, Ed Miliband was photographed failing to look normal while eating a bacon sandwich and his fate was truly sealed. What a pair those brothers are, eh? One stabs the other in the back, they had a rabid Marxist father who tried to bring down the country that took him in, one couldn't eat a bacon sandwich properly and the other couldn't handle a banana.

A man sat down opposite me with a pint of lager, and rolled up a cigarette.

'All bollocks that, ain't it?' he said to me, pointing at the paper.

'Which bit?' I asked.

'All of it,' he said.

He looked as if he was in his mid-forties, his face hard, pulled in a tight scowl, with eyes darting around in a kind of hypervigilance that would make you nervous if he was standing behind you at a cashpoint.

That feeling was not helped by the spider-web tattoo covering the entire left side of his face. On his head he wore a tight beanie hat.

'I've been in and out of prison,' he said, apropos of nothing. 'Assault, GBH, you name it.'

He fixed me with a cold stare. I shifted slightly in my seat, sitting more upright, suddenly paying close attention.

'Oh, yeah,' I said, not really sure what to say, but trying to sound casual.

'Cut your throat in prison for what you've got there, mate,' he said, pointing to my phone on the table. 'Seriously. Ha, ha, ha.'

'Ha, ha, ha,' I laughed back, sounding like a scared functionary responding to a mad dictator's joke.

'My life's been all over the place,' he said. 'Survived attempted murders. Want to see?'

He ripped off his hat. The top of his shaved head was like nothing I'd ever seen before. It was corrugated, rippled, like a crinkle-cut crisp.

'Jesus!' I said. 'What happened?'

'Hammers, baseball bats, mate,' he said. 'Don't really want to talk about it.'

He put his hat back on, tugged on his roll-up, took a long sip of his pint. He picked up his phone, looked at it, as if willing it to ring, and put it back down on the table.

'I'm waiting for a call,' he said. 'Then I'll have to go.'

'Business?' I asked, in the sort of shit Ray Winstone voice that I always seem to adopt in situations like that.

'Nah,' he said. 'Waiting for a call from my ex. My son, the school he's at had a water leak this morning, closed the school down, I don't really know him, know what I'm saying, want to learn more about him, I'm waffling on about my son now, sorry about that, just trying to give you a little insight into my life, I've had it pretty negative, you know, I've only got myself to blame for most of it, bad company, sometimes I'm the bad company, know what I mean, ha, ha, ha, ha.'

'Ha, ha, ha, ha,' I laughed back.

He'd kept his nose clean for the last eighteen months, he said. No trouble, nothing. He had five kids with three different women. None of them would have anything to do with him. He looked sad when he said that. His youngest, the one at the school with the water leak, was his last chance. He was going to really try with him. 'That's him,' he said, holding up a picture on his phone of a cute, smiling little blond boy. 'Six in July.'

He was trying to get his life straight. He'd lost his mum. 'That's why I've got her there,' he said, showing me a tattoo on his arm. And his dad had died recently too, and one of his best friends. 'It's just been one bad thing after another.'

His dad had moved to Coventry from Nuneaton as a young man.

'It was like that song by The Specials, weren't it, Boom Town?' he said.

'Ghost Town,' I said.

'You what?'

'It was called Ghost Town,' I said again, though I was wishing I hadn't, really, as he looked a bit angry now.

'Yeah, yeah, Ghost Town,' he said. 'You're the clever one, ain't ya? What I was trying to say was that it was a boom town, all the industry, cars and all that, me mum and dad did very well, started a furniture business, but Cov is a ghost town now, I were there yesterday, dead, shithole.'

His parents had moved back to Nuneaton when they'd retired, and he'd followed.

'I had nowhere else to go,' he said. He wasn't working at the moment, but had dreams of going into business with one of his brothers. 'Building,' he said.

'I'll probably be doing the labouring, ha, ha, ha, filling skips or whatever, it's just boredom with my mental health, I don't know what to do with myself half the time.'

Did he feel that the system had supported him, I asked. Less Ray Winstone now, more Robert Winston.

'It's me that's let the system down,' he said. 'I can blame it sometimes, but I'm human. We're all human, ain't we? We all mess up.'

He pointed at the *Daily Mail*.

'We should go back the way we were, we're an island, we do our thing, we stick up for the world, everyone comes running to us, don't they, when there's a problem, that's true, even the Americans, I dunno, two worst things you can talk about, politics and religion, the two things that start wars.'

What did he think about all of the jobs that had been lost locally?

'Lots of jobs going to China, India, they reckon India's going to be one of the most powerful economies in the world, imagine that!' he said. 'You make a phone call, and it goes to India and back to here and that, it doesn't bother me, as long as I get through, I'm not a racist, raised in an area of Cov that's very multiracial, people from all over the world, that's where I grew up, one thing I won't stand for is racism and all that.'

We sat there quietly for a minute. He had been checking his phone every few seconds.

'Last thing I got done for was twocking,' he said. 'Know what that is?'

'Nicking cars?' I said. I was back to Ray Winstone.

'Very good,' he said. 'Remember that guy what used to do that TV thing about criminals, news presenter weren't he, smug-looking fuck, he ended up getting done for drink-driving, and he's there slagging everyone off and he gets done himself, fucking funny that was, ha, ha, ha, ha.'

'Ha, ha, ha, ha,' I laughed back.

He wasn't driving at the moment, he said. He liked a drink too much. 'I wouldn't say I was an alcoholic, but I'm a bit of a binger. Easier just walking, or getting the bus, so I'm not hurting nobody.'

He'd been speaking to one of his brothers about going into rehab. 'I'm going to go and see them this week. I want to get my life sorted, for him mostly,' and he lifted up his phone again, found the picture of his son, showed it to me again.

His phone rang. He pulled it to his ear.

'OK,' he said into the phone. 'See you there.'

He stood up, smiling, but looked a little anxious too, as he put his tobacco and his phone into his pocket.

'Nice talking to you, mate,' he said.

'Good luck,' I said.

And with that he was away, out onto the street, walking under the pub sign from which George Eliot gazed down, off to meet his son. 'What we call our despair,' the author had written in *Middlemarch*, 'is often only the painful eagerness of unfed hope.'

17

THE DECLINE AND FALL
(NUNEATON TO COVENTRY)

I saw Jimmy at a distance, picked him out instantly among the crowd of people getting off the train. We'd known each other for over forty years, since our first day of secondary school in Tyseley, Birmingham. Everything about him was immediately recognisable: the way he took a minute, when he first stepped off the train, to straighten himself up, looking around, like a visiting dignitary; the way he slung his bag over his shoulder in an exaggerated gesture; the way he walked, with a kind of military stiffness. These things were part of me. I knew them on a cellular level.

My heart always leapt when I saw Jimmy. He'd been the punctuation marks in my life, the constant presence. We grew up in each other's houses. We spent endless hours fishing together. We had played for the same cricket teams, and rugby teams, in school and out. We'd shared sporting triumphs and disasters. We'd got drunk together for the first time, aged thirteen, on a trip to a youth hostel, and got banned from the YHA together as a result of the vomit-covered sheets that ensued.

We'd had an argument only once, but I couldn't even recall what that was about. Jimmy supported Aston Villa. And because of him, and despite the traditional rivalries between that club and West Brom, I always felt happy when Villa did well.

We'd seen each other grow from boy to man, through those

first awkward dates with girls, and the heartbreaks. We had gone to the same sixth-form college. Had both moved to London in our twenties. We had carried each other's parents' coffins. We had spent endless hours on the phone, or in the pub, talking about our successes and setbacks. In the mental photo album of my life, Jimmy was in nearly every frame. I did have a map, after all, and Jimmy was all over it.

'Hello, Mick,' Jimmy said, stiffly holding out his hand.

That was another thing that spoke of our lifelong bond. Being called Mick, for sure, took me right back. But whereas I hugged all of the friends I'd made in adulthood, with Jimmy it was always a handshake. We'd never hugged. Not once. That kind of thing had not been invented when we were eleven years old, or at least not in inner-city Birmingham.

Now it was too late to change. In some weird way, it was comforting, a ritual that wordlessly connected us to another place, another time, but also to here, now.

We walked away from the station. I got us a bit lost trying to find the canal that would take us to Coventry.

'Idiot,' Jimmy said.

'At least I'm not a Villa fan,' I said.

'At least we've won the European Cup, you wanker,' he said.

Minutes. That's all it took. We'd become eleven years old again.

We found the canal. It felt great to be on a towpath again.

'Heron!' Jimmy said. 'One-nil.' And he gave me the V-sign.

At some time in the past, exactly when neither of us could remember, we'd started playing the heron game. It was a stupid game, which involved spotting herons and shouting 'one-nil', 'two-nil' and giving the V-sign to the other person as you shouted. And that was it. But, like the manly handshake, it was what we did – what we would always do.

Jimmy grew up in a council house in Sparkhill, a mile from the house where I lived. His mum and dad had moved to England in the early 1960s, from Cork and Limerick respectively, because there was no work in Ireland. Jimmy's dad got a job as a bus conductor for Birmingham City Council. He'd loved it, Jimmy said, collecting fares, having a chat to the passengers. It had been a social thing and everybody seemed to like it, having a conductor in a smart uniform walking around. 'It made people feel safer,' Jimmy's dad would say.

One day, he came home from work in a panic. They were sacking all of the conductors; the driver would now be collecting the fares.

'Even back then, councils were under financial pressure,' Jimmy said. 'Somebody came up with the bright idea of halving the workforce overnight, losing what must have been thousands and thousands of jobs at a stroke.'

Jimmy's dad told the family he was going to apply for a job as a bus driver. 'He'd never even driven a car,' Jimmy laughed. But his dad passed the test. At first it was all OK, but then the assaults on drivers started, robberies, so they put them behind a cage. I remembered that happening when I was young: the cages, first a metal grille and then a Perspex shield, with a driver imprisoned behind it. If he was now safe, what did that make us passengers?

Jimmy said his father's greatest sadness on the driver-only buses was the loneliness he felt – not only on the job, shut up inside a cage for hours, but at the terminus, where previously the driver and conductor would have had a cup of tea and a chat.

'He'd loved that,' Jimmy said. 'It was good for him, that contact. He'd always have great stories about what such and such was up to.'

We had a similar transformation happening now on the trains

on which I travelled to work. The franchise owners were trying to get rid of the guards and have driver-only-operated services. Aside from all of the union arguments about safety, and the franchise's arguments about 'efficiency' (for which read 'profit'), there was just something humanly reassuring about having somebody in uniform walking up and down the carriages. It couldn't be explained to accountants. But it just made the whole business of being human slightly more, well, human.

'Heron!' yelled Jimmy.

'Where?' I asked.

'There,' he said, pointing to the huge bird sitting by the side of the towpath up ahead.

'Two-nil. Ha.'

In the margins at the edge of the towpath were clusters of wild garlic and cow parsley. On the water, behind two Canada geese were their goslings, seven grey fluffballs, all in a straight line.

I asked Jimmy about growing up in a council house. Fine in those days, he said. No stigma at all. You just took the word 'council' out, and that's what you had: a house. Most of the people we were at school with lived in council houses.

'Hardly anybody thought about owning their own home,' he said. 'Didn't occur to them. Would have been like going to the moon.' Why would they have wanted to, Jimmy said – why shell out all that money when they had affordable rents?

'My dad was a bus driver, normal job, and my mum never had to work. There was my brother and me, in a three-bedroom house with a decent garden,' Jimmy said. 'That would be impossible now on a bus driver's salary. Both parents would have to work and you'd be living in a two-bed flat with a private landlord. We call that progress!'

Jimmy talked about the sense of protection you felt living in a house owned by the council.

'Anything went wrong, you'd ring them up and the next day somebody would turn up and fix it. That sort of protection was factored into your rent. All seems a long time ago now.'

It reminded me of what Sean in Walsall had talked about, the way cash-strapped councils were no longer seen as benevolent, but there to frustrate you.

Jimmy had worshipped his dad for the quiet, dignified way he'd got on with his life, raising a family, watching Villa at the weekends, having a few pints with his mates from the buses, never complaining. He found it hard to imagine his dad living in a world where that wasn't enough.

'I never had the sense that our working-class, inner-city upbringing was something bad and had to be escaped from,' he said. 'You could become a teacher or work in a bank or something, but there was nothing wrong with the way we grew up.

'Your dad, Mick, was a bricklayer, mine was a bus driver. There was nothing wrong with living in a council house, nothing wrong with going to a state school. Somehow the message now is that being working class is quite shameful. What's wrong with being average, the average man in the street? Everybody wants to be above average now. Statistically, how can that happen?'

Jimmy went quiet, gathering his thoughts, trawling through his memories, looking for ways to make sense of it all.

'At my dad's funeral, one of his best mates came up to me,' Jimmy said. I remembered Jimmy's dad's funeral as if it was yesterday. I had never seen anybody as physically affected by grief as Jimmy that day. His face was so red it looked as if it had been boiled, his features blurred almost beyond recognition. He'd sat there in front of me during the service, his arms wrapped around himself.

'His mate said to me, "You know what was the best thing about your dad? He was really happy with what he had." It was true. My dad was one of the happiest people I ever knew. He didn't want a bigger house, or more clothes or anything. Happy with his job, wife and kids, a few pints with his mates, watching the Villa.'

But it was complicated, though, wasn't it, I said to him. Both of us had turned our backs on all of that. Why hadn't that been enough for us?

'We laugh,' he said, 'when we see the pictures from North Korea. "Look at how brainwashed they are. They lead terrible lives but now their leader's dead and they're all crying in the street." I don't think there's a bigger con going on in the world than what's happening in the UK and the US. "You can be anybody you want to be." Not really. Let one or two through every now and again, but the majority of you won't be moving up the ladder.

'You and me, we sit there on the sidelines moaning about it all. But we're not doing anything about it. We're not knocking on doors, selling newspapers, making speeches, like your dad did. We just sit there, angry. I don't know where to turn to, where to put this anger. Every other person I speak to about this thinks I'm mad. "Shut up", "Corbyn's a tosser", "We've never had it so good".

'I don't know what the answer is. But I do know that my dad was happier than I've ever been. He never let anything bother him. Not like me. It bothers me. My dad used to follow the news and read the papers but it was very hard to rile him. I wish I could be more like him.'

In 1983, the first election in which we could vote, Jimmy had put his cross in the box for the Tories, helping to give them the most decisive election victory since Labour's landslide in 1945, when Clement Attlee's government had founded the welfare state and the NHS. Jimmy might have been winning in the heron-spotting contest, but I would always have that. Who knows, maybe that was why we'd had our only fight.

'You always bring that up!' he said. 'I was only nineteen for God's sake.'

He said he thought things like buying your own council house would be a way forward for working-class people.

'If I knew then what I know now,' he said, 'then obviously I would never have voted Tory.'

I spotted a heron up ahead, but didn't say anything, didn't want to stop Jimmy's flow.

'On paper it sounded amazing. Owning your own home, owning shares, ordinary people,' Jimmy said. 'There were multinationals around, but they didn't have the control and power over government that they do now. There were no zero-hours contracts. Our public services were still good. This was against a backdrop of inefficient state industries, crippled by unions, massively subsidised by the taxpayer. Somebody came along and said it's better if the citizens are the shareholders of a country. I was one of the mugs who believed it.'

We came to a junction in the canal. Turn left to London via the Oxford Canal, or straight on to our evening's destination at the end of the Coventry Canal, which, a signpost said, was only five miles away.

At the junction was a lovely looking pub, the Greyhound, with tables set outside overlooking the water. We stopped for a drink. Jimmy went inside and came back to the table with two pints of Pedigree.

I told him I had seen a heron while he'd been talking. He believed me, he said, but competition rules meant heron-spottings could not be claimed retrospectively. I told him I didn't know there were such things as competition rules. Of course there were rules, he said, or else there would be anarchy. During our discussion about the finer points of heron-spotting, I had been removing my boots and my socks.

'Phew! Who ordered the cheese?' said a voice from behind me. I turned around. There were two women sitting on the next table, around our age, maybe a little older, both with glasses of rosé in front of them, beside which was a half-empty bottle and, next to the half-empty bottle, a completely empty bottle.

'I said, "Who ordered the cheese?"' the same woman repeated, pointing at my feet, in case I hadn't understood.

'Ha,' I said. 'We've been walking. Just giving them some air.'

I sensed that she wanted to talk. And maybe it was the empty bottle-and-a-half of rosé on their table, but I had a feeling of dread inside me.

'Where you from, then?' the woman asked me.

'I work in London now, my mate lives just outside Birmingham.'

'London!' she shrieked. 'You've only gone and voted for a Muslim mayor. Where will it all end?'

I shrugged my shoulders in that ambiguous way where you hope the other person thinks you are expressing sympathy for their views, while you know that your shoulders are really saying 'what the fuck, you racist cow!' It was cowardly, but it usually helped avoid confrontation.

'What do you think about this Europe thing, then?' she said.

I opened my mouth . . .

'All the foreign paedophiles coming over here. Fiddling with our kids. They let them all in,' she said. Clearly my shoulder action needed some work. 'We're bloody soft, that's the problem. Taking all that rubbish. Foreigners coming here to scrounge off the rest of us. Send 'em all home.'

Jimmy put his pint down on the table. He listed the positive things about the European Union, the protection of the environment, free movement, providing nearly 60 per cent of our trade, access to a seven-hundred-million-strong market, an end to centuries of bloodshed, workers' rights, human rights . . .

'Don't talk to me about all that stuff,' the woman spat back. 'Workers have far too much bloody protection now. I run a business and I have to pay everything.'

Jimmy stared at her, then picked up his pint and didn't say another word. I just shrugged my shoulders at her. I knew what I was saying.

We finished our pints and left. Once onto the Coventry Canal, we replayed the conversation. 'Foreign paedophiles! Coming here to fiddle with our kids. What's wrong with our paedophiles doing it? A Muslim mayor!' I said, mimicking her accent. 'Where will it all end?'

'You laugh, Mick,' Jimmy said. 'But I hear that kind of thing a lot.'

In 1980, after Jimmy had taken his O-levels, his parents wanted him to get a trade. He got himself on a plumbing apprenticeship, and they were very proud of him. But he hated it and quit. Jimmy returned to school to do A-levels, the first in his family to do so. His parents were mystified, angry. Why would anybody give up an apprenticeship? Jimmy went to university, where he studied economics. By this stage his parents thought he'd been taken over by aliens.

He moved to London, where he worked for an accountancy firm, which seemed to make him no less miserable than the plumbing apprenticeship. After a few years, he jacked that in as well and returned to the Midlands, where he enrolled on a PGCE course, to train as an economics teacher.

By 1993 he was teaching in a sixth-form college. It was there that Jimmy had witnessed, just like David in Macclesfield, the marketisation of the FE system, the driving down of standards on vocational courses, the grade inflation, the competition among colleges to attract more and more students to keep the money rolling in, the increasing pressure on teachers to pass the students, the ever-increasing teaching hours.

'All the good teachers, who wanted to be prepared properly, deliver good, stimulating classes and push kids,' Jimmy said, 'they grew very depressed and disillusioned. Those that could leave did; but those with financial commitments, families, they had no choice but to stay. Many of them hated every minute of it.'

Jimmy, without any such commitment, left after six years.

'I couldn't stand it any more,' he said. 'Couldn't live with myself. A once-great job turned into a load of bollocks. It is now just one big money-making machine.'

Jimmy talked about the pass rate of A-levels today.

'It's 98 per cent! Did you know that? Ninety-eight fucking per cent,' he said, and held up his hands as if in supplication.

Back in 2012, Glenys Stacey, the head of the exams watchdog Ofqual, had admitted that A-level grade inflation was a huge problem.

'We have seen persistent grade inflation for these key qualifications for at least a decade,' she said in an interview with the *Sunday Telegraph*. '[It] is virtually impossible to justify and it has done more than anything, in my view, to undermine confidence in the value of those qualifications.'

How handy, Jimmy said, that all those students were passing A-levels in a society obsessed with sending half of its young people to university, a society that had built a multi-billion-pound industry out of it. I'd lost count of the times I'd heard people tell me that on my walk.

Jimmy's phone rang. He looked at the screen. It was a Birmingham number.

'I should get this, just in case it's work,' he said.

'Hello,' Jimmy said into the phone. 'No, I haven't been involved in a bloody accident.'

After Jimmy left teaching, he picked up a succession of jobs, in IT and sales and other things, before landing a job with Birmingham City Council. At first that had been a fabulous job, and he thought he'd found the place he wanted to spend the rest of his working life. But after the election of 2010, when central government's funding cuts really kicked in, everything started to change, just like it had done in education.

'It's like a cancer spreading through society,' Jimmy said. 'Efficiency, cuts, do more with less, that's the constant mantra. It will never end until there's nothing left.'

It was wearing him out, he said. He didn't know where to go, what to do to escape from it all. Morale among his colleagues was terrible. Every year they had to sign new contracts, and every year they involved more hours, and demanded more flexibility. He was now doing a job previously done by three people.

He gave me an example of these new practices. By law you had to register a new baby. But the council had closed down its register office in Sutton Coldfield because of the budget cuts and removed registration from hospitals. Now everybody had to go to the register office in Birmingham. Demand there had shot up massively, but they got no more staff. The front page of the *Birmingham Mail*, Jimmy told me, ran a headline that said the register office was failing to meet its legal requirements. All of the blame, Jimmy said, fell on the staff and management of the register office.

People went in there complaining, because they would get into trouble as parents for not registering their child's birth within the legal time limit, but every slot was taken and they couldn't get an appointment for six weeks. So the parents would be breaking the law.

'That's how those bastards get things ready for privatisation,' Jimmy said. He was right, of course. That's exactly how it worked: public services were run into the ground so that nobody could object when the private sector was given the opportunity to 'fix' them. The easiest game in the world.

We walked through Coventry, past the former Royal Mail sorting office, which was being demolished to make way for student flats for Coventry University. Two months before my walk, it had been announced that the city's two universities, Coventry and Warwick, with 52,000 students out of the city's population of 345,000, were to invest over £1 billion in Coventry, into a range of academic, commercial and accommodation buildings.

The skyline of Coventry was busy with cranes, and from reading the hoardings around the bases of the rising buildings, I saw that many of them were university developments.

Back in the mid-twentieth century, Coventry's economy was very different. Daimler had built Britain's first ever car plant there in 1897, and after that the manufacturing industry had grown and grown. It reached a peak in the fifties and sixties, when the UK was the second-biggest carmaker in the world, with Coventry at the centre of that industry. Factories including Triumph and Daimler, Rootes and Peugeot had seen it dubbed 'Britain's Detroit'. The average wage in the city was 25 per cent higher than in the rest of the country.

'The industry *was* Coventry,' recalled Geoff Wise, a retired car plant worker, in an interview with the *Daily Telegraph*. 'Most factories had a social club – they brought families together. It was part of the fabric of society.'

With the global oil crisis of the 1970s, industrial strife and the destruction of the UK's manufacturing base in the 1980s, Coventry was devastated, as the top fifteen employers in the city cut almost 50 per cent of their workforce.

That was the time of The Specials' 'Ghost Town', released in

June 1981 by the Coventry band, the month after the People's March for Jobs had passed through. The song's lyrics spoke of urban decline, deindustrialisation, unemployment and the inner-city violence that was to infect thirty-five communities up and down the country that summer. The song went to number one.

Jerry Dammers, founder of The Specials, has said that the song was inspired by the things the band was seeing on tour. 'You travelled from town to town and what was happening was terrible . . . everything was closing down,' he told the pop critic Alexis Petridis in 2002. 'You could see that frustration and anger in the audience . . . It was clear that something was very, very wrong.'

By the time I had walked into the city thirty-five years later, the only plant still making cars in Coventry was The London Taxi Company, now owned by Geely, a Chinese firm. British Leyland closed its Canley factory in 1980. Massey Ferguson's vast tractor production line closed in 2002, after three million machines had rolled off it since the plant's opening in 1946. Its American owners, Agco Corporation, who'd bought Massey Ferguson in 1994, decided to concentrate their business on specialist machines they built in plants in France and Brazil. Over a thousand people at the factory were made redundant.

Jaguar stopped making cars at its Browns Lane plant in 2005, and Peugeot's Ryton factory was wound up in 2006. Another of the city's big employers, Marconi, axed hundreds of jobs at its Coventry facilities in 2005.

In 2016, Coventry was on the verge of partly rejuvenating its automotive heritage at two new hi-tech design centres. Coventry University was planning to open its £7 million National Transport Design Centre in the summer of 2017, while Warwick University, in a joint venture with Jaguar Land Rover and Tata

Motors, was planning to open the £150 million National Automotive Innovation Centre in 2018, bringing together students, academics and industry in a cutting-edge research and development facility.

Looking at those figures, there could be no doubt that the universities were playing a big part in the regeneration of Coventry. But a look at the letters pages of the local paper showed that this drive to attract more and more students to boost the local economy was dividing opinion.

In the students' defence, a Danielle Rose had written that she couldn't understand what many local people had against them. 'They spend their money in shops, cafes, at the cinema and in nightclubs,' she wrote. 'Without this income, new shops and businesses cannot be developed and this is the reason why so many shops in Coventry are closed down . . . why can't the people of this city be proud of its accomplishments? What would be so bad about being a city that bases its success and growth on the faces and names of the future?'

A Joe Reynolds had responded to Ms Rose. As a former student himself, with all of his children having gone to university too, he had no problems with students per se. What he objected to was 'the growth of the university at the expense of the people of Coventry . . . my problem is the balance of non-council-tax-paying students against those of us living and working in the city who would like some of the facilities that other cities enjoy . . . The only area that looks appealing is the area around the university. The rest of us have to put up with poor-quality roads and pavements and second-rate amenities.'

Under an article about another new student accommodation block, many readers echoed Joe Reynolds' views. 'Surely the people of Coventry should have a say on what things are built in Coventry,' wrote Mary Fisher; 'The city centre is now a university campus,' wrote Pat Mock; 'Can't we just make it a nice place to live for everyone already here?' asked Becky Hinson; 'Please, no more students. They're taking over,' wrote Tony Fulford.

Jimmy and I walked along Market Way, with its Poundland and pawnbrokers and betting shops. The British Heart Foundation had a sprawling megastore, selling furniture and electrical goods. On a bench, two young men with bulging holdalls sat drinking cans of Special Brew and shouting at each other. We passed a pub, busy in the late afternoon. People glided past us on mobility scooters, or hobbled past on walking frames.

'Have you heard from Anders recently?' Jimmy asked.

I had, I said. I'd spoken to him on the phone about two months before.

Anders was a mate of ours from Stockholm. He had been to London many times, so when he came to visit me and Jimmy a couple of years ago we decided to take him to Blackpool to see a different side of the UK's cultural life – a place where Jimmy and I had spent many happy days as youths on day trips from Brum.

We'd walked around Blackpool with Anders, gone to the Pleasure Beach, wandered along the Golden Mile. It was now a town where the average life expectancy was five years lower than the UK's average, and where alcoholism, drug abuse, violence and self-harming was rife.

Part of Blackpool's problem was its houses of multiple occupation, often bedsits converted from guesthouses by landlords, which attracted a lot of people on incapacity benefit. This had made Blackpool a net importer of ill health, pushing public support provision to its limits.

Perversely, too, because accommodation in Blackpool was relatively cheap, standardised housing benefit, combined with the low price of alcohol in the UK, had made the seaside resort something of a 'boom town' in attracting those with drink problems. It was easy to see how poverty became entrenched.

As we'd walked around that day with Anders, all I'd really seen was the Blackpool of my youth, the fairground, the Tower, the amusement arcades, the trams. Jimmy and I had become inured, perhaps, to the poverty and the dysfunction.

'What do you think about Blackpool?' I asked Anders.

'What is this place?' he had said. 'What has happened to these people?'

Jimmy and I arrived at Coventry station. It was early evening, and a train arrived from London, weary-looking men and women in suits detraining and heading off to the car park. A friend of mine who lived in the city had told me that an increasing number of Coventrians, faced with the shortage of well-paid jobs, were now commuting daily to jobs in London, with Euston just an hour's train ride away. What he'd told me echoed similar observations from along my walk.

Despite an annual season ticket costing £9,000, the difference in accommodation prices between Coventry and the capital meant it could be economically worth the commute. Although for that money, you weren't guaranteed a seat. For that, you would have to stump up £15,000 a year to travel in first class.

In 2010, Philip Hammond, the then Transport Secretary, had told MPs that HS2, the new £33 billion high-speed rail line, was about 'long-distance commuting. Places like Milton Keynes and Coventry will find they are well within commuting distance of London', helping to address the north-south economic divide. (And suck more and more people into the south-east economy, he didn't say.)

There have been so many studies into the deleterious effects of long journeys to work. A report for the Royal Society for Public Health in 2016 found that the stress of long-distance commuting, with overcrowding and journey delays, was a ticking time bomb for commuters' physical and psychological wellbeing.

A US study in 2004 found long-distance commuters suffered from a host of issues, including feelings of impatience and fatigue, increased blood pressure, musculoskeletal problems, lower frustration tolerance, and higher levels of anxiety and hostility.

Combine this with the UK's increasing working hours. The European working time directive, which aimed to limit hours to 48 or under a week, had been largely ineffective. According to a TUC analysis in 2015, the number of employees working beyond that limit had reached 3.4 million, up by 450,000 since 2010.

At the time, Frances O'Grady, the TUC general secretary, said: 'Britain's long-hours culture is hitting productivity and putting workers' health at risk. Working more than 48 hours a week massively increases the risk of strokes, heart disease and diabetes.

'We need stronger rules around excessive working, not an opt-out of the working time directive. David Cameron will not convince people to vote yes in the EU referendum if all he's offering is "Burnout Britain".'

All of this was set against stagnant wages in the UK since the financial crisis and a freeze on public-sector pay. In a 2015 report, the Institute for Fiscal Studies found that British workers were taking home less in real terms than when Tony Blair won his second election in 2001. Between 2008 and 2014, the IFS said, women's average hourly pay had fallen 2.5 per cent in real terms, while men's had fallen a whopping 7.3 per cent, a squeeze that

Frances O'Grady described as the longest fall in living standards since the Victorian era.

It all seemed a long way from the spirit of my degree, preparing us for a world in which we would have so much free time, and no reduction in wealth as a nation. Could that have been only thirty years before?

Jimmy's train pulled in, and as it left with him on board I stood there outside the carriage window, waving. I watched the train until it became a tiny speck in the distance and disappeared around a corner. I stood there for a moment longer, feeling so happy that Jimmy had been in my life for almost as long as I had.

18

THE PUNK ROCK PRIEST
(COVENTRY TO RUGBY)

The next day I made short work of the twelve-mile walk to Rugby, out along the A428, following the River Avon and the Coventry to Rugby railway line, through the villages of Brandon, with its proud little war memorial, and then Bretford. It was raining heavily and the flat Warwickshire countryside reflected my mood.

Just outside Church Lawford, a car stopped and a man asked if I would like a lift. It had been the first time on the walk that anybody had offered, and it took me by surprise. I hadn't experienced any unfriendliness, far from it, but I was a burly, middle-aged bloke tramping along main roads with a large backpack and, to be honest, I wouldn't have stopped for me either.

No, thank you, I said. You sure, he said, it's pouring with rain. And it was, absolutely bucketing down. I had the thought that nobody need ever know. I remembered Chris Jones, the People's March first-aid man, telling me about the 'sicknotes', as he called them, littering up the support van. But then I remembered him telling me of that feeling, of arriving at Trafalgar Square having walked every single inch of the route. How that had felt, to have walked the entire way. I also thought about my dad, about what I was trying to prove, to him. No, really, I said to the nice man in the car, I'm OK, and he drove off, shaking his head.

In the distance I could see the familiar shape of Rugby's cement works, its giant silo and chimneys poking out of the greenery like the launch pads of the Kennedy Space Center. In fact, locals call it Cape Canaveral. Still the rain fell, as the tendrils of Rugby came to greet me.

I walked into the lovely old town, past Rugby School, established in 1567, one of the oldest independent schools in Britain. Outside St Andrew's Church, I saw a man standing in a doorway. He looked as if he was in his early twenties. He was wearing smart black trousers and a bright red polo shirt, over which he wore a bright red fleece. On his head was a red baseball cap. I thought he might be on his break from the nearby McDonald's, but as I walked past I saw that he had an earpiece in, and in his hand he was clutching a walkie-talkie. On his fleece was a logo, a rugby-ball shape, within which were the words 'Rugby First'.

'Hello,' I said.

He raised his forefinger, as if to indicate that he was listening to something in his ear, and then confirmed this by pressing the same finger against the earpiece and tilting his head.

'Hello,' he said, finally. 'How can I help you?'

'What's Rugby First?' I asked, pointing to the logo.

It was an initiative paid for by a group of businesses in Rugby town centre, the man said. It ran the CCTV cameras, for which it received contributions from Rugby Borough Council, for whom it worked as an agent. He'd been talking to the CCTV room just then, he told me, about a couple of vagrants he'd seen hanging around the churchyard. I hadn't heard the word 'vagrant' used in a while.

The Town Rangers – for that's what he was, he said – patrolled the town centre six days a week, between 8 a.m. and 6 p.m., assisting with shoplifting incidents, antisocial behaviour, vulnerable people, rough sleepers, that kind of thing. After 6 p.m., police community support officers took over.

Could he arrest people, I asked.

No, he said, and he looked a little bit downcast. If he spotted anything, he would radio the CCTV room, and they would call the police. Rugby First had been going since 2005, he said, and had huge support among the community.

'We ensure that Rugby is safe. People do seem to like a uniformed presence on the street,' he said.

Like the police, I said.

There was a beat. He straightened up a little bit, folded his arms across his chest.

'The police think we're doing a great job,' he said. 'Frees them up to do their proper job.'

I asked him what he thought the proper job of the police was if it wasn't to patrol our streets, deterring crime, clamping down on antisocial behaviour, helping the vulnerable. You know, policing.

He raised his forefinger again, put it to his ear.

'Sorry, mate, I've got to go,' he said, and walked off down the street.

According to a Home Office report, between 2009 and 2016 the number of police officers in England and Wales had fallen by nearly twenty thousand, from 143,769 to 124,066, with police budgets seeing an overall reduction of 18 per cent in real terms between 2011 and 2016.

The report showed that the number of officers involved in front-line policing had fallen by nearly 4,500 in just a year and that nearly 2,500 officers – about 2 per cent of the total workforce – were on long-term sick leave.

In 2015, the then Home Secretary, Theresa May, addressed the Police Federation's annual conference in Bournemouth. There she was told repeatedly by police officers about the effect the cuts were having on their ability to do their jobs and on staff morale.

The Federation's chairman, Steve White, whose organisation represents rank and file police officers, had told the conference that the bobby on the beat was becoming an 'endangered species' and that neighbourhood policing was under serious threat in the 'new, barren policing landscape'.

A survey for the Federation suggested that thirty-three out of the forty-three English and Welsh forces had scrapped, reduced or merged their neighbourhood policing teams since 2010.

They had warned that this diminished force would soon only be able to carry out a paramilitary style of policing, increasingly reactive in nature. With the loss of the 'eyes and ears on the ground' of community policing, there were dire warnings about the impact on security – about the force's inability, for example, to police and monitor the radicalising of some young Muslim men.

In a remarkably bullish speech for a minister whose party had long claimed the mantle of law and order, and which during the great industrial conflicts and riots of the 1980s had always ensured that the police were well looked after, Theresa May told the conference to stop 'scaremongering'.

'I have to tell you,' she said, in the tone of a junior school headmistress talking to naughty eight-year-olds, 'that this kind of scaremongering does nobody any good – it doesn't serve you, it doesn't serve the officers you represent, and it doesn't serve the public . . . So please – for your sake and for the thousands of police officers who work so hard every day – this crying wolf has to stop.'

Whether or not she then sent a letter home to their parents is not recorded. But all of this might help partly explain why we have young people dressed as if they should be serving burgers policing the streets of Rugby, paid for by contributions from local businesses. Was this, perhaps, another step on the road to a fully privatised police force, with all of the terrifying consequences of arbitrariness that might entail?

Feeling hungry, I popped into a 'Polski sklep' – one of the many Polish shops that have opened up across the country in recent years. There was a young woman behind the deli counter. I looked at the food under the glass, and asked her what was good. Her English was not so great and she didn't know how to describe the items. She'd only just arrived in the UK, she told me in broken English.

'I come improve life,' she said. 'Learn English quick.'

She went off to get a colleague.

'I'm sorry,' the colleague said. 'We don't get many non-Poles in here.'

She pointed to some pancakes.

'These are fantastic,' she said. 'In Poland they are called *naleśniki*. These are stuffed with curds.'

A woman in the queue behind me pointed at some cooked meat. 'You should try that as well,' she said. 'Polish ham is the best in the whole world.'

I took my pancakes and ham, and a small loaf of Polish Village rye bread, to the till, behind which sat a man with dark olive skin.

'You are not Polish?' he asked. He spoke softly, shyly, as if he was trying not to take up too much space. 'No,' I said, 'are you?'

'Kurdish,' he said.

'From where?' I asked.

'Iraq.'

'Ah,' I said, 'I have been to Kurdish Iraq.'

His face lit up. 'Where?' he asked.

'Irbil, Sulaymaniyah,' I said.

'I am from Sulaymaniyah!' he said. 'Did you like it?'

'Very much,' I said.

'We love Bush and Blair for what they did for us,' he said. 'Freed us from Saddam.'

So why was he here now, not at home?

'Corruption, the police are terrible, brutal,' he said. 'If you are poor there, they treat you like a dog.'

I left the shop feeling like I'd had an amazing adventure in my own country. I wondered why everybody didn't feel the way I felt about immigration. But then, with a job at a national newspaper in London, with a strong trade union, it was unlikely that I was ever going to turn up one day and find somebody else doing my job for half of my wages.

I checked in to the Travelodge by the station.

'How has your day been?' the man behind the desk asked me.

'Pretty good,' I said. I was still floating from the exchanges in the Polski sklep.

I watched as he punched my details into the computer.

Surely it wouldn't be too long before hotel receptionists would be done away with, I thought. Quick scan of the credit card on a reader. A card key delivered through a slot. A secure door from the reception to the rooms, accessed with a swipe of your room key. This was probably already happening somewhere. There were fewer manned ticket halls in railway stations; more self-service tills in supermarkets; self-service check-ins at airports; driverless cars were on the way. It was as if humans were absolutely determined to render themselves obsolete. I'd seen a picture recently of a robot in America being taught to shoot a gun. There you go, I'd thought: that's how it all ends.

The historian Yuval Noah Harari has written a terrifying essay about one particular version of our future, drawing a timeline beginning at the transition of our egalitarian ancestors from hunter-gathering to farming. It was the agricultural revolution,

Harari argues, that heralded the arrival of the whole concept of property, as humans gained 'ownership' of land, animals, plants etc. Money had been introduced as a trading tool.

With this change in human organisation, rigid hierarchical societies had emerged. This new world needed order. Equality would bring chaos. Small elites monopolised power for generation after generation.

With the Industrial Revolution, this had all started to change. Industrial economies relied on masses of workers, and their vast armies needed a ready supply of fighting men. The health of the masses became important, as did better industrial relations between those supplying the labour and the owning classes, who relied on the workers' labour to create their wealth.

The late modern era, then, had been one of pragmatism on behalf of the rich. They, often begrudgingly, had given away concessions to workers' organisations such as trade unions, and supported a more equal society, because they needed the labour. The reforms were often slow and hard-fought-for, but the direction of travel was very much towards more and more equality.

People like me, born in 1964, had no reason to believe that this would not continue indefinitely. And this history of progress would also help explain the optimism of Pete, and those on the People's March for Jobs in 1981. But then came increasing automation and globalisation and the post-industrial landscape we saw in many developed nations today.

Those masses, so indispensable just fifty years before, were now becoming irrelevant. Even modern hi-tech armies didn't need them, with their unmanned drones, special forces units and IT specialists to fight the growing wars in cyberspace.

'As some groups increasingly monopolise the fruits of globalisation,' Harari wrote, 'billions are left behind.'

As power and leverage drift away from the masses – witness the emasculation of trade unions and disillusionment with the political process – so more and more of the world's wealth gets appropriated by those at the top.

In 2015, according to a report published by the Equality Trust, the average FTSE 100 chief executive was earning 386 times more than a worker on the minimum wage for over-25s, pocketing an average pay packet of £5.3 million a year.

Those chief executives, the report calculated, were paid 132 times more than a police officer (and goodness knows how many more times than a Rugby Town Ranger), 140 times more than a teacher, 165 times more than a nurse and 312 times more than a care worker.

A 2016 report by Credit Suisse found that 1 per cent of people in the UK now owned 24 per cent of the country's wealth, and that the richest 5 per cent owned 44 per cent. An Oxfam report in January 2016 showed that the sixty-two richest people in the world owned as much wealth as the poorest half of the world's population. That's sixty-two people, less than the capacity of a double-decker bus, owning as much as 3.6 billion people. In 2010, the charity said, that figure had been the richest 388, and the wealth of the poorest 50 per cent in the world had dropped 38 per cent between 2010 and 2015. In the same period, the wealth of the richest sixty-two people had increased by $500 billion (£350 billion) to $1.76 trillion.

Such growing inequality has profound effects on society, according to extensive global studies by the British epidemiologists Kate Pickett and Richard Wilkinson, documented in their superb 2009 book *The Spirit Level: Why Equality is Better for Everyone*. So many aspects of life, they found, from life expectancy to mental illness, violence to illiteracy, trust in communities to drug and alcohol abuse, teenage pregnancies to social anxiety, prison populations and even obesity rates, were affected not by how rich a society was but by how unequal it was.

The most unequal societies in terms of income differential consistently scored worst in all of these factors. The USA was at the top of the tree, followed by Portugal, the UK, New Zealand, Greece, Australia, Ireland, Italy, France and Canada. Bottom of the list, in reverse order, were Japan, Sweden, Norway, Finland and Denmark, countries where progressive taxation regimes kept income differentials the lowest.

The conclusion of the book was stark and simple: societies do better when they're more equal; human beings are fundamentally disturbed by inequality and unfairness.

From this perspective, it is possible to see why Britain, where social mobility has been in reverse since 1976, has become an angrier, fractured little island, with epidemics in obesity and mental ill health.

Much of the wealth that had accrued to the global financial elite was now sequestered in offshore tax havens, of course, where it was beyond the taxation regimes of sovereign governments. But in the UK, the Tories were still blaming the last Labour government for the banking crisis and saying that we must cut the deficit by slashing public services and reducing the welfare bill. This from a government led by a man whose father had his money in a bank account in Panama.

If this shift of the globe's wealth into fewer and fewer hands isn't worrying enough, Yuval Noah Harari thinks that what might come next, with the rise of artificial intelligence and more and more sophisticated automation, could be even more frightening.

As humans get outperformed by AI in more and more skills, it is likely to replace more and more of our jobs. We might retrain, but AI will always be ahead of us. Subsequently, billions of humans might become unemployable. Harari calls this 'the useless class'.

He uses the rise of self-driving vehicles as an example. In thirty years' time or sooner, all vehicles could be self-driving. All of those millions and millions of bus, lorry, taxi and ambulance drivers the world over will be out of a job.

Harari outlines a scenario where one organisation might own the algorithm that controls the entire transport market. 'All the economic and political power which was previously shared by thousands is now in the hands of a single corporation,' he writes, 'owned by a handful of billionaires.'

Here's where Harari's vision gets particularly scary. Once the masses are stripped of their economic importance and political power, what incentive will the state have to invest in their health, education and welfare? What price the social contract then, when people's future depends on the largesse of a small elite, beyond democracy?

It might be argued that this is where we were back in Victorian England, before any state welfare provision, where the idea prevailed that moral courage and enterprise alone could secure people's freedom from want, ignorance and disease. But there were a lot of jobs around for the unskilled and semi-skilled in Victorian England.

In countries such as the UK, with a long tradition of philanthropy, the new elites might continue to look after the useless class even though they didn't need to (if only to stop us revolting). And perhaps our country's nascent thinking about a citizen's basic income is a part of that process. But the rich in other countries might have a different attitude.

'What would the Indian, Chinese, South African or Brazilian elite prefer to do in the coming century?' Harari asks. 'Invest in fixing the problems of hundreds of millions of useless poor – or in upgrading a few million rich?'

We'd seen popular mass movements flare up to challenge the new world order, such as Occupy and Spain's Indignados and Greece's Syriza. I thought I'd seen an inchoate form of such a movement on my walk – that when ordinary people talked about 'taking back control', Brussels was mostly a proxy. Our wealthy and political elites were appropriating the language of sticking it to the Man, when they were in fact the Man. More worryingly, there seemed to be a deep cultural conservatism underpinning much of the rhetoric.

In my room, I ate my Polish pancakes, which were heaven, then sliced the bread with my penknife and layered it with the Polish ham. The woman in the shop hadn't been wrong. The ham was delicious – thick and salty.

I looked at my watch, logged my tablet onto the Wi-Fi, and dialled a number. I'd managed to track down another one of the originals from the People's March for Jobs. It hadn't been easy. Numerous bands had played for the march in the towns and cities on the way, and at the end-of-march party in Brockwell Park, south London, where the line-up included Pete Townshend, Aswad and the jazzman George Melly.

But only one band had marched all the way from Liverpool to London: a punk outfit called The Quads, Brummie lads who'd briefly hit the heights in 1979 when John Peel named their record 'There Must Be Thousands' his single of the decade. In 1981, The Quads had brought out a song called 'Gotta Get a Job', and it had joined UB40's 'One in Ten' and The Specials' 'Ghost Town' as anthems in that summer of urban rage.

After that, The Quads disappeared without a trace. All of my investigations came to nothing, until one day I got an email from Big Bear, a record company in Birmingham, with a New Zealand telephone number for the band's lead singer, Josh Jones.

The phone was ringing. There was a plink and a plonk, and there was Josh Jones, looking back at me on the screen.

'Good evening, Mike,' he said.

'Good morning, Josh,' I said.

The little bit I knew about Josh was that he'd been born in 1954. Could that be true? He looked very fit and younger than me, much younger.

'It's true, it's true,' Josh laughed. He spoke with that mid-Atlantic rock and roll twang, with a hint of Brummie thrown in. Josh told me how he'd grown up in Acocks Green, south Birmingham, and had gone to Severne Road Junior, where he passed his eleven-plus, 'one of only three in the school that did'.

He'd loved his childhood. His parents had been dirt poor, his dad unable to read or write. His mum had grown up in the old back-to-backs in Digbeth, and as a child she used to go around the market in the Bull Ring picking up all the leftover vegetables at the end of the day to feed the family.

Josh remembered the times his dad would come home from work early because he'd got the sack, again, and his mum saying, 'Why didn't you just keep your mouth shut?'

'But my dad couldn't help himself. He hated injustice,' Josh said. 'If he saw the bosses taking the piss with workers, he would speak up. Always getting the sack. In those days, Brum still had a big manufacturing base, so he'd always walk into a job. He could challenge authority without too much fear.'

I thought about Dave the pigeon man back in Stoke, when he'd told me about his colleagues at Wedgwood being too terrified to protest against ever-worsening terms and conditions for fear of losing their jobs.

Josh told me that it was what was happening in the wider world when he was growing up that really opened his eyes to the possibilities out there.

'It was the sixties,' he said. 'The world suddenly became colour, on your TV screens and in real life. Psychedelia, man! The Beatles got me interested in music. They epitomised so much about working-class aspiration.

'You woke up every day and here was the new Rolling Stones record, or the new Beach Boys. Or The Kinks. This was the soundtrack to my youth,' Josh said. 'There was a working-class revolution, the start of social mobility. Michael Caine. Rachel Roberts. Peter O'Toole. Albert Finney. Tom Courtenay. Suddenly it was sexy and cool to have an accent.'

'Probably not a Brummie one, though,' I said.

'Ha, ha, Brummie never quite made it to sexy, did it?' Josh laughed. 'We only had Benny from *Crossroads*. With his woolly hat!'

He'd left school and drifted for a while before forming the band in 1975 with his two brothers, Terry and Colin, and a mate called Jim.

'We dyed our hair black because we wanted to look so "quad",' he told me, laughing. 'We were called Josh, Jim, Johnny and Jack. Terry was Johnny and Colin was Jack.'

They'd played pub gigs around Birmingham until John Peel picked up their song. After that things had started to take off.

The Quads looked set for the big time, but it never happened. 'We thought, "This is our moment,"' said Josh. 'But it all turned to custard for various reasons. UB40 supported us at a gig, in Derby, and six months later they cracked it and went on tour with The Pretenders and never looked back. We just stumbled from one bad moment to another.'

Josh didn't sound bitter or angry about it. I noticed that by now he was sounding more and more Brummie, and I noticed too that so was I. This always happened when I spoke to someone from 'home', and it always felt lovely, like putting on a pair of comfy slippers.

All the members of the band had been on the dole in 1981. 'We saw signing on as a kind of arts grant,' Josh laughed. 'And we'd play this game with social security, "Yeah, yeah, I'm looking for a job," but really all we wanted to do was make and play music.'

He had sensed that the system was being tightened up. 'I think it's much harder now for working-class kids to escape that background through music.'

Josh mentioned interviews he'd seen with the comedians Alexei Sayle and Stewart Lee. 'They were saying that, from a comedy perspective, those opportunities for working-class kids have shrunk,' he said.

'Alexei Sayle said that as a working-class kid from Liverpool, with unemployment benefit and free university, it afforded him the opportunity to follow something other than the usual trajectory for working-class kids. It's the same with bands. That was the thing for us: you're either gonna be a footballer or join a rock and roll band. I spent my youth trying to get out of the framework of what I existed in. I wanted to get out of that.'

After releasing 'Gotta Get a Job', the band had been approached by the organisers of the People's March for Jobs.

'That's when I met your dad,' Josh said.

Ah, Pete. He'd once persuaded The Kinks at the height of their fame in the mid-1960s to play a festival for the Young Communist League. He'd had a lot of charm.

Josh remembered being in a room with a bunch of guys from the march's organising committee. At that stage they were trying to get The Quads to play at certain points along the way, but when Josh and the rest of the band decided to walk the whole thing, the organisers said they could play in Brockwell Park as well. Josh and his two brothers and Jim set off with the march on 2 May 1981.

He remembered their pride when they walked into Birmingham from West Bromwich. 'We were like troubadours. We had walked all the bloody way from Liverpool, and there were our families waiting for us.'

He recalled the blisters, how he'd been prone to them, how some people would be showing off theirs at the end of a day 'like they'd come through a war'.

Josh started laughing to himself. 'Remember that Monty Python film *Life of Brian*, Mike?' Josh asked me. 'Brian wants to join the revolution against the Romans. He says, "Are you the Judean People's Front?" and they go "Fack off, we're the People's Front of Judea," and they all end up fighting each other in front of the Romans.

'I think that summed up so much about the left. We were on the march, and there was the Socialist Workers Party and the Workers Revolutionary Party and the Communist Party, and the Socialist Party of Great Britain, and the Revolutionary Communist Group, and the Revolutionary Communist Party of Britain. I remember going, "So, are you guys the Socialist Workers Party?" and they'd say, "Nah! Fack off! We're the Workers Revolutionary Party!" They all hated each other. That only seems to afflict the left, and I'm not sure why. I used to say to them, "Isn't Thatcher the enemy?" and they'd say, "Yeah, but we hate those fuckers over there more."'

When they got to London, Josh remembered, the Metropolitan Police were out in force, 'looking as if they wanted to beat the shit out of us'; arriving in Trafalgar Square, there were a hundred thousand people there to greet them. That was so emotional, Josh said. All four of the band sat on one of the lions. The next day, they went to Brockwell Park for the People's March concert.

'I think the organisers thought they would squeeze on The Quads, just because we'd done the whole march,' Josh said.

'We were backstage, and Pete Townshend came towards us. Of course, we were like, "It's Pete Townshend from The Who."

'He said, "Hi lads. I just wanted to say how much I admire what you've done, to walk all the way from Liverpool." We got very emotional. To have Pete Townshend, who I'd grown up listening to, come up and speak to us. A big moment.'

So how long had Josh been in New Zealand, and what had taken him there?

He smiled, a little sheepishly.

'Well,' he said, 'I've been here about six years and it's a long road from being a punk rocker in Birmingham, but I am now . . . a priest, in a rural parish in Auckland.'

'A priest!' I said.

'I know!' Josh laughed. 'But don't let that put you off!'

Josh told me about how his first marriage had collapsed in the late 1980s. He'd had something of a breakdown. One night, full of anger and fear, he sat on the floor and started crying.

'I wasn't religious. Hated all that stuff. But I found myself saying, "Dear God. I might be talking to myself, I don't know if you exist, but please help. I'm on the precipice here."'

Josh said that he'd instantly felt a sense of peace.

'I want to say I heard a voice, but it wasn't that really. It was a calm. Something inside me was deeply touched.'

Josh told me that he had still been a long way from Christianity, though. He still had his battles to fight. Ten years later, and remarried with a young child, Josh met another parent at the nursery school gates. They got chatting, and shared a love of sport and real ale. He turned out to be a priest, and eventually invited Josh along to church.

'I was like, no, no, I hate religion. But Kim, my wife, and I started going. It was St Martin in the Bull Ring, and I started playing my music in the church.'

St Martin's had been doing a lot of work with the homeless. 'I was captured by their mission,' Josh said, 'which was all about social justice. I got drawn in.' The long road to priesthood had begun.

The priest Josh had met was South African, his wife a Kiwi. After three or four years at St Martin's, the priest's wife grew homesick, so they moved to Auckland. Around 2010, he phoned Josh and asked him to join them. Josh wasn't yet a priest, but was well on the way to becoming one.

'We jumped on a plane and headed for New Zealand,' Josh told me. 'I was ordained the year after.'

They were loving their time in New Zealand. It was a stunning country; every day they woke up feeling blessed.

'It's a baby country,' said Josh. 'Only 4.5 million people.' But it wasn't immune from the market forces shaking the rest of the world. Josh could have bought a house in Auckland for £125,000 when they first got there. They didn't, and now that same house would cost £450,000.

'That's in just over five years,' Josh said. 'We've been priced out of a house. I don't know where we're going to live in our old age.'

They felt very distant from the ructions going on in Britain and in the US, but followed the politics closely.

'Community, Mike, is what's core to everything. That's the biggest thing I've learned about being in the Church. A church community doing things the way they should be done is one of the most authentic communities you will ever encounter, where people can find a common purpose for the common good, of finding meaning together.

'If you take that away . . . look at the miners. I knew a copper in the early eighties, and he said they were just going up to Yorkshire the next day to beat up a load of miners. He was looking forward to it, the thug. They went in and destroyed those communities. Thatcher's puppets.'

Josh looked exasperated. But it was wonderful to hear so much passion, so much anger. His journey from punk rocker to priest made a lot of sense to me.

'Remember me talking about the *Life of Brian*?' Josh said. 'And the factions within the left, railing against each other and not the common enemy? Well I see a lot of that in Christianity as well. We've got ecological disaster on our doorsteps, migrants drowning in the seas, sexual exploitation, corporates getting their tentacles into every aspect of life. And what do we spend all our time debating? Whether somebody from the same sex can get married! We have these earnest doctrinal discussions about whether this is where the devil's got his tentacles into the world. Gay marriage! You're talking six verses from the Bible compared with thousands that talk about the poor and oppressed. Am I missing something here?'

So why did Josh think the Church got bogged down in these issues?

'I think it's got a lot to do with Christianity feeling increasingly irrelevant in the world, feeling impotent against the bigger issues,' he said. 'So it flexes its muscles against things it can have control over, and it picks on the small guy, who is the gay guy, because we've got no chance in other areas.

Josh wondered if that's why the left got so bogged down in all the petty squabbles too. 'They feel they can never really take on and defeat the forces of the markets and the corporations – they're just too powerful. So they get involved in doctrinal detail and at least then they feel as if they are winning a cause, achieving something.'

It was thrilling to talk to someone in their sixties whose fire in the belly still burned so fiercely. And I loved talking to Josh about the neighbouring parts of Brum where we'd both grown up; the same pubs and nightclubs we'd gone to; the schools; our shared cultural hinterland. We'd travelled around the landscape of our youths on a magic carpet, our accents syncing, our conversation bringing us home, to that place somewhere inside where we belonged, even though I was in Rugby and he was on the other side of the world, where his day had just started as mine was drawing to a close.

I had a long, long walk the day after, to Northampton, twenty-six miles away.

'I remember that stretch,' Josh said, laughing. 'Brutal.'

'Cheers for that, mate,' I said.

'You're welcome,' Josh laughed.

'Keep walking, Mike.'

'And you, Josh, and you.'

19

A TOUCH OF CLASS
(RUGBY TO NORTHAMPTON TO BEDFORD)

In the little cafe at Rugby railway station I scanned across the Sunday newspapers in the rack. The *Sunday Express* headline read '12m Turks say they'll come to UK'.

I walked out of Rugby, past Tom Brown Street, onto the Lower Hillmorton Road, tree-lined, with neat semis, quiet on that Sunday morning, most curtains still closed. Then onto the main road out of town, where the ribbon of Rugby gradually thinned out until I was once more in open countryside.

I crossed over the M1, passing a sign that read 'Welcome to Northamptonshire: John Clare Country', and walked through the lovely little village of Crick, with its thatched cottages and fifteenth-century church with coursed ironstone walls. And then on to the village of West Haddon, whose outlying fields in 1765 had been the scene of an enclosure riot, where a crowd had torn down fences, protesting against laws that were being enacted allowing rich landowners to lay claim to land that had once been in common ownership. Nothing seemed to change.

On and on I walked, lost in that almost drunken reverie that comes with long-distance walking, the gentle folds of the green land rising and falling under my feet. I felt like I could carry on forever, not remotely concerned about where I was going.

'The beauty is in the walking,' wrote the Welsh author Gwyn Thomas. 'We are betrayed by destinations.'

As I walked, I pondered over my conversation with Josh Jones, the Acocks Green punk rocker turned New Zealand priest. I recalled him talking about growing up in the 1960s and 1970s, and the cultural flowering of that era that had seen the rise to prominence of working-class people in the arts.

That was something else which seemed to be in reverse in 2016. That year, academics from the London School of Economics and Goldsmiths, University of London, had published a report which found that only 27 per cent of actors now came from a working-class background and that the profession was 'heavily skewed towards the privileged'.

At the time, *The Night Manager* was the hottest thing on the telly, and its three stars, Hugh Laurie, Tom Hiddleston and Tom Hollander, had all been to the same private prep school – the Dragon School, in Oxford, fees £28,000 a year. After finishing prep school, Laurie and Hiddleston had both gone to Eton, the alma mater also of Dominic West, Eddie Redmayne and Damian Lewis. Benedict Cumberbatch, another of the industry's current leading lights, had gone to Harrow.

In February 2016, the Sutton Trust think tank found that 67 per cent of UK Oscar winners and 42 per cent of Bafta winners had been to private schools. Extraordinary figures when only 7 per cent of the UK's population is privately educated.

In a piece for the *Observer* in 2016, Carole Cadwalladr, herself state-school educated, argued that this takeover of the acting world by the privileged had huge wider significance.

'What has happened in acting and therefore what we see on our screens is intimately connected to what is happening in Britain,' she wrote. 'Acting, culture, identity, representation and politics are all inextricably entwined. The actors on our screens, the dramas that are commissioned, the way we view ourselves, the politicians we vote for, our ability to empathise with people from other parts of our culture, are all of a piece . . . Acting has changed because Britain has changed. And money, and its Great British handmaidens – inequality, privilege, class – is at the heart of it.'

When tertiary education was free, young people from working-class backgrounds could go to university or drama school and then enter a famously insecure industry where, in 2013, according to the actors' union Equity, 56 per cent of its members earned less than £10,000 a year from acting work. But who from a poorer background would look at those figures and think it worth accruing the £27,000 tuition fees that drama school would now entail?

The actress Julie Walters, a Black Country girl who'd grown up in Smethwick with a postal clerk mother and builder father, told a *Guardian* interviewer in January 2015, 'People like me wouldn't have been able to go to college today. I could because I got a full grant . . . Working-class kids aren't represented [in dramas being written today]. Working-class life is not referred to. It's really sad.'

David Morrissey, born in 1964 in inner-city Liverpool, was inspired to become an actor after seeing *Kes*, a film about a boy's relationship with a kestrel, set in a Yorkshire mining community and made by Ken Loach. It was the first time he'd seen his background reflected on screen, he told Cadwalladr.

'It's about young people from working-class backgrounds not being able to get on the first rung. Not being able to take a risk,' Morrissey said of the current climate. 'The creativity that comes from suburban bedrooms. That world has gone and that has enormous consequences for our nation. If you look at how important the creative industries are to Britain, how much things like The Beatles and Harry Potter have formed our national identity, it's like we're going around tarmacking over the oil wells.'

Cadwalladr also spoke to Jessica Hynes, who won a Bafta for her role in *WIA*, and who was raised in a working-class single-parent family on the south coast of England.

'The worst thing is the academy system, which has monetised all subjects and schools simply don't receive any money from arts subjects, so they've become incredibly difficult to justify,' Hynes said. But drama as a school subject, she told Cadwalladr, was not just all about 'prancing around or finding the next Orlando Bloom. It's about how you build confidence, how you connect with other people. It's about coming into a class where you feel different. Where you feel able to express yourself in another way.'

Hynes read out a mission statement from Eton's drama department, with its two professionally staffed theatres, including a flying system, orchestra pit and revolving stage: 'The aim is to provide the boys with a safe and stimulating environment in which to develop skills not easily learned in the schoolroom: physical and vocal self-confidence; the social disciplines of group work; imaginative spontaneity and the disciplines required to channel it; an extended emotional range; the power of their own creativity and a respect for that of others.'

'Don't all children deserve that?' Hynes asked. 'Not just Etonians?'

Our privately educated acting elite was not about to take such criticism lying down. In 2015, Rupert Everett (alma mater Ampleforth College, annual fees £34,000) claimed that posh British actors were dominating because US audiences 'don't want to see snaggle-toothed working-class people, obviously'. He told the *Radio Times* that we should celebrate the success of Eddie Redmayne and Benedict Cumberbatch instead of griping about it.

'The upper-class people are making the films that the Americans like, but that's how it is. There's nothing we can do about that . . . but we could also just not be so envious and bitter about it.'

In February 2015, Benedict Cumberbatch's old drama teacher at Harrow, Martin Tyrell, had claimed that coming from a public-school background actually worked against those in the acting profession.

'I feel that they are being limited [from playing certain parts] by critics and audiences as a result of what their parents did for them at the age of thirteen,' Tyrell told the *Radio Times*. 'That seems to me very unfair.'

If acting was getting more elitist and the working class more excluded, what did that mean for the kind of films and TV programmes being made?

Rupert Everett argued that the rise of programmes such as *Downton Abbey* and *The Night Manager* simply reflected the kind of thing people wanted to see. But as the comedian Josie Long told the *Observer*, 'When you don't have different voices coming through . . . posh fetishisation, posh as aspiration' becomes a defining feature of our culture.

Interestingly, in 1981 too there was something of a wave of cultural posh fetishisation. The TV blockbuster that year was *Brideshead Revisited*, adapted from an Evelyn Waugh novel, which charted the decadent lives of aristocrats living in a palatial mansion. In the cinema, it was *Chariots of Fire*, set in the rarefied, privileged world of Cambridge University in the 1920s. In real life, we had the obsession with Sloane Rangers, and one in particular, Lady Diana Spencer. Was all of that, then as now, somehow connected to a right-wing government claiming the cultural narrative?

There was another nasty consequence to the current rise of the elite in the arts, too, according to Owen Jones, in his 2011 book *Chavs: The Demonization of the Working Class*. For not only were artistic representations of the working class disappearing from our screens, but those that remained portrayed an 'underclass' to be despised and feared.

No more sympathetic representations such as *Boys From the Blackstuff*, or *Kes*, or *Brassed Off*, tales of human struggle and dignity against the odds. Today we got *Benefits Street*, *Saints and Scroungers*, *Skint*, *The Jeremy Kyle Show* and *Little Britain*, in which two privately educated comedians mocked the weakest and most vulnerable people in the UK: the poor, the disabled, the elderly and the overweight.

And with Tory austerity budgets, and arts funding cut to the bone, one could only imagine that working-class access to the arts and music was going to get more and more circumscribed.

The same thing has been happening in popular music, now dominated by the alumni of fee-paying schools – bands such as Mumford & Sons, Coldplay and Radiohead, and artists such as Lily Allen, Eliza Doolittle, Florence Welch, Mark Ronson. The musician James Blunt, who went to Harrow, responded to the Labour MP Chris Bryant's comments about the rise of the privately educated in the arts by calling him a 'classist gimp'.

In sport, too, the working class were being edged out. In October 2015, following England's ignominious exit from the rugby union World Cup, the *New Statesman* published an article highlighting the issue. In the 2003 World Cup (which England won), only eleven members of the thirty-one-man England squad had attended fee-paying schools. In 2015, that number had risen to twenty of the thirty-one-man squad. (In the Welsh squad, incidentally, only five of the thirty-one-man 2015 squad had been to private schools. Since control of education was devolved to the Welsh Assembly in 1999, Wales had largely remained committed to the concept of community-based comprehensive schools.)

In the England cricket team, the picture was largely the same.

Eight of the eleven who played the first Test against the West Indies in April 2015 had been privately educated. In 2005, in the Ashes series that gripped the nation, nine of the twelve-player squad who'd beaten the Aussies had been to state school. (Critics say that the England and Wales Cricket Board's exclusive TV deal with Rupert Murdoch's Sky Sports, which had begun after that Ashes series, has had some impact. The 2005 series had been free to view on Channel 4. An average of 2.5 million people had watched each of the five Tests. England's victory in the first Ashes Test of the 2015 series, screened on Sky, had been watched by just 467,000 people.)

Asked about the decline in state school players representing England, Iain Simpson, director of sport at the private Oakham School, told the BBC: 'My great sadness is that state school sport has gone downhill in the last twenty years. We don't play any state schools, because they don't offer the right level or quantity of competition. For lots of state schools, sport just isn't important.'

Phil DeFreitas, an Ashes-winning bowler with forty-four England Test caps, and an alumnus of Willesden High School, a north London comp, also believed the lack of opportunities to play cricket at state schools was behind the shift. 'It won't be long before everyone in the England side is privately educated,' DeFreitas, now cricket coach at Magdalen College School in Oxford (fees £18,000 per year), told the *Daily Telegraph* in 2015. 'There's no arguing with the facilities and the coaching [we have] . . . At MCS, we are very proud of what we offer our pupils, but I do feel for those who miss out on the opportunities I had as a boy.'

Millfield, one of the country's leading private schools for sport (fees up to £34,650 per annum), has twelve teachers coaching its fifteen cricket squads, headed up by Richard Ellison, another former England international. It also has a performance analyst, two strength and conditioning coaches, a sports psychologist, two physiotherapists, and nutritionists on call. Facilities outside cricket include an Olympic-sized swimming pool, a nine-hole golf course, thirteen tennis courts, an equestrian cross-country course, and specialist coaches across those sports to match.

Nearly fifty Millfield alumni play international sport every year, including England's 2015 rugby union captain Chris Robshaw.

It was all in stark contrast to Phil DeFreitas's alma mater. 'Now Willesden is an academy,' he told the *Telegraph*, 'and it certainly doesn't have a cricket field any more.'

As the 2015 *New Statesman* article affirmed, during the time of the Tory governments between 1979 and 1997, more than ten thousand state school playing fields were sold off, often to developers for private housing. A further two hundred were sold off by New Labour between 1997 and 2010. Education budget cuts since 2015 have seen state school sports provision cut back to the bone.

Obesity, especially among the UK's poorer people, has reached epidemic proportions. But just as acting is about more than learning lines and playing a character, so sport is about far more than just running around, getting exercise. At my state school in the 1970s, there were still playing fields, and still teachers willing and able to coach. I was introduced to rugby, a game that I loved and went on to play for nearly thirty years. I learned about teamwork and sharing and co-operation, about the sweetness of victory and the bitterness of defeat, about drinking beer through a muddy sock. I learned that there was a role for everybody, the swift and the not so swift, the tall and the short, those who were strong and those for whom determination made up for any athletic shortfalls. I made friends for life, from all backgrounds, from all over the world. Like Phil DeFreitas, I felt sad that so many working-class kids might never experience that. What a terrible waste.

The major exception to the rise of the privately educated in elite sport was professional football, which remained resolutely working class. According to a 2014 report by the schools watchdog Ofsted, 94 per cent of English players in the Premier League had received a state school education. And only three footballers in England's twenty-three-man World Cup squad that year had been privately educated.

Perhaps it was football's organisational simplicity, the fact that you just needed a ball and a bit of space to play, that had largely immunised it from the creep of private-school domination. Maybe there were much deeper cultural forces at play. But who would bet against the number of privately educated players in the Premier League starting to rise in the near future?

After East Haddon, Northamptonshire's gentle folds gave way to short, deep clefts, my calves burning as I pressed on. The urgent alarm calls of skylarks filled the air, rich with the dungy, cloying smell of oilseed rape.

Chris Jones remembered the People's March leg from Rugby to Northampton as being particularly tough, with his medicine chest getting a hammering and the support van filling up with blistered feet and torn muscles.

'I couldn't be arsed to bollock them any longer,' he had told me. 'There were serious problems starting to emerge, among the diabetics and the asthmatics.'

Like Josh Jones, Chris had also told me that once they got to this part of the world, he noticed a difference in the way they were treated.

'If it was a local authority that was Labour-controlled, you'd get a school and all the dinner ladies would be called in on over-time to give you a good meal,' Chris said. 'And after the speeches were done, and you'd go out for a beer, you get, "Hey, lad, are you of them marchers? Come here, lad," and that would be it. You couldn't put your hand in your pocket. But once you got to Northamptonshire, all they gave you was a big line of coppers! And in the Tory areas, instead of your bed and meals being organised, you'd get handed out to a hotchpotch of trade unionists' houses, like refugee children.'

I walked into Northampton, past the enormous Church's shoe factory. The town had once been the centre of shoemaking in Britain – it was an ideal place, with a plentiful supply of oak bark and water for tanning, an abundant supply of leather from local cattle markets, and a central location with good trading links.

Northamptonshire shoemakers had made the county famous around the world, providing boots for the British forces during the American War of Independence and more than half of the seventy million pairs of footwear made for UK and allied servicemen during the First World War. The Queen got some of her footwear from Northampton, as did Pierce Brosnan's James Bond – and Daniel Craig's 007 too. Tony Blair had a 'lucky pair' of Church's black brogues that he wore to every session of Prime Minister's Questions.

Today, many of the shoemakers were gone, but there was still a thriving industry in specialist and high-end footwear. Church's remained a big player, but in 1999 the company fell under the control of the Italian luxury goods manufacturer Prada, who bought it for £106 million. In 2003 Prada sold a 55 per cent stake to Equinox, a private equity firm, before buying the shares back in 2006, benefiting from a surge in demand for its luxury goods from big emerging economies such as China – overall, Asia accounted for 35 per cent of sales made by Prada companies worldwide.

In April 2016, Prada released its 2015 accounts, showing that its profits had dropped 27 per cent. This was on the back of a difficult 2014. The company blamed declining sales on the slowing of GDP growth in China to its lowest level since 1990.

It all reminded me of the potteries industry back in Stoke-on-Trent, a dizzying procession of sell-offs to foreign multinationals and private equity firms, and the constant uncertainties that came with it.

I walked into the centre of the town – Northampton, after Reading and Dudley, was the third-largest town in the UK, turned down for city status in 2002 – past the twelfth-century Holy Sepulchre, one of the best-preserved and oldest round churches in England, through little backstreets of lovely Georgian houses and along Derngate where, at No 73, stood the only house in England designed by Charles Rennie Mackintosh.

The Guildhall in St Giles' Square was magnificent as well, a neo-Gothic mid-Victorian municipal pile decorated with friezes and statues as impressive as any I'd seen on the walk. Northampton seemed a quietly confident kind of place, experiencing one of the highest population growths in the UK between 2004 and 2013 at 11 per cent, the expansion partly explained by London being only fifty-six minutes away by train.

I passed the headquarters of Northamptonshire County Council in George Row. Like most other councils, this one was making huge cuts, in its case £143 million worth by 2020. Its budget figures had shown that the cost of providing services was expected to rise by £104 million over the next four years, while money received from central government would fall by £79 million.

A report by the Local Government Association in 2014 had suggested that of the twenty-seven county councils in England,

Tory-run Northamptonshire was 'least able to fund itself', in part because it charged the lowest council tax of any shire authority; its fast-growing population exacerbated the problem.

In 2015, instead of raising council tax to help cover the costs, the council voted to outsource all of its services – all of them – to third parties, in the process reducing core staff from more than four thousand to a hundred and fifty. Its 'Next Generation' model had created four new 'service providers', autonomous bodies responsible to the council but managed as commercial enterprises.

The council had already been outsourcing street lighting to Balfour Beatty and road maintenance to Kier. But these new bodies would be separately responsible for much more delicate services, among them child protection, care for vulnerable adults and health services.

'How can people hold these bodies to account?' the Northamptonshire Labour spokesman Mick Scrimshaw said to the BBC.

Northamptonshire had followed the lead of Barnet Council in north London – whose spokesman had unofficially named its policy 'easyCouncil', drawing a parallel with no-frills airlines such as easyJet that charge extra for things that were once included in the fare – and other local authorities with major outsourcing programmes such as Essex, Southampton and Suffolk. But Northamptonshire was going further than any of them, in effect reduced to the role of commissioning body, buying in all of its services.

This extraordinary revolution in how our local authorities are being run, migrating power away from democratically elected bodies to the private sector, is based almost entirely on the ideological obsession with the idea that the private sector can do the job more cheaply (often the case as services are debased) and better (often not the case for the selfsame reason).

*

The next day was hot again, probably in the mid-twenties, as I left Northampton to walk the twenty-one miles to Bedford. The most direct route between the towns was the murderously busy A428. I looked at the OS map. There were no obvious country lanes or footpaths to take me cross-country that wouldn't add miles and miles to my journey, so I had to press on. Sometimes, where the pavement ran out, I was forced into the road, just one lane either way. The hedgerows in late May were tall and solid and right against the carriageway. All I could do was walk when there was a gap in traffic and then hurl myself against the hedgerow to avoid being run over.

A cough I'd developed earlier in the walk had gone from being mildly irritating at first to a full-blown, hacking number that made my whole body shake and shudder. I wondered whether it had anything to do with the three weeks I'd spent gulping down the traffic fumes.

The year before, the Volkswagen Group, which included Audi, Porsche, Skoda and SEAT, had admitted cheating on its emissions tests in the US. A so-called 'defeat device' – a piece of software – had been put in its diesel vehicles so that in test laboratory conditions they complied with environmental standards, with the engine running below normal power and performance. But once out in the real world, the engines switched out of this test mode. The result? The engines emitted nitrogen oxide pollutants up to forty times above what was allowed in the US.

'We've totally screwed up,' said VW America boss Michael Horn. The group's CEO, Martin Winterkorn, said that his company had 'broken the trust of our customers' and resigned. Jos

Dings, from the pressure group Transport & Environment, said that diesel cars in Europe operated with even worse technology than in the US. 'Our latest report demonstrated that almost 90 per cent of diesel vehicles didn't meet emission limits when they drive on the road,' he told the BBC in December 2015.

A 2016 study by the European Environment Agency claimed that nitrogen dioxide had caused about 71,000 premature deaths in Europe in a single year, and that the UK had experienced 11,940 annual premature deaths, second only to Italy.

You want to believe that car manufacturers had been caught out by this as much as anyone, that it had all been some terrible mistake. But the idea that people knew about the disastrous impact on public health of this technology, but that profits and shareholders took precedence? What was the endgame of all that? Societies where you must assume by default that corporations are lying?

The diesel scandal certainly had a long way to run. Defra, the UK government department responsible for the environment, had long resisted the idea of setting up a national system of clean-air zones, and admitted in September 2015 that it expected seven major UK urban areas to still be breaking EU pollution laws by 2020.

'We want local authorities and members of the public to come forward and share ideas on action to be taken at national and local level to make our nation cleaner,' the Environment Secretary Elizabeth Truss said.

In April 2015 the Supreme Court had ruled that the government's plan to tackle air pollution was unacceptable and that it should urgently come up with new proposals. But for now Defra seemed happier to put the onus onto local authorities – to incentivise people to use electric, hydrogen and ultra-low-emission vehicles and to penalise individual drivers of polluting vehicles via emissions charging zones – than to commit itself legally to act: as if it expected the death of diesel not through regulation but consumer action. It would in many ways be the perfect parable for our times.

Coughing merrily away, I got into route-march mentality. I put in my earphones, put on my music loudly and started singing away at the top of my voice. I wasn't remotely worried that people driving along would think I was mad. I was walking along a murderous A-road with no pavements in the middle of nowhere. If that didn't already say mad, what would?

The miles slipped by, the monotony only broken by the occasional little village, the buildings mostly made from blocks of the gorgeous local Blisworth limestone, so called because it was first studied during the digging of the nearby Blisworth Tunnel for the Grand Union Canal in the late eighteenth and early nineteenth century.

In Lavendon, with its village signpost illustrated with rural scenes of wheat and sheep and horses, I passed St Michael's Church. The entrance to the cemetery was a lovely lychgate, under the eaves of which was the inscription 'Death – the Gate of Life'.

A little further along the churchyard wall was a small plaque set in the stone. I bent down to read it. It was put there to commemorate the Jarrow March, which had passed through Lavendon on 26 October 1936.

'Made desperate by the State's neglect of their plight, the workless of Jarrow are marching to London,' the inscription read. 'They hope that by their presence in London they can make the Government do something positive to bring back work and wages to towns that have known little enough of either since the war. Their grandparents built up the nation's wealth in the boom days of Scotland and the industrial North. Little enough of that wealth stuck to their fingers. Now, when industrial methods have changed, their descendants are left as so much human scrap.'

I left Lavendon and walked off the edge of OS Landranger map number 152. That was always a delight, walking off the map. Just as it was a delight to open a fresh map and see that your destination was just two folds away. By my calculations, I had only three maps to go before Trafalgar Square.

I arrived at the River Great Ouse at Bromham Mill, a late eighteenth-century watermill of brick, timber and stone, and crossed the river itself on a narrow, twenty-six-arch bridge, which didn't have a pavement but had regularly spaced little pedestrian refuges where the bridge parapet jutted out a little wider; I'm assuming these were originally to let horse-drawn traffic pass, but they suited this walker just fine as cars sped by.

Shortly afterwards I entered Bedford itself, and paused by a handsome bronze statue of John Bunyan, Bedford's most famous son, on St Peter's Green at the top of the high street, standing nine feet tall and perched upon a plinth with three bas-relief scenes from his most famous work.

In *The Pilgrim's Progress*, Bunyan said it was often hard to see the meaning of wanderings through a wilderness until they were over. Standing there in Bedford, with tired limbs, nowhere to sleep, and the evening drawing in, I was hoping my wanderings would indeed one day make some sense to me.

I walked along Dame Alice Street, lined on one side by a row of lovely little mock-Tudor almshouses, all their doors painted cobalt blue, their chimneys all pointing in unison to the darkening heavens, now all lemony puffballs and shadows, like a Turner sky.

The almshouses were built in 1802 by the Harpur Trust, the street itself named after Sir William Harpur's wife, and had been used as homes for older couples, with applicants having to be at least sixty years of age. If Bedford had a founding father, then that man is William Harpur, who lived between 1497 and 1574, and who rose from a humble background to become one of the country's leading merchants, in 1561 becoming Lord Mayor of London.

Today his name is everywhere in the town. In 1566, he, along with Dame Alice, created an endowment to sustain a grammar school. That endowment had also made provision for the award of dowries on the marriage of 'poor maids' of the town, for poor children to be 'nourished and informed', and for any residue to be distributed among the poor. The fund was still going strong today, and in 2013–14 it was valued at £72 million.

I turned down Harpur Street, looking for somewhere to stay the night, but it didn't look as if I'd find anything there. I saw a building with a sign outside reading 'Bedford Guild House – Looking after older people in Bedfordshire', and popped in to ask if they might know of somewhere.

The woman behind the desk took a look at my rucksack and said that they didn't do accommodation. I was somewhat wounded, because I'd rather hoped that I didn't look like an older person who needed looking after.

'No,' I said to the woman, 'I was wondering if you knew of anywhere central that might have a room.' She mentioned a pub in the centre of town that she thought did cheap rooms. She asked me what I was up to and I told her about my walk.

'Do you want to have a look around?' she asked. 'There's a line-dancing class starting upstairs.'

As we walked, she told me a little about the place. It was a drop-in centre for the over-fifties. So that was official, then: I was an older person. Her name was Sonia, she was seventy-five, and she had been working here for the past seventeen years.

'I only came for two years!' she laughed.

The month before, the centre had lost its statutory funding

from the council, some £25,000 a year, a fortune for the Guild House. A Bedford homelessness charity had also lost its funding at the same time. The building was old, she said, it went wrong, 'just like the people!' They got their money now from private grant-making trusts.

'You have to grow a thick skin,' Sonia said. 'You court them and they say no. You just have to keep going. We do everything but sell our bodies.'

Sonia was Bedford born and bred, she said. The town had changed a lot in her lifetime, the biggest change being the ethnic mix. When she was at school, at Dame Alice, it was very unusual to see anyone of an ethnic minority background. But she didn't have any problems with it at all.

The only thing she would say is that it would all be a lot easier if people from other ethnic groups would integrate more. 'The ones that have integrated are almost English themselves. I don't mean that nastily,' she said.

Did they have many ethnic minority guests at the centre? Not really, she said, they have their own groups and day centres. Besides, Asians wouldn't like the food they served there.

I wondered if there might be something else culturally in the lack of people from ethnic minorities using the centre – people from cultures where older people might be more looked after by the family.

'Families are much more spread out now,' Sonia said. 'I mean, I've got a son in Australia. I can't expect him to look after me. None of my children can afford to buy a house round here, so they've all moved. It's a bit cheaper up Northampton way. I do think a lot of white British do tend to use residential care homes more than the others – we don't look after our elderly as much. That's just the way we've gone. People move away.'

Sonia said she often felt quite jealous when she saw people

whose children lived two or three doors away. If something happened to her, she said, with nobody locally to look after her, she'd probably end up in a home.

'Would people move away if Bedford still had a lot of good jobs?' I asked.

'No,' she said, emphatically. She told me that her grandfather had moved to Bedford from Bermondsey when his factory had relocated. Sonia's brother and nephew had both worked at a local factory making engines for ships. That had closed thirty years ago. She went through a long list of long-gone factories. It was the type of speech I'd heard a lot on my walk.

They had about four hundred people through the centre every week. A lot of them were very isolated at home. The centre didn't fit into the social services spectrum because they couldn't take people with disabilities.

'We stop our guests becoming the type of people that social services need to help,' she said. 'But that is difficult to prove, so we don't get the funding.'

They used to deliver meals at one stage, but that stopped with the cuts. 'That was a shame because it wasn't just about food. The people delivering it knew the recipients and stopped for a chat. That's all gone. I get people coming up to me saying they don't know what they'd do if it wasn't for this place.'

I left Guild House and walked back down Harpur Street. At the top of a pedestrianised shopping street was a large modern sculpture, maybe twenty feet high, of two faces staring at each other, the faces lined with brick shapes so that the steel looked like cracked marble, electric-blue lights reflecting off the chins so that they had the appearance of angry gods. It was rather beautiful.

I walked past a coffee shop upon whose entire side wall was a mural of Michelangelo's *Libyan Sibyl*. Bedford had a really lovely feel to it.

I stopped by the pub Sonia had mentioned and asked if they had rooms. They did. The Irish landlord showed me upstairs, past a sign that read 'remove work boots'. I always like a place with signs like that.

My room was tiny, just space for a single bed and a side table and a TV on a little shelf screwed to the wall. There were communal toilets and showers at the end of the hall. I went and had a stand-up wash and returned to the bar, where I ordered a pint of lager and stared at it for a moment sitting on the counter, at the dancing bubbles and the perfect white head. It had cost more than a pint in Birmingham, and that in turn had cost more than a pint in Stoke. I calculated that beer was going up in price at roughly a penny a mile.

*

The next morning, I had an appointment with a woman called Glenda who worked for a local non-profit, POhWER. She had clear memories of the People's March coming through Bedford in 1981, and was happy to talk to me.

We met at her office, where she explained that POhWER stood for People of Hertfordshire Want Equal Rights. It had started out in Hertfordshire as an organisation to support vulnerable people, and as demand had grown for its services, so POhWER had expanded. They'd moved into Bedfordshire five years ago and now had contracts all over the country. Most of their funding came from local authorities, she told me, but the money available to them had been severely reduced and they would have to start seeking other funding streams. I felt my heart sink. I had spent three weeks listening to variations of the same story.

Glenda talked about the People's March for Jobs. She had

taken part, meeting the marchers at the Northamptonshire county border and walking with them all the way to Bedford. She recalled the banners and the chanting and the huge turnout from Bedford to greet the marchers. They looked pretty road-weary by then, she said. The next day she walked with them out of Bedford, through Stotfold and into Letchworth, providing the marchers with food and drinks. The local Labour Party had really got behind it all.

'I've been on a few marches in my time,' Glenda said. 'But that was a particularly poignant one at a very poignant time.'

I told her that it had perhaps been my dad's proudest achievement. 'I'm not surprised,' she said. She didn't think that people would be very interested in such a march today. The Iraq war demo had been her last. 'I felt that if you ignore a million people,' she said, 'then what's the point? I think that sapped the life out of a lot of us.'

Glenda talked about the work of POhWER, how cuts had put the squeeze on what her organisation called the preventative work, the community engagement, the advocacy for people who don't quite hit that shifting statutory threshold.

Glenda gave me an example of a recent client. She had bipolar disorder – 'about half of our clients have got some kind of mental health issue' – and problems with drugs. Her children had been 'removed' and she was now asking to downsize because the bedroom tax had made her two-bedroom flat unaffordable and she'd fallen into arrears.

The mental health team had closed the woman's case and discharged her because she was unable to keep appointments due to memory issues. She had also been unable to remember her appointments with the Department for Work and Pensions (DWP), so she had been sanctioned. 'So everything was being removed from her,' Glenda said.

To compound this client's problems, she had been taken off the old Disability Living Allowance and put on the new Personal Independence Payment (PIP). Glenda said that a lot of POhWER's clients were being rejected for PIP, with over 50 per cent of applications refused. On appeal, 60 per cent of the refusals were overturned.

Glenda told me of cases where people living in Bedford had been given a PIP assessment appointment in Milton Keynes at 9 a.m.

'You know they can't get there,' she said. 'So they get sanctioned as well.'

What she heard time and again from people working for the DWP was that they were just 'following procedures'.

'I don't know how people do these jobs, when they're imposing these sanctions or issuing the eviction notices through the housing associations,' Glenda said. 'They must just shut down, put up a kind of shell around themselves to survive.'

If clients decided to appeal against a sanction, it took a long time. It was fortunate that this particular client Glenda was telling me about had been referred to POhWER, and they'd been able to work with the local housing association. Otherwise she'd have been evicted and homeless.

'If we didn't exist, these people would struggle on their own,' Glenda said. 'There's very little support left. We're a shrinking pool of services and we beat ourselves up because we think we are only scratching the surface of the problem.' Glenda smiled at me, held up her hands and shrugged her shoulders.

Her team, she said, were the most dedicated people she knew, working many more hours than they should to help support people. 'But we're often saying to each other, "What's happening to the people we're not getting to? What's happening to those people? Where are they going?"'

Increasingly, Glenda said, there were obvious signs in Bedford as the number of homeless people on the streets had spiked. 'They weren't there two or three years ago,' she said.

Many more people were being evicted, and housing associations were becoming increasingly draconian with the penalties they were imposing. Universal Credit was just being rolled out in Bedford, which Glenda predicted would lead to another sharp spike in desperation.

'It places a huge burden on people,' she said, 'because they've got this lump of money and, quite frankly, they are not going to pay their council tax if they're short of food or whatever. So they get into arrears and end up being evicted.'

POhWER had recently been told that they couldn't take any more self-referrals. They'd had their funding for a drop-in service for the deaf community cut, so they were unable to offer that any more. Glenda listed the other local organisations that had had their funding slashed or cut altogether: the Alzheimer's Society, the Deaf Society, Sight Concern. 'Don't be blind, poor, old, deaf, disabled or have a mental health problem and live in Bedford,' Glenda said.

She was in no doubt that it was being driven by Westminster, that because of the government's agenda, they now saw people at the bottom of the pile – 'probably disabled, probably got mental health issues' – routinely portrayed as lazy, feckless and not worth supporting. 'How did we become so uncompassionate and cruel?' she asked. 'It's just so shocking.'

One of their mantras as an organisation, she said, was that this could happen to anybody. POhWER had helped plenty of people who had never dreamed that they would need somebody to support them.

'They've fallen ill, long-term sickness, had to give up their jobs,' Glenda said. 'And had no idea how the benefits system worked. They come to us completely bewildered that they are now in this lump of people deemed to be undeserving.'

This desensitisation to the suffering of others had led to a surge in hate crimes in Bedford against people with disabilities, Glenda said. A report from the Attorney General's Office in 2016 revealed that hate crimes against people with disabilities across the country had soared, with the number of prosecutions in 2015–16 up by 41.3 per cent on the year before.

'People seem more emboldened to say what they like these days, less afraid of making comments,' Glenda said. 'We've had people tipped out of their wheelchairs in Bedford.' She shook her head. 'I don't know, Mike. You blink, and here we are.'

As I walked through Bedford, I thought about what Glenda had said, about the UK having become less compassionate over the years. A good place to see that shift is in the British Attitudes Survey, where every year people are asked the same series of questions. It has been running since 1983, and its longitudinal nature meant changes could be comprehensively tracked.

In 1983, when asked if unemployment benefits were too high and discouraged the unemployed from finding jobs, 35 per cent of respondents agreed. In 2012, that number rose to 54 per cent, even though in real terms unemployment benefit had gone down. Somewhere in that thirty or so years, we have become a lot less charitable as a nation.

I walked south, through the pedestrianised shopping centre, and into a beautiful little square where the town's Harpur Centre stood, its shops behind a fine Gothic Revival facade in Bath stone. I walked towards a cafe on one side of the square and ordered a cappuccino at the counter. The man serving me had a faint Italian accent. I got chatting to him, told him about my walk. Other customers were queuing up. He turned to the other two men behind the counter. 'I'll be a few minutes,' he said to them. Then to me: 'I'll come out.'

We sat down. He told me that his name was Liberato Lionetti, but that everyone called him Libby. He was fifty. He was tall and strong-looking, and appeared much younger. That's the Italian blood, he said.

He patted his stomach and told me he had to be careful these days, especially with all the pastries in the cafe, which he owned. He had volunteered as a special constable for fourteen years, and was due to have his annual police fitness test that evening.

Libby was born in Bedford in 1966. 'A good year for England. I am a lucky mascot!'

He explained how, just after the war, his father had come to Bedford from a tiny village in Puglia, in Italy's impoverished south, to work for the London Brick Company in its nearby Marston Vale plant. Devastated in the war, Britain needed a supply of fit labour to replace all those killed and injured, to help rebuild the country, physically and emotionally.

'They looked at France, but it had its own problems,' said Libby. 'Spain, Greece, same thing. Italy had surrendered in 1943, so they had a lot of young men left over.'

The brick company had set up a recruiting office in Naples, and in the following decade recruited over 7,500 men on four-year contracts. Each was given a medical examination, a ticket to England and a bed, often in a converted prisoner-of-war camp. Loneliness, cold, damp weather and awful food meant some of the men didn't last, and soon returned home. But many settled, bought houses and paid their families' passage to come and join them. Today, of Bedford's population of 80,000 people, around 14,000 have Italian ancestry, the highest concentration of Italian families in the UK.

'My father had a choice between coming to the UK and

337

going to Australia,' Libby said. 'He always told me that the main reason he chose the UK and not Australia was so that he could walk home to Italy if it didn't work out.'

'Walk home!' I said.

'I know,' replied Libby. 'Imagine.'

But it had worked out. Libby said that word got out back in Italy that the UK wasn't such a bad place. 'What they'd thought were the enemy, who they'd been fighting a few years before, were just ordinary human beings.'

Libby's dad worked in the brick factory until his contract expired. After that there had been a steady run of different jobs, 'because there was lots of work in those days'. He'd been employed at the ironworks – 'that's a housing estate now' – and then he worked in Letchworth, where he made furniture. After that he spent the rest of his working life at Vauxhall Motors in Luton.

'That was his favourite job,' Libby said. 'He loved that journey, the mates, the different people working there. When he was at London Brick, it was all Italians. But Italy's weird, because even though we're all Italian, it's all "yeah, but you're from Naples and I'm from Milan". Romans think of themselves as the fathers, caught in the middle of the squabbling children. "Come on, calm down, everybody!"' Libby laughed and made that lovely Italian gesture of clamping his fingers together on his right hand and moving it up and down, as if tugging on a thread from the ceiling.

Libby talked about growing up in Bedford, in Queen's Park, 'basically a little Italy'. When you came over the bridge, all you'd see was Italian shops and cafes. But the area also housed a lot of the other early immigrant communities, also attracted to Bedford by the abundance of work – the Irish, the Indians from Punjab, people from Grenada and Barbados in the Caribbean, the Polish.

'A lovely big mix of everybody, but not a lot of too many, if you know what I'm saying,' Libby said. 'As kids, we always used to play Brazil v Italy in the park. All Italians against everybody else.'

Who would win?

'It would always end up in a big fight!' Libby said, and laughed again.

Libby told me a story about his dad, who'd recently died, and the passport he'd had when he first arrived in the UK. It was a green Italian passport and it had the word 'Alien' stamped on the cover.

'Alien,' Libby said. 'Can you imagine? It had this lovely black and white photograph, Gregory Peck style. It had been Sellotaped so many times because it was falling apart.'

Libby had always loved that passport. One day, he went round to his dad's house and noticed that it was gone. 'Bubba, where's that thing you had in the cupboard?' Libby asked. His dad said that he had thrown it away as he didn't need it any more. Then he pulled out his new EU passport.

'We don't need anything like that now. We're safe,' Libby's father said.

'I'll never forget how proud my dad was of his EU passport,' Libby told me. 'Like it had unified a continent. When he first came here, people still said stuff like, "You bastards, you're the ones that killed my cousin in the desert." And now they were unified. He died a happy man, knowing of unity, a black president in America, the Berlin Wall coming down. He couldn't believe that: communism thrown out of the window. He just thought, "This is fucking brilliant. This is fantastic." No more fascism or bullshit like that. All gone in his lifetime.'

Libby had retained his own Italian passport, he told me; his parents' generation had tended to register everybody in Italy, 'just in case we have to go back'. His own three children had also been registered in Italy, 'so they have a right to go back as well'. Did that sense of 'going back' ever leave any of us?

His dad was buried in the local cemetery. There, Libby told me, you could see all these Italian names, from the same little villages in southern Italy. It was the same with people from the Punjab, or Jamaica, or Poland, all clustered together in death.

I asked Libby what the atmosphere in Bedford was like, with the EU referendum looming. Lots of people seemed to be pro-Brexit, he said, blaming everything on foreign people in the UK. He was a little afraid, he said, having a foreign name, of not being welcome in the UK any more.

Some of his customers from Eastern Europe were worried, too. They'd had people saying to them, 'We don't need you any more. Off you go.'

'They've bought houses here, started businesses, sold up everything in Poland,' Libby said. 'They've come here to give Britain the rest of their lives, and probably their children's lives as well. They want to be here forever. And people say things like that . . .'

Libby challenged people when he heard that sort of talk. 'Have they come to take up your houses, or build them? Have they come to steal from your hospitals, or clean them or tend to the sick?' he would say.

He had spent time in the army when he was younger and liked to visit the battlefields of the First World War.

'There's a little cemetery in Belgium that has eighty-one Italian soldiers buried there, guys taken from the Italian front to dig the trenches for the Germans,' he said. 'They all died and nobody knew where to put them. So the Belgians said, "We'll bury them with us." I go round these places and think "what a waste". Working-class kids just slaughtered.'

It had been a hundred years since that war, Libby said, and he feared that we could go straight back.

'That's why when they took down the borders in Europe, it's so my daughter can marry your son,' Libby said. 'Fantastic. You do that for long enough and soon everybody's speaking everybody else's language. Do you know what other country's done that? Great Britain. When you had borders with Scotland and Wales, you were killing each other left, right and centre. Soon as borders go up, that's what happens.

'Just think about what our parents had to go through to make it good for us. And now we've got to make it good for our children. Our hair is tied in with everybody else's. To release it you've got to cut it. But who keeps the knot? It's mine as well. It's got my hair in it too.'

Bedford, Libby told me, was an extraordinarily diverse place. 'We've all got a friend who's from somewhere else,' he said. 'There's no picking on somebody because of the colour of their skin, or their religion. We've all been mixed together for so long that it's impossible not to know somebody from India, or Italy, or Poland, whose dad was here on the Spitfires. You only know he's Polish because of his surname – it's got about fifteen consonants in it! That's all you know. It's like every Italian's got a vowel at the end of their name because that's-a how-a we-a talk-a. Ha! Honestly, Bedford's one of the coolest places in Britain. Peterborough's pretty cool as well. They've got a big Italian community too.'

So it's all down to the Italians, I said to Libby.

'It's all about the Italians!' he said, laughing. 'Espresso, a little bit of vino, gorgeous women. We just need a little bit of Italy everywhere in the world. We all just need to slow down a bit more, that's all.'

20

STATUS ANXIETY
(BEDFORD TO LUTON TO HEMEL HEMPSTEAD)

I walked across St Paul's Square, heading south. By this point, I didn't need a map to know which way I should leave Bedford: when you walk into a town, you instinctively know which way is out.

I crossed the slow, wide Great Ouse on Bedford Bridge, with its lovely balustrades. Looking behind me, on the north bank I saw the stunning Gothic Revival building which housed the town's magistrates' court. The spire of St Paul's loomed above it.

Soon after that I was on the road out of town. I passed a grave-yard where an eviscerated mobility scooter was neatly folded up at the foot of a gravestone like a puja offering. Just along from there I came across a well-worn desire path that cut all of three feet from the journey around the edge of the grass. That was perhaps my favourite desire path of the entire walk, for it made no sense at all, in terms of a short cut. It just spoke of humans' determination to go where they go. I took it, of course.

On the outskirts of Luton, I stopped for some water at a newsagent. The *Daily Telegraph* was reporting that Britain topped the foreign aid spending league, spending twice as much of its wealth on aid to the world's poorest countries as any other G7 nation. In 2014 the figure, up 144 per cent in a decade, had reached £13.2 billion, representing the UN-recommended target of 0.7 per cent of GDP.

The issue of foreign aid had become another front in the attack against EU membership, with the promulgation of the idea that whether it was Brussels or the developing world, Britain paid much more than it received, or more than other countries.

'We are clearly the mugs of the world,' the Tory MP Philip Davies had told the *Telegraph*. 'The Prime Minister might think it makes us look compassionate to spend more and more money when we're in debt – to hand it over to some fantastically corrupt countries around the world. I personally think it makes us look stupid.'

Fellow Tory MP Peter Bone was quoted as saying that the UK should 'learn a lesson from other countries that put their populations first and decide to spend money at home'.

Next to the *Telegraph* was the *Guardian*. It had a big picture of the luxury St George Wharf Tower in Vauxhall, with the headline 'Revealed: The London skyscraper that is a stark symbol of the housing crisis'.

I bought a copy and sat on a wall, reading the story. It reported that almost two-thirds of the 210 apartments in the tower, opened in 2013, were in foreign ownership, with a quarter of them held through secretive offshore companies based in tax havens.

At least thirty-one of the apartments had been sold to buyers in the East Asian markets of Hong Kong, Singapore, Malaysia and China; fifteen to buyers from Saudi Arabia and the United Arab Emirates; and others to buyers from Russia, India, Iraq, Qatar and Switzerland.

Among the alleged owners were a Russian billionaire, the former chairman of a defunct Nigerian bank, a Kyrgyz vodka tycoon, a Kurdish oil magnate, an Indonesian banker and any number of Singaporean millionaires. Town hall records obtained by the *Guardian* had shown that nobody was registered to vote at 184 of the apartments, and the paper reported that many of them were unoccupied for most of the year.

The five-storey £51 million penthouse, twenty-four times larger than the average new three-bedroom home in the UK, was thought to be ultimately owned by the family of the former Russian senator Andrei Guriev.

Next door to St George Wharf at the Nine Elms development and the former Battersea Power Station, as at most of the new luxury developments across the capital, the story was the same. Foreign money had poured in to the city, to be parked in property investment.

The juxtaposition of the foreign aid story and the luxury flats story seemed stark. For what was modern London's property market if not some form of international aid, transferring assets from the UK to 'some fantastically corrupt countries around the world' and impoverishing many in the UK in the process?

The ripple effect of that building boom in luxury property was spreading quickly, as house prices skyrocketed across the capital, forcing ordinary people to spend more and more of their salaries on rent or mortgages.

In January 2016 the *London Evening Standard* reported that private-sector rent had gone up from 49 per cent of average pre-tax income in 2010 – already pretty eye-watering – to 62 per cent. In 2010 tenants spent more than half their income on rent in only five of London's thirty-two boroughs. That number had now increased to twenty. Stories were legion of rogue landlords renting out garden sheds for the poor to sleep in, or people living in the most unimaginably dangerous, cramped and squalid conditions, about hard-pressed councils cutting corners on safety regulations in their properties.

I thought about all the homeless people I'd seen on my walk, sleeping in doorways, or in tented villages in the cities, the numbers growing all the time. And I thought about all of the property speculators, from the south-east, and from overseas, building their portfolios in the poverty of Stoke-on-Trent or Liverpool. It was like the Wild West.

'It can't last, can it?' Annie had said to me back in Salford.

On the walk into Luton town centre, there were Vote Leave posters everywhere. A pub had the flag of St George flying out-side, and a cartoon drawing of a British bulldog draped in the union flag in one of its windows.

I walked into the centre around mid-afternoon. I went into a pub, and told the woman behind the bar that I'd booked a room by phone the day before. What I didn't tell her was that I'd called twice.

The first time I'd been told to call back later, because the man on the end of the phone said that he wouldn't remember because he was too pissed.

The woman behind the bar didn't seem to care much. She told me that the room wasn't ready and went off to serve people. It was 3 p.m., midweek, but the bar was already quite lively – mostly men, all white, many Irish by the sound of it, from teenage to elderly.

When she walked back past me, I asked her when she thought the room might be ready. She told me she didn't know, maybe an hour. I ordered a pint and sat at the only empty table, next to the pool table, where two men were playing for a fiver sitting on the table's edge, their faces a study in grim determination.

After an hour, I returned to the bar. The woman had gone, replaced by a man who looked to be in his sixties. 'Any news on the room?' I asked. 'What room?' the man replied. I explained that I had booked a room the day before. I recognised his voice from the phone call. He'd been the man who was too pissed to take a booking.

'It's not ready,' he said. 'How long?' I asked. About an hour, he replied. Could I leave my bag behind the bar? 'Sure,' he said.

I walked around Luton town centre. There didn't seem to be much logic to it at all, no obvious middle, just a series of streets where people hurried along between the railway station and a vast shopping centre called The Mall. I was disappointed that it hadn't been named after Luton's famous car industry.

I walked up to the railway station and stood outside the entrance where, at 7.21 a.m. on 7 July 2005, CCTV cameras had captured Hasib Hussain, Germaine Lindsay, Mohammad Sidique Khan and Shehzad Tanweer walking calmly past wearing backpacks to board a train to London.

British-born Khan, thirty, Tanweer, twenty-two, and Hussain, just eighteen, had travelled to Luton from their native Yorkshire. Lindsay, nineteen, Jamaican-born, had travelled from his home in Aylesbury, Buckinghamshire.

By 9.47 a.m., fifty-two people were dead, and seven hundred seriously injured, blown up on three tube trains and a bus. Among the dead were thirty-two British nationals, and victims from Afghanistan, Ghana, India, Iran, Israel, Romania, Sri Lanka and Turkey. The UK had experienced its first ever Islamist suicide attack, by four young homegrown jihadis. Our country had changed forever.

A few days later I got on the tube, and a young man in a white dishdasha with a beard and a small pack on his back boarded and sat opposite me. He looked nervous, as well you might if the whole world was suddenly terrified of you. To my shame, I got off at the next stop and waited for the following train.

On 1 September 2005, al-Jazeera broadcast a videotape of Mohammad Sidique Khan, a learning mentor at a Leeds primary school and married with a young child. In it, Khan calmly looks into the camera, as if recording a birthday message, and says:

'I and thousands like me are forsaking everything for what we believe . . . Your democratically elected governments continuously perpetuate atrocities against my people all over the world. And your support of them makes you directly responsible . . . We are at war and I am a soldier.'

Pete had been working near Edgware Road station on the day of the bombings. He'd helped out as the victims emerged into the street, bloodied and bewildered. When I next met up with him, a few months later, he was still shaken up by what he had seen.

'It's all connected, Mick,' he said. 'Everything.'

I went back to the pub. The same guy was behind the bar, by now looking rather glassy-eyed. I asked if my room was ready. He said it wasn't; it would probably be another twenty minutes. So I ordered another pint and sat down by the pool table, where the same two men were still playing.

Eventually, the man behind the bar beckoned me and lifted up the hatch so that I could walk through, and then led me up some narrow stairs, and then some more stairs, until we were in the attic. He opened a door and showed me into a little room, where there were three sets of bunk beds crammed into the little space, with a mini fridge that whirred loudly, and a kettle but no cups or sachets of tea or coffee. Dotted around the room were little piles of clothes.

'Am I the only one sleeping here?' I asked, looking around at all the beds.

'You are,' he replied.

He left, and I lay down on one of the lower bunks. Below me, in the bar, the music had been cranked up, and even right up there, at the top of the building, it seemed as if the floors were bouncing up and down.

I'd just drifted off to sleep when there was a knock on the

door. I opened it and there was an elderly man standing there in a greying vest. He smelled heavily of drink. He was wondering whether he'd left his phone charger behind. There it was, he said, pointing over my shoulder, and he walked past me to retrieve it.

Was this his room?

'Usually,' he said.

I walked back through the pub, now heaving and raucous, and set off to find something to eat. Around the corner, there was a steakhouse. The place was as loud and busy and raucous as the pub, but in the steakhouse I seemed to be the only white person.

There was laughter everywhere, loud blues music playing over the speaker system. Young women in headscarves applied lipstick at the tables using their phones as mirrors. The waitress brought me a menu. 'All halal,' she said. I looked down the drinks menu of alcohol-free cocktails. 'What's good?' I asked. 'The mojitos are to die for,' she said. 'I'll have one of those, then,' I said, 'and a sirloin steak, please, medium rare.'

She tapped my order into an iPad, then danced her way back through the heaving tables of laughing people to the counter. I ended up having three of those virgin mojitos, and by the time I left I'd convinced myself that I was quite drunk.

Back at the pub, nobody needed convincing that they were drunk. I ordered a pint and went out into the tiny courtyard. There was only one other person outside, a tiny, birdlike man, perhaps in his seventies. He wore a suit and a tie and two-tone brogues. His eyes had a faraway look and he was a little unsteady, swaying this way and that, as though on the deck of a gently rolling ship.

'I only come in on Mondays, Wednesdays and Fridays,' he said in a Cockney accent. 'Never go anywhere else.'

He asked me what I was doing in Luton and I told him I was walking from Liverpool to London. I didn't go into any detail.

He looked down at my feet, stared at them for a bit, and then looked back up at me.

'Like that bloke in the marathon, who died,' he said.

'What?' I said.

'You know, that bloke. He died.'

'Kind of,' I said, although I had no idea what he was talking about.

'When I saw his family doing the finish for him . . . I had tears,' and he stroked his cheek where the tears would have been if he had actually been crying.

*

Nearly all of the newspapers the next morning carried the same horrific picture on their front pages of a migrant ship capsizing in the Mediterranean, with terrified people leaping into the sea as it rolled over. The *Daily Mail* and the *Telegraph* both had banner headlines about how the UK's population was due to rise by four million over the next eight years.

I walked up a steep hill out of the town, and then through Stockwood Park. A funfair was being assembled for the upcoming bank holiday. By the time the fair opened, I would be in London, now just five walking days away.

Overhead, planes taking off from Luton Airport passed by every few minutes, most from the low-cost airlines, but also many sleek executive jets; airports serving the London region now had more private jet traffic than any other European destination, and Luton, with nearly thirty thousand private flights a year – or over eighty a day – was the busiest of all, and growing fast.

Luton had just opened its third private terminal to meet the growing expectations of the super-rich, who preferred not to have to mix with ordinary travellers, being whisked from car to private jet and into the air in as little as ten minutes.

The increase in the private jet market was just another symptom of the aftermath of the 2008 financial crash. For the majority, austerity was the prescribed corrective so that the economy could recover. But as income inequality steadily rose, and more and more people slipped into poverty or grimly hung on, the luxury market, serving people whose great wealth had largely left them unscathed, had flourished.

In August 2014, the *Financial Times* reported that the market in luxury superyachts was booming, with sales hitting their highest levels since the recession struck. Sales figures for luxury cars, watches, handbags and clothing were also buoyant.

Ben Perkins, a research director for consumer goods at Deloitte, told the *Guardian* in 2013 that the world's super-rich would not have been hurt by the recession at all.

'They won't have noticed the change,' he said. 'It tends to be the middle that gets squeezed during the times of economic hardship. They [luxury goods companies] might have lost the luxury shopper that would buy one Louis Vuitton handbag a year, but they've kept the ones that buy one a month.'

I looked up at another sleek executive jet taking to the skies. These days, every time I encountered such obvious manifestations of obscene wealth – seeing the man who drove around west London in a gold-plated Ferrari, or reading about the Mayfair restaurant selling a £9,000 cocktail with 'lashings' of gold leaf in it, or finding out about the tax-dodging exploits of the rich – I felt a tightening in my chest, a visceral anger rising. That feeling seemed to have got much worse in recent years, as if the flaunting of such wealth is now accompanied by a giant two-fingered salute. It is hard to escape the conclusion that the reason the rich have now got so much more is that everybody else has got so much less.

There is some science behind those feelings of anger that arise when we are forced to stare at grotesque inequality. And there is a common confined space in modern life where there's no escaping close proximity to huge wealth disparity. That world is the increasingly stratified one of commercial airliners, and a group of academics who've studied it were blaming it for a huge increase in violence and distress in the skies. 'We have lots of surveys that say in a very general way [that] people are already upset about the current levels of inequality in the United States,' said Michael Norton, a social psychologist at Harvard Business School, in 2016. 'But the question is, how does that play out in everyday life?'

In 1994, according to the International Air Transport Association, globally there were just 1,132 reported incidents of air rage. By 2015, that number had risen to 10,854 – an 858 per cent increase in just over twenty years. In 2016, the Civil Aviation Authority, the UK airspace regulator, reported a sharp rise in air rage on flights involving British airlines, with 386 dangerous incidents in 2015 compared with just eighty-five in 2013, a 354 per cent increase in two years.

There are several factors. The sheer number of aircraft in the sky has increased hugely since 1994, and airlines these days are far less likely to tolerate antisocial behaviour on board, as concerns over safety and security have increased. Add to that the increasingly long check-in queues, flight delays, overcrowding, rising charges for once-free courtesies such as a luggage allowance, and shrinking seats – the deregulation of airlines in 1978, which at first led to increased competition, has now produced a race to the bottom, where an absence of consumer protection laws means there is no statutory limit on how small seats or legroom can get – and you might get closer to explaining the explosion of air rage.

352

One might also assume that alcohol was a significant culprit in this spike in incidents. But of those 10,854 reported incidents of air rage in 2015, in only 23 per cent of the cases was alcohol identified as a factor.

So what was driving this epidemic of air rage? In 2016, Norton and Katherine DeCelles, a professor of organisational behaviour at the University of Toronto, published their study of the phenomenon, using data from a major international airline spanning several years. Their findings were sensational.

Aeroplanes with first-class cabins – that is, those where passengers were segregated by ticket price, which the academics called 'physical inequality' – were four times more likely to report an air-rage incident on board than those without one.

Further, Norton and DeCelles found that air rage was also more probable when what they called 'situational inequality' occurred during boarding – that is, when economy passengers had to wait until first-class ticket holders had boarded and then were forced to walk through the luxurious first-class area to get to their tiny, cramped seats, thus heightening the awareness of the inequality.

'We've all experienced that feeling,' said Norton. 'When you walk through first class and see people with champagne, of course you're upset. So we wanted to document that kind of emotional reaction.'

The breakdown of the air-rage events was also instructive. Whereas incidents in economy were most often the result of emotional outbursts, such as panic attacks or fear, in first class arrogance and belligerence were much more common. The academics said that those with lower status could feel aggravated because they lacked the resources to have any agency over tightly controlled and increasingly debased circumstances, while those in first class could become irritated or angry when even the most trivial of things didn't meet their expectations because they felt their power and status deserved more.

When an aeroplane's economy passengers loaded through the first-class cabin, as opposed to a door in the middle of the plane, first-class passengers were twelve times more likely to indulge in air rage, as if being reminded of their superiority 'triggers entitled behaviour', according to DeCelles.

'We certainly don't sit around all day thinking about inequality and being upset about it, because we're living our lives,' Norton said. And yet airlines had become a highly visible microcosm of income inequality, one that we had little choice but to stare at.

Norton didn't have an easy answer to the problem. On the one hand, he said, airlines want people to see how great first class is (and, through lived experience, how bad economy is) so that passengers might upgrade the next time; the same principle was at play in our degraded public services, reinforced by every glossy brochure for a private hospital or school.

'But you might also ruin the experience of everyone who could've had an OK time, but now all they're thinking about is the rich people having an even better time,' Norton said.

And what of the psychology of this status anxiety? Could exposure to extremes of inequality have a profound and deleterious impact on us as animals?

Definitely, according to Robert Sapolsky, a professor of neurology at Stanford University. He had studied baboons, considered the primates most closely related to humans in their responses to stress, because, like us, they had almost no natural predators and hence the majority of their stress derived from their social functioning.

Observing these animals in their hierarchical troops in Kenya, Sapolsky saw the ranking systems they used to put others in their place. Measuring their stress hormones through blood samples, he found that stress echoed down the hierarchy through bullying: the alpha male hit a lower-status male, who would then harry a weaker male, who would take it out in turn on a female, who might then bite a younger, even lower-status female.

Sapolsky found that those at the top of the hierarchy had the lowest levels of stress (except when there was disorder in the troop). In stark contrast, he found that the lowest-ranked baboons were almost constantly overwhelmed by their stress hormones, which affected their health. The lower-ranked the animal, the worse they scored on cholesterol levels, impaired immune systems and blood pressure, all risks for illnesses such as heart disease, cancers and infectious diseases, not to mention mental health problems. Of course, baboons don't smoke or drink, eat junk food or take drugs, all things that were often cited as causal factors in studies about human health, status and social class.

In humans, Sapolsky claimed, most of us manage to avoid getting bitten or beaten up on a daily basis, but status stress was much more acute than it was for baboons.

'There's just endless reminders [of your status],' he told the neuroscience writer Maia Szalavitz. 'Someone passes you on the street and you're reminded of your low status by the expensiveness of their clothing. You go for a job interview and try to regulate that accent of yours that gives away your low [status] roots.'

Sapolsky's findings with baboons tied in with a study by Sir Michael Marmot, a British professor of epidemiology who examined data from a longitudinal survey of eighteen thousand male civil servants in the UK, known as the Whitehall Study, conducted over a ten-year period beginning in 1967. He found a threefold difference in mortality between the top-ranking and lowest-ranking civil servants, none of whom was exactly subsisting on poverty wages.

Marmot found that while lower grades of jobs were associated with obesity, smoking, lower levels of physical activity, higher blood pressure and even shorter height, these risk factors accounted for no more than 40 per cent of the differences between civil service grades in coronary heart disease mortality.

'The striking thing was not just the difference between top and bottom but the gradient,' Marmot said.

'From failure will flow humiliation,' Alain de Botton wrote in his 2004 book *Status Anxiety*, 'a corroding awareness that we have been unable to convince the world of our value and are henceforth condemned to consider the successful with bitterness and ourselves with shame.'

Little wonder that the wealth and status divisions inside a narrow fuselage should engender such feelings in us. And who should be surprised if, as differences in comfort and security become ever greater in so many other areas of our lives, our anger and distress keep rising too?

I walked out of Stockwood Park, and onto a busy road with no pavement, my feet treading carefully between the poppies and the cowslips and the vetches, the empty beer cans and the scrunched-up fag packets.

I loved those verges on my walk, the places most of us only ever got to see blurrily flashing by out of the corner of our eye – dull, inconsequential spaces that, if they did ever come into focus, it would only be when we were stuck in traffic, where no amount of beauty could ameliorate the frustrations.

But beauty there is. For roadside verges are a haven for seven hundred species of wildflower, 45 per cent of the UK's entire flora, many of which have been pushed out of the wider countryside by intensive farming and urbanisation: 97 per cent of our wildflower meadows have been lost since the 1930s.

On the forgotten margins, they could still thrive: the bird's-foot trefoil, the ox-eye daisy, the yellow rattle, the greater butterfly-orchid, the meadow crane's-bill, the spiked rampion. Or at least you would think so.

In May, when I was walking, the verges were at their best, bursting with colour and life, the bees and the butterflies – those pollinators whose numbers had seen huge declines in recent years – hard at work.

But in a week or so, Central Bedfordshire Council, if they were like most local authorities in the UK, would cut down this green strip I was now on, citing line-of-sight safety concerns for motorists and pressure from local communities to maintain certain aesthetic appearances.

This 'neat and tidy' approach, says the charity Plantlife, is a disaster for these precious linear nature reserves, a sort of Noah's Ark for our wildflowers.

'Yes, the verges need management and you have to have an annual cut,' Trevor Dines, a botanical specialist at Plantlife, told the *Observer* in 2016. 'But what we're finding is species being mown down in their prime.'

Plantlife says that such brutal cutting tends to favour those plants that are quick to colonise newly mown ground, such as stinging nettles. And plants such as fen ragwort and wood calamint, already pushed to the edge of extinction by our management of the land, are now clinging on for dear life on just a handful of verges.

The remedy is easy, according to Plantlife: local authorities should cut only twice a year – once early on, before the growing season gets going, and once in the late summer, when the flowers have finished blooming and the seeds have been distributed.

Perhaps these verges and our imperilled wildflowers might end up being unintended beneficiaries of austerity, as councils struggling to cope with slashed budgets have to cut back on their grass-cutting operations. As man steps back, nature reclaims. Perhaps in this there would be a much bigger lesson.

I walked past a little encampment of Travellers' caravans tucked right beside the M1, another group surviving on the margins. Then under the motorway, through the village of Slip End, with its neat rows of terraced houses, and then back out into the open countryside, on narrow lanes cradled by trees, moving gently in the breeze, the dappled light dancing on the ground as if from a disco glitterball, picking out the bluebells and the late celandines.

Wood pigeons flew out of the trees and showered me with blossom. The lane turned off to the left, but I carried straight on, along my desire path, a public footpath through a field of oilseed rape, the yellow so brilliant in the sunshine that it hurt my eyes, the air dense with that mustardy, musky scent.

My walk had opened my eyes, and ears, to a lot of things. Above all, it had been the pace of it – the slow, measured way the natural world gradually revealed herself to me, as if she had her ancient metabolic rate, and me too, that rate being three miles an hour. It had been like pulling the focus on a camera.

A pheasant, flushed out of the rape by my footsteps, stood on the little path in front of me, clucking explosively, flapping his wings in panic. I stared at his mottled brown plumage, his long, elegant tail, the brilliant viridescence of his neck, his scarlet wattle. The more I stared, the more that common bird looked like the most otherworldly, exotic thing I had ever seen.

I came to the old A5 – the Roman Iter II route which later took the Anglo-Saxon name Watling Street – with cars and trucks flashing past so fast and frequently that it made me feel a little queasy. Once safely across, I entered the lovely village of Flamstead, with its tidy cottages and gardens, framed by little stone walls or white posts and chains, and a row of neat almshouses, the village dominated by the parish church of St Leonard, with its 'Hertfordshire Spike' spire. Hertfordshire! I had crossed another boundary.

Swallows and swifts danced overhead. I went into a pub and ordered a coffee. While waiting, I read a little sign on the counter that told me the ingredients on the pub's menu were sourced locally, with meat from a local butcher, the minimum food miles possible. They banked with the village post office, employed local staff, used low-energy equipment where possible, and used recycled furniture and interior fittings. Their regular beers were brewed nearby in Tring, and their wines were sourced from a family-run business in Leighton Buzzard. A noticeboard had details of the many local clubs and events. A few days before I was there, the village had held its annual Books in the Belfry literary festival.

There you go, said the young woman behind the counter, putting my coffee gently on it, lest she disturb the delicate leaf she'd drawn in the foam. I sat down and opened my OS map. What a pleasure that always was, sitting down with an OS map, running your finger along the route you'd followed and then running it along the route ahead.

The door opened and a group of middle-aged men and women came fussily into the room. They ordered their coffees and all sat on a large table quite close to me. From the snatched fragments of conversations I could pick up, they were all locals, the meet-up a regular thing, a chance to catch up, talk about politics and books, and gossip and laugh. What fun they were having. For probably the first time on my walk, I felt a pang of loneliness.

I walked on, the rumbling hiss of the M1 in the distance, spooked occasionally by a racing cyclist whooshing by. On the edge of Hemel Hempstead, I picked up the Nickey Line, a former railway track that once linked the town with Harpenden, now a lovely trail for walkers and cyclists, running through dense woodlands of yew trees, and cutting through the middle of Hemel Hempstead like some green secret passageway. My spirits soared in that verdant heaven. My feet did too. They knew that the end of the walk would be coming soon enough; they knew they were going to make it to London.

I emerged from the Nickey trail close to the old town in Hemel, and stopped at a bus stop for a rest. Soon a man joined me, and asked what time the bus was due. I told him that I didn't know, that I was walking, had just stopped to take the weight off my feet for a while.

Opposite the bus stop was a modern red-brick semi-detached house, with a giant Vote Leave sign pasted onto the gable end and another one on a post in the garden. No doubt what they thought, I said to the man, who was in his sixties, I'd guess, with grey stubble on his chin.

'He's right, too,' the man said. He told me that all his friends would be voting to leave the EU, and not just his friends. Everybody he'd spoken to about it was of the same view. He mentioned the £350 million we sent the EU every week. He'd seen it on the news, on the side of Vote Leave's battlebus, with the slogan 'Let's fund our NHS instead'. He'd heard Boris Johnson and Michael Gove say that Britain was being royally ripped off by Brussels.

You couldn't argue with that, could you, the man said. Think of all those nurses and doctors we could pay, and the operations for our old folk. And foreign aid, he said. Why should we spend all that money on foreigners? We should look after our own. There were too many foreigners coming here. He wasn't racist, he said, but enough was enough. Our culture was being destroyed by immigration. He wanted his country back.

Let me tell you a story, he said. There'd been a local woman raped and murdered. They'd caught the killer. He was a Pole. What else did you need to know?

21

VIRTUOUS CIRCLE
(HEMEL HEMPSTEAD TO WATFORD
TO WEMBLEY TO SOUTHALL)

A sprinkling of stardust fell on Hemel Hempstead in 1959, when the Hollywood actress Lauren Bacall laid the foundation stone for the town's new cinema. Hemel had been part of the wave of planned new towns built under statute after the Second World War to create better living spaces for communities from the big cities ravaged by poverty or bombs. The new towns were another legacy of Clement Attlee's reforming government, along with the National Health Service and the welfare state.

Like all of the first-generation new towns, Hemel Hempstead, designed by the architect Geoffrey Jellicoe, was divided into residential neighbourhoods, each with its own 'village centre', serviced by schools, shops, pubs and other amenities. The town centre had a new theatre and library as well as the cinema. There were plenty of other celebrity openings of shops and businesses, too, by the showbiz royalty of the day, Frankie Vaughan, Benny Hill and Terry-Thomas among them.

The neighbourhoods had each been designed around a few major feeder roads with myriad cul-de-sacs and crescents coming off them, intended by the planners to minimise traffic noise and nuisance. Parks and other green spaces were built into the scheme. No wonder the waiting list to move there from London stretched into the tens of thousands – people desperate to move from the blighted capital and out into leafy Hertfordshire. In the space of sixty years, Hemel had grown from a small village to a town of nearly a hundred thousand people.

Today, walking through the centre, the place still carries a sense of planned optimism. Waterhouse Street follows the line of the River Gade, the far bank made up of landscaped gardens. The wide pedestrianised high street, with sculptures and water fountains, is fronted by modernist buildings that look as if they could have leapt straight off a utopian architect's drawing board in the sixties. Only the ubiquity of payday loan shops, pawnbrokers and betting shops grounded today's Hemel Hempstead firmly in the twenty-first century.

I popped into a newsagent for my daily ritual of looking at the front pages. The *Express* screamed that 'EU migrant numbers soar yet again', while the *Daily Mail* headline ran 'Record number of jobless EU migrants in Britain'. The *Telegraph* was reporting on the 'Details of 800 terror suspects destroyed'. I imagined the man at the bus stop from the day before reading these headlines. The *Guardian* was splashing with a story about foreign companies investing heavily in the London property market, under a headline which read 'Offshore London: secretive firms buying up the capital'. I looked back at the *Express* and saw that, above the splash headline about migrant numbers, it was trailing another story: 'Donald Trump on course for White House'. Inside, the report said that the New York property magnate had just secured enough delegate votes to win the Republican Party's presidential nomination. Trump had been storming it in America's post-industrial rust belt, using the same language as the Brexit campaigners: taking back control, making the US great again, putting white Americans first. After my experiences in Britain's post-industrial forgotten towns, it wasn't hard to see how attractive Trump's message was.

I walked up a little path and knocked on a door.

A man in his late fifties with grey hair and a rugged, handsome face answered the door. 'Come in, Mike,' he said with a broad, warm smile.

It was Kerry Underwood. Back in 1981 Kerry was a Labour councillor in Harrow, north London, and he remembered clearly the day the People's March for Jobs had passed through. He was out on the street, cheering them on.

'I am the classic Londoner moving out,' he said. Born in Ruislip, west London, he had started up a firm of solicitors in St Albans before moving it to Hemel Hempstead in 1988. 'My guess is that four-fifths of people living here have London origins.'

The town was still growing – five thousand houses were currently being built – but despite its proximity to London, just twenty-five minutes away by train, it wasn't a particularly big commuter town, unlike nearby St Albans and Berkhamsted.

This, Kerry told me, was mainly down to the vast industrial estate on the edge of town – another cornerstone of new-town planning – that employed fifteen thousand people. Up to 50 per cent of the working population of Hemel were employed in the town, and this had all kinds of knock-on effects. One was that house prices were relatively low, especially compared with St Albans and Berkhamsted.

In turn, that meant people with more ordinary backgrounds were likely to move there; the sense of community was strong; the town centre was busy because there were more people around during the day.

'There's plenty of thriving cafes and lunchtime food because there are loads of people here,' Kerry said. 'The evenings are busy too. There's low crime, excellent community relations, a low rate of drug problems, you don't get bouncers on pub doors, you can wander around and not feel uncomfortable. I'm not saying it's paradise, but it's a place that feels comfortable with itself. It's got an identity.'

It all added up, Kerry said, to a feeling of vibrancy. Kerry told me that when he ran his firm in the commuter hotspot of St Albans, they used to open late into the evenings because nobody would be back in town until then. In Hemel, they came in at lunchtime, or straight after work.

That core spirit of community in Hemel had helped it weather the tough times. There had been a deliberate policy not to let the high street get eviscerated, and to maintain the common spaces, with 'a lot of investment, a lot of encouragement'. The local MP, Mike Penning, Kerry said, was amazing.

'He's a Tory from a working-class background and I'm a socialist,' he said. 'But we do things together because we both really like the town. Anyone who is part of the town and keen to help will get support.'

Kerry was a business ambassador for Hemel, and put his money where his mouth was. His firm, Underwoods, was the main sponsor of the local football club and shirt sponsor of the rugby league club.

The way Kerry described Hemel reminded me of the way David had spoken about Macclesfield: both towns with a steady supply of decent jobs and a strong sense of community.

'Because we were a new town, we were lucky that when the Maylands industrial estate was being planned, it wasn't around heavy industry, locked into the declining industries like steel or mining,' Kerry said, 'but rather technology-based industry and modern light manufacturing.'

It was a virtuous circle. Unemployment was almost non-existent (in 2016 the figure was 1.6 per cent of the population aged sixteen to sixty-four), so if people were unhappy with the way they were treated at work, they could always get another job. In fact, one of Hemel's major problems was a skills shortage. Most of the firms on the industrial estate were relatively small, Kerry told me, with few multinationals, so they didn't have the constant threat of them moving to cheaper countries. These firms, he said, had invested heavily in the *idea* of Hemel Hempstead, tended to be in it for the long run.

Kerry thought that the demographics of Hemel, the fact that it was mostly populated with working-class Londoners, also had a big impact on the cohesiveness of the place. 'There's a sense that this is an improvement on the life they had before, or the life that their parents had. People in Hemel feel that, overall, they are moving forwards.'

He thought that there was 'an ugly mood out there in the country at the moment', and that this was largely down to people feeling that they lacked meaningful control over the direction the country was going in.

Kerry told me about a friend who had recently been at a meeting in Germany. 'A senior German politician said to him, "How on earth have you got into a situation where your core utilities like power and water are owned by foreign companies – and often by state-owned foreign companies?"'

I asked Kerry what would improve the quality of life in Hemel Hempstead, and the country at large. Localism, he thought, must be a big part of the future.

'I hope the argument that economic efficiency is the only marker is being lost,' he said. Local hospitals, courtrooms, police stations, they were all vitally important presences for communities. 'Those things are both a symbol of authority and places where, in people's minds, they can think that there is somebody looking out for them, making decisions locally to keep them safe. Those things are very important psychologically.'

Kerry railed against tax offices spread out across the country. 'All this "your tax is dealt with in Glasgow, or Newcastle"! It's crazy. It just alienates people. We should try to get the day-to-day things that affect your life dealt with locally. Most reasonable-sized towns could manage that,' he said.

It infuriated him that there was so little joined-up thinking in local government. He cited Norway, where schools' facilities were used in the evenings by the adult population.

'Here, all the schools stand empty in the evenings. We've got a football ground and two rugby grounds, but none of them are big enough. So why can't we have a policy where every town has a five-thousand-capacity sports and entertainment complex that the whole community can use for everything?'

Where might the money come from? When Kerry started working, he said, the basic rate of income tax was 35p in the pound as opposed to 20p as it was now.

'The assumption is that no one will ever agree to tax rises,' he said. 'I'm not sure that's correct at all, as long as people can see where their money is being spent. That's key.'

Kerry was optimistic that proper progressive politics was making a mainstream comeback. He thought that the right-wing press's influence on the country was on the wane. 'Wilson had all of this in the sixties. Labour has won elections in the past,' he said. 'A party that comes up with some properly progressive politics will do well. One of the few benefits in getting older is that you know that what goes around comes around. I think that's the stage we're reaching now. The establishment in general is getting very worried.'

I left Kerry. As I walked through the centre of Hemel, I thought about what he said at the end, about things changing. The Labour leader James Callaghan had said something similar in 1979.

'There are times, perhaps once every thirty years, when there is a sea change in politics,' he said, days before being ousted from No 10 by Margaret Thatcher. 'It then does not matter what you say or what you do. There is a shift in what the public wants and what it approves of.'

Callaghan thought thirty years. Naomi Klein reckoned it took thirty-five years for a nation to begin recovering from shock-doctrine economics. Could real, meaningful change really be around the corner?

I found the towpath of the Grand Union Canal, turned right and started walking towards Watford – or so I thought. After about thirty minutes, passing Bourne End, I realised I was walking in the wrong direction, and turned around. I calculated that I had covered nearly three hundred miles by that point. A few extra miles wasn't going to upset me.

I passed Hemel Hempstead, again, then Kings Langley, and shortly after that, the canal towpath took me under the M25, London's orbital motorway. The M25! I really was on the home stretch now.

A familiar shudder ran through me. I had always found endings very difficult, from jobs to relationships, even reading a book. Pete always used to leave a little bit of work unfinished on his building jobs. I used to think it was a pathology particular to him. Now I knew differently: there was something about keeping things open that meant the story couldn't end; and something in the finality of endings that spoke of oblivion.

And although I was hopeful my walk wouldn't end in oblivion, I was pretty sure it would mean finally letting go of my story of Pete – a story that had defined me for as long as I could remember.

A lovely old restored working boat chugged past, carrying the red, green and yellow livery of the famous Black Country canal-transportation firm Fellows Morton & Clayton.

Up and down the canals on my walk, I had seen, among the usual holiday hire boats and old restored working boats, plenty of boats that looked as if they were being lived on permanently, moored up alone, or more usually in clusters, like little floating villages.

It was easy to spot the houseboats: they'd have little generators chugging away on the forepeak, or solar panels or little wind turbines on the roof, next to a huge stack of logs for the wood-burning stove.

There was usually a cat or a dog, too, and the boat's name would often reflect the spirit of the endeavour, from *Dream Catcher* to *Narrow Escape*, from *Impulse* to *Up Yaws*, from *Cirrhosis of the River* to *Argee Bargee* and, my personal favourite, *She Got the House*.

As I'd got closer to London, I had started to see more and more of these liveaboards.

This phenomenon of people living on canal boats had grown enormously in the UK since the financial crisis. Previously it had been the preserve of those choosing the lifestyle of living afloat, like Pete – most of whom, like him, had a permanent mooring and access to services such as water and electricity and a pump-out for sewage.

But with the loss of social housing and the cost of homes and private rents soaring, people had latched onto the idea that you could buy an old canal boat for as little as £15,000 and live on it full-time.

The *Guardian* office where I worked in King's Cross overlooked the Regent's Canal. There was now an almost continual line of boats, often moored two or three deep, from the mouth of the Islington Tunnel right up to Camden, one-and-a-half miles away, from traditional narrowboats to converted lifeboats to what look like garden sheds on hulls. In London alone, it is estimated that more than ten thousand people live on boats on the capital's one hundred miles of canals. When the *Guardian* first moved to its canalside location in 2008, there were far fewer boats. It was a stark reminder of the housing crisis.

Every time I passed a community of houseboats on the canals, I couldn't help but think about the wildflowers pushed out from the countryside and surviving on roadside verges, or the countless desire paths I'd found and followed – that dynamic force, speaking of adaptation, survival, defiance.

I thought about Pete, living out his final years on a canal boat, his home tethered to the land by a flimsy rope. And I thought about those last few visits, when the end was in sight, when the pressure to finally cement that connection as the clock ticked down to zero felt unendurable to me. I thought about the very last visit, when Sue had called me to say that Pete was very ill, when I'd sat opposite Pete, rasping and skeletal, and he had poured me a glass of wine and then warned me about my drinking, and those caring words had felt like a punch to the heart. I'd let him have it with both barrels and Pete had leaned over and turned on the radio to drown me out. When I leaned over and turned it off, he put his fingers in his ears. So there we were: a forty-seven-year-old man screaming at his father; a seventy-three-year-old dying man with his fingers in his ears.

In May 2016, as I stood there by the Grand Union Canal, I was beginning to think I'd worked out just why I had been so angry with him that last time on the boat. There he was, riddled with cancer – the fighter who'd never given up the struggle, losing. Looking at him that day, there had no longer been an impenetrable fortress to conquer, no colossal walls to scale, just a dying, helpless old man. And perhaps that had been the biggest betrayal of all.

*

Going through Pete's box before my walk, I'd found photographs of him as a baby, on a sandy beach clutching his little bucket and spade, smiling at the camera, or being held by his own father, in smart military uniform – the same father who, according to Pete, had been an alcoholic and emotionally unavailable.

I'd also found a copy of a love letter he'd written to a girlfriend some time after he left my mum. It started with 'Colours' by the Soviet poet Yevgeny Yevtushenko. 'When your face / appeared over my crumpled life / at first I understood / only the poverty of what I have. / . . . / I am so frightened, I am so frightened, / of the unexpected sunrise finishing, / . . . / I don't fight it, my love is this fear, / I nourish it who can nourish nothing, / love's slipshod watchman. / Fear hems me in.'

Underneath, Pete had written: 'You have confronted me about relationships like no other person . . . to an understanding that when we love, nothing is base or tasteless. Nothing is shameful. There is freedom within, that liberates from bondage.'

He went on: 'My problem is that I have not worked out how this all works in practice. The wounds go deep. I suppose I can best be described as an adult desperately trying to find the key . . . Please understand that my actions over the past two weeks have had more to do with protecting myself than with rejecting you . . . My way of dealing with things has been attack being the best form of defence. It worked in the past, and I feel very vulnerable in having to admit that it's failing me badly with you . . . I've really been thinking hard, because I sense that time is running out and I do hope that too much damage has not been done . . . Lots of love and comradeship. Your best mate, Pete.'

I treasure that letter, that gift from beyond the grave, for the glimpse of the inner workings, Pete's and mine – for the sad realisation that his struggle to trust love had been a lifelong one, had not been my fault.

I got off the canal and walked through Cassiobury Park, with its many fine trees. Another funfair was setting up ahead of the bank holiday. A hoarding next to a children's playground read 'We have lots to be happy about. We are Watford'. I saw my first tube train and my first red bus.

For the next two days I walked. First through Sir John Betjeman's Metro-Land, through Moor Park and Northwood, past golf courses and along endless avenues of mock-Tudor houses. Once farmland, it had been bought by the Metropolitan Railway and developed after the First World War, as a rapidly growing London started to stretch north. 'A land where the wild flowers grow,' the railway company's marketing brochures had promised, adorned with pictures of idyllic cottages and women gathering posies in fields under endless blue skies. The building boom of the 1930s had produced more than half a million homes in the capital, almost all of them in outer London.

To Pinner and to Harrow, where suddenly the streets looked poorer. For as London's inner boroughs had become gentrified, poorer people priced out of those areas – the Brixtons, the Hackneys, the Elephant and Castles – have headed to the Metro-lands. It was the usual pattern of urban socio-economic ecology – the poorest people in the centre, a crescendo of wealth radiating outwards – turned on its head. The *Economist* had dubbed it 'the great inversion'.

A former leader of Harrow Council had been alarmed at the fast-changing nature of the borough's demographics. 'It's dreadful,' Susan Hall told the *Guardian* in 2015. 'I've seen five or six people living in one room. I've seen some rooms that are complete slums. People are being exploited by landlords. And it's not fair to the neighbours. It's wrong on every level . . . Harrow has always been lovely, but certain parts of it are going downhill.'

Harrow had been one of the London boroughs reporting a growing problem with 'beds in sheds'. In 2014, Hall had ordered a thermal-imaging plane to fly over the area and create a heat map of where people were living. Over three hundred occupied outbuildings had been discovered.

Outside West Harrow station, on the Metropolitan line, I passed a group of Sheffield Wednesday fans who had just parked their car in a nearby street and were heading to Wembley, where their team would be attempting to gain promotion to the Premier League in the Championship play-off final against Hull. It had been dubbed the £200 million game, because of the money the winners would get from the Premier League's new £5 billion TV deal the following season.

Several of the Wednesday fans carried giant inflatable owls – the club's nickname is The Owls – or sex dolls, and all wore the club's blue-and-white-striped replica shirts so that they looked a bit like walking Tesco bags. By the time I'd reached Wembley, the game was under way and the streets around the stadium were deserted, strewn with bottles and food wrappers from the pre-match bacchanal.

I walked along the new pedestrianised street running right outside the ground, part of the Wembley stadium complex. Next to the fan zones, where supporters gather before a match, were food chains such as Pret A Manger, Costa and TGI Fridays. There was the London Designer Outlet, Sunglass Hut, Next and a Nike superstore. How football had changed.

One thing that would never change, though, was what was going on inside the stadium, from where I could hear the agonies and the ecstasies, rising and falling in waves. I stood there remembering being inside Wembley in 2007 on the exact same date, 28 May, watching West Brom lose to Derby County in the Championship play-off final. At the time, it was dubbed the £52 million game. It still hurt to think about it, even nine years on. As I'm sure it would for those Wednesday fans, even a decade later, after their team lost 1-0 to Hull and they made their way back to Yorkshire with their deflated owls.

From Wembley I headed south, along the Ealing Road – like any high street in India, really, with the pavements outside grocery shops stacked with boxes stuffed with gourds and okra, coriander and ginger, jackfruit and plantains. I stopped in a cafe for a lamb seekh kebab on flatbread, drizzled with garlic, chilli and mint sauce.

Afterwards I stood outside the extraordinary Shree Sanatan Hindu temple, made entirely of imported Indian limestone, symmetrically perfect, with its broad staircase ascending to the temple's entrance, where carved figures standing atop richly decorated columns represented the four Hindu principles of human life: the pursuits of prosperity, pleasure, virtue and liberation. On the temple's roof were exquisitely carved domes and spires. How lucky I felt to live in a country where I could walk around the world.

I walked past an estate of self-storage units – just like payday loan shops, a business that had grown from almost nothing a few years ago. In 2015, total turnover for the industry in the UK reached £440 million. Industry experts had their own four principles of human life to explain the self-storage phenomenon, the four Ds: death, divorce, downsizing and dislocation.

I reached the busy A40, six lanes of fumes and fug, and found a narrow little tunnel of an underpass, stinking of urine, with murals of exotic birds on the tiled walls. On the other side

I walked alongside the A40. On the opposite side of the road was the stunning Hoover Building, dating from the early thirties, which was one of my favourite structures in London, and which Sir John Betjeman once described as a 'sort of Art-Deco Wentworth Woodhouse – with whizzing window curves derived from Erich Mendelsohn's work in Germany, and splashes of primary colour from the Aztec or Mayan fashions at the 1925 Paris Exhibition'. It looked like a palace, the kind of place in which a pharaoh might live.

In 1981, when the People's March for Jobs passed by, the Hoover factory was still making cleaners. Many of the workers were on their week's spring holiday, but two thousand of them turned out at the factory to greet the march and walk with them to Southall. Vacuum-cleaner production at the site ceased the year after and the factory closed down. After lying empty for a decade it was bought by Tesco, who redeveloped the rear of the site as a supermarket and restored the main building at the front. Today it was being converted into luxury apartments.

I found a tree-lined, sun-dappled footpath, which funnelled between a golf course and allotments; just ahead, nestling in the trees, was St Mary's Perivale, a beautiful little twelfth-century church of ragstone and flint with a tower clad in white weatherboarding. It looked as if it should be in an Amish village in Pennsylvania, not Perivale.

The church fell out of use in 1972 after becoming separated from its parish by the heavy traffic on the A40. Today it was a music venue, maintained by the trustees of the Friends of St Mary's. I'd never known it was there, and had I not been walking, I'd probably still not know.

I walked through the seemingly endless suburban streets of Greenford and Southall, where more or less every front garden had been concreted over for car parking. I emerged onto The Broadway, Southall's high street, and it was like walking into a carnival. The pavements were packed, and pimped-up cars with low suspension, full of young men with loud stereos, cruised up and down, blasting out grime or bhangra music. The smell of grilling meat filled the air. Crowds of people stood around, talking animatedly. It was quite overwhelming, an assault on the senses. I had lived in London for thirty years of my adult life, yet had never been to Southall, this extraordinary place, right on my doorstep.

I found a bench, took off my pack and sat down to take it all in. An elderly woman sitting next to me with a golden scarf around her neck and a bindi on her forehead said hello and asked where I'd walked from.

I told her that I had walked from Liverpool and a little about the People's March – how they had stayed overnight in Southall on 29 May 1981, had been given food and beds for the night at the Sikh temples, how the Indian Workers' Association had looked after them, and joined them on the final day's walk into London.

'It's true,' said the woman, whose name was Ansuya. 'Southall is small, like the Punjab. People here have very wide hearts. We welcome all.'

A small crowd had gathered round. They'd been listening to what I was telling Ansuya. They asked me questions about what I had seen on the road, what the mood of the country had been. One woman in a veil told me she would be voting out in the EU referendum. 'We are full,' she said.

Two women who looked as if they were together, one with a full-face veil, the other bare-headed, talked about the casual racism they experienced every day in their jobs with the NHS. The covered-up woman said she too would be voting to leave the EU. 'Too many immigrants,' she said.

They were sisters-in-law. The covered woman had to go, and said goodbye. I got up to shake her hand, but she didn't extend hers. 'It is *haram*,' she said, and then, laughing, 'You probably think I am a suicide bomber now!'

The other woman sat down next to me. He name was Saara. She talked about the veil, said that she had been in Britain a lot longer than her sister-in-law, so was 'a little bit freer with things like that'. She told me that her family was devout but that 'if you have a good heart and you are kind to people, I think religion comes after that'. Her mum had recently become much more religious. 'She says, "You need to start hitting the mat,"' Saara laughed. 'That's what we say in our family, "hitting the mat".'

Saara was forty-seven, with four kids. She worked as a care assistant for Hounslow Council, looking after a disabled woman in her forties. The woman lived with her elderly mother, who had dementia, and her father, who had severe kidney problems.

I asked Saara whether the cuts to the care budget had affected her work. Yes, she said, but she thought that families needed to step up as well. 'If you have a disabled person in the house, it should be just like having a child,' she said. 'People can make a rota: "Today I look after her, you can do it tomorrow." Why should it be all the state's responsibility? Britain is too nice for its own good.'

Not everyone had the time, I said, especially these days. I suppose not, Saara said. But you still didn't see many Asians in care homes. 'We still look after our elderly,' she said.

Saara and her parents had come to England in 1972 from Uganda when Idi Amin expelled the country's Asians. Her ancestry went back to Gujarat in India. She talked about the close-knit nature of the community in Southall, how people looked out for each other. She mentioned the racial tensions in Southall in 1979, when the National Front held an election meeting in the town hall and it all kicked off. Blair Peach, a teacher taking part in a demonstration against the meeting, was killed that day, felled by a police baton.

'The 1970s were very frightening for us,' Saara said. 'Skinheads everywhere in Southall.' She'd had to cross the road when she saw them. Day in, day out, she would get racially abused on the street, told to go home. White parents had objected to the rising number of Asian children being taught at local schools, and limits were placed on the proportion of immigrant pupils any particular school should take. 'We used to get bussed off to a school in Greenford. Southall was like Victoria coach station every morning. We didn't understand why we were taken to schools miles away when there was a school opposite.'

The atmosphere started to change when the Southall community – Sikhs, Muslims and Hindus – came together in the late 1970s and stood up to the racist thugs, drove them out of town. 'Everyone really pulled together and that's what made us strong,' Saara told me. 'After that, we never saw skinheads around for miles. It was great, Mike. We never had anyone to stand up for us. The police weren't much help. So we did it ourselves. Nobody messes with Southall now.'

That progress had come at a cost, Saara said. In Southall today and the areas around it, you didn't see many white people. 'I think that's sad,' she said. 'England isn't England without white people. It's like we've taken over, you know, and it's their territory, their country. Some of the things that Ukip says, I can relate to, though I'd never vote for them. Immigration, the floodgates are open. There's not enough space or resources for everybody for the government to keep bringing people in.'

Saara talked about the changing nature of Southall. Where once the shops had been run mostly by Indians, these days many of them had been taken over by Afghan Sikhs, who had fled the Taliban.

'They are clever people, Mike,' Saara said. 'Excellent businessmen. They can just look at you and know how much you're going to spend. The Asian community here has had to relearn how to haggle, which had been lost. My mum used to do it and we'd say, "Mum, this is embarrassing, the price is that much. We are not in India or Africa."'

Saara talked about the wave of Somalis that arrived in Southall in the 1990s. She said that when her father's generation came in the 1970s, they had all worked hard at the airport, or in her father's case at the Quaker Oats factory. 'They worked. They didn't take a single penny of benefits. We lived in private rented accommodation.'

Then they saw the Somalis arrive. 'They got the nicest council houses, disability benefits. Just like that. That's how we used to see them. I thought, "Right, now I know what the English meant about us, telling us to go home."'

The influx of Eastern Europeans, she said, had only increased the pressures, although Saara said that she admired their work ethic.

'They're not looking for handouts,' she said. 'They work hard, live in private rented accommodation. It's more the crime we're worried about with the East Europeans – burglaries, fights, pickpocketing, you know.'

So how was she planning to vote in the EU referendum? Definitely out, she said. Too many immigrants.

She had been to visit her son at university in Coventry and it was like a ghost town. 'Not enough nice shops or outdoor spaces or community centres or anything,' she said. 'They just huddle at home watching TV all day. It's a shame.

'In the north, it's basically dead. All those factories closed down. I see that stuff on TV, *Benefits Britain*, stuff like that. These people who live in the north, they're on the scrapheap.

They're the people the government should be looking after. Not new immigrants. The government needs to reach out to these people. Saying we can re-educate you, retrain you. They're going to these food banks. In this rich country! My heart sank when I saw that. Is this what it's come to?'

I walked along The Broadway, stopping at Southall Town Hall, where the People's March for Jobs had held their rally, as had the National Front two years before them. The building has long been at the centre of the community, in recent years housing a migrant advisory and advocacy service, providing legal help for those who could not afford it, and a group offering support to the elderly. Not long after I walked through Southall, Ealing Council, no longer able to afford the upkeep of the town hall, announced that the lease would be put up for sale. A range of options being considered for the building included luxury flats, a restaurant and a bar.

I sat on the steps, thinking about the complex story of immigration, about the layers of it. I had not heard much racist sentiment on my walk. What I'd heard was fear – fear of the changes being too big, too fast, too overwhelming for communities to cope, to keep their shape; ancient fears. But if that was part of the story, in Southall and around the UK, then the closing down of the town hall was another, for no community could hope to keep its shape if all of its common spaces were sold off.

I remembered what some of the original marchers had said about Southall. For them, arriving there had been one of the highlights of the whole journey. Chris Jones had said that Southall's Asian community couldn't do enough for them.

'All these stallholders were running over, putting apples and oranges in our hands,' he said. 'And they made you wear this cheesecloth-type thing on your head in the temples. Not a drop of alcohol to drink. Just men on this side of the room and women on the other. Then the music kicked off and it was all fellas dancing!'

I'd asked him if he'd ever experienced a multicultural community before. 'In Kirkby?' he said. 'Are ya mad?!'

Tara had spoken of the kindness she'd experienced in Southall, 'a humbling experience, which renewed my faith in humanity, or at least reminded me that humanity did exist.' Kim Laycock had said her three greatest memories of the march were Stoke, walking into Trafalgar Square, and Southall. 'Southall was spectacular,' she said. 'What a welcome we had from the community there.'

As I sat on the steps, an elderly, frail white woman came up to me. Could I spare £4 to help her out with her electricity bill? She held out a prepayment key for me to see, as if I wouldn't have believed her otherwise. In 2013, David Cameron's spokesman had suggested that people struggling to pay their energy bills should put on an extra jumper at home.

'Of course,' I said, and handed her a fiver.

'Bless you,' she said.

22

THE END OF THE ROAD
(SOUTHALL TO TRAFALGAR SQUARE)

And so, four weeks and 330 miles after putting one foot in front of the other on the steps of St George's Hall, Liverpool, my last day on the road had arrived. It would be thirteen miles to Trafalgar Square.

I walked out of Southall, heading east. From the low, thick cloud, the spectral shape of an aeroplane emerged briefly, before being swallowed up again, on its final approach to Heathrow. I passed Ealing Hospital, where, at the base of a tree by the roadside, lay a few stuffed children's toys and a bunch of dried, dead flowers left by grieving parents along with a fading note that spoke of their great loss and their gratitude to the staff for everything they'd done. Nearby was a sign saying that children's A&E and inpatient services at Ealing Hospital would be closing down in a month's time.

I crossed the River Brent on an elegant balustraded bridge, and looked down to the dark, oleaginous waters, where a garland of marigolds had become snagged on a low-hanging alder branch. Nearby, a board outside a state primary school was asking parents for donations to make up for the shortfall in its budget.

I walked south, following the line of the ancient Brent as it headed towards the Thames, under the elevated M4, with its phalanx of huge advertising boards that saluted people on the way into London from the airport. I crossed the A4 and was soon standing at the gate to the little community of boats where I used to live, on an island in the Thames; that private island.

I stood there looking at it, remembering some of the happiest days of my life. That early excitement about living on the boat had been short-lived, before the realisation kicked in that I was trapped on an island, with no protections, with ever-rising bills and a landlord who seemed driven purely by profit and power, with nothing I could do about it – a recipe for emotional and spiritual meltdown.

I thought back to Sean and Mark in Walsall and their warnings about the end of local authorities, and about Northamptonshire County Council, who had privatised all of their services, and the many who were on the brink of following suit. I thought about the private parks I had seen, and the private railways, and the closed libraries and the shuttered museums, and the food banks and the tented homeless cities and the ubiquity of shrunken human forms huddled under blankets in shop doorways in benighted northern and Midlands towns. I thought about the high street money-lenders charging 5,000 per cent interest, and the pawn shops and bookmakers, and the artery-clogging fast-food shops that now filled our streets. And I thought about the buy-to-let investors devouring whole streets in our struggling communities.

In his book *Man's Search for Meaning*, the Holocaust survivor and psychiatrist Viktor Frankl described how he'd witnessed prisoners will themselves to death when all hope had finally been extinguished. By contrast, those who told themselves stories of a life after the camp, of a future, who clung on to an idea of man's basic goodness, might will themselves to survive the horrors. Frankl wrote that survivors of the camps could remember 'the men who walked through the huts comforting others, giving away their last piece of bread. They may have been few in number, but they offer sufficient proof that everything can be taken from a man but one thing: the last of the human freedoms – to choose one's attitude in any given set of circumstances, to choose one's own way.' Later on, Frankl wrote: 'Life is never made unbearable by circumstances, but only by lack of meaning and purpose.'

I headed towards central London, back under the M4 and along Chiswick High Road, lined with expensive restaurants and delicatessens and little coffee shops where people sat outside sipping lattes, and past furniture shops flogging sofas and beds for thousands of pounds. I stopped and looked in the window of an estate agency, where one-bedroom flats were on sale for £500,000 and nondescript family homes for a couple of million. I thought about Salford and Stoke and Walsall and Nuneaton. I was in another world.

It was while walking this route to work that I'd often seen a man drive past in his gold-plated Ferrari. I'd always remembered what my Swedish friend Anders had told me about Stockholm – how it was one of the richest cities in the world, but that you would never generally see Swedes flaunting their wealth in public. 'People would laugh at them,' he'd told me. 'They'd think it was pathetic and disrespectful.'

I thought about how the difference in life expectancy between the richest and the poorest in Britain had been growing alarmingly. A 2015 study in the *Lancet* had found that men in Blackpool could expect to live 75.2 years, while those in the City of London, where life expectancy was highest, could expect to live for an average of 83.4 years. That eight-year differential was as high as the gap between the UK and Sri Lanka or Vietnam.

I walked on, through Hammersmith and then Kensington, one of London's richest boroughs, where women could expect to live for 87.3 years, according to that *Lancet* study. I walked along Kensington High Street, past the offices of the *Daily Mail*, and then into Kensington Gardens, where the nation had grieved for Princess Diana in 1997, and then past her memorial fountain in Hyde Park, where children from a nearby private prep school were playing football in bright red caps and what looked like pantaloons. I passed the luxury apartment complex One Hyde Park, where in 2014 a penthouse had been sold for £140 million. 'We're in boom-time prices,' the developer Nick Candy had said, 'more expensive than we've ever been in the history of mankind.'

In 2011 the *Observer* reported that only nine of the sixty-two homes that had been sold in the block were registered for council tax. In 2012 an investigation by the *Guardian* discovered that almost 80 per cent of the residences had been bought by anonymous offshore firms – a majority of them registered in the British Virgin Islands. Every time I'd passed it at night, there would be hardly a light on. Meanwhile, in 2015, over a quarter of a million households in London were on local authority waiting lists for housing. In Westminster, where One Hyde Park was located, over half the families waiting for social housing were homeless.

At Hyde Park Corner, I walked through the Wellington Arch, celebrating Wellington's victory over Napoleon, crowned by the largest bronze sculpture in Europe, the Angel of Peace descending on a four-horsed chariot of war. Just across the way was the Royal Artillery Memorial, in honour of that regiment's fallen in the First World War. It was after that war that the ambitious Housing Act of 1919 had been passed, promising 'homes fit for heroes'. Also nearby were the Machine Gun Corps Memorial, monuments honouring the war dead of Australia and New Zealand, and one commemorating the crews of RAF Bomber Command. Mostly working-class kids, I'd imagine.

Past Buckingham Palace, and through St James's Park, full

of happy-looking tourists taking photographs. In my lifetime, central London had become more and more like a theme park, and less and less like a working city: ordinary Londoners priced out of the centre, whole swathes of housing bought as investments and lying empty; our shops and nightclubs and top-end restaurants the playgrounds of the world's mega-wealthy; a simulacrum of a city, really, a soulless plutocrat's Potemkin village, for tourists and gawpers and those with deep pockets.

I walked into Parliament Square, with its statues of Disraeli, Palmerston, Churchill, Lloyd George. Every few years there is a campaign to get a statue of Margaret Thatcher erected; and every few years it gets refused for fear that it will be vandalised.

I looked over at Parliament. There's a story told by Thatcher scholars that in 1975, after becoming leader of the Conservative Party, she opened her handbag at a meeting of senior Tory colleagues, and slammed a well-thumbed copy of a book on the table. The book was the economist Friedrich Hayek's *The Constitution of Liberty*, published in 1960. 'This,' Thatcher allegedly said, 'is what we believe.'

In it, Hayek had outlined a philosophy that would become known as neoliberalism. He believed that competition was the guiding principle of human motivation. Any state intervention at all – through taxes, or legislation, or provision of essential services – could only act as a drag on progress. If the market is allowed to perform in its purest form, then a natural hierarchy of winners and losers will emerge. Hayek thought ideas such as trade unions, political freedom, human equality, universal human rights and a more equitable distribution of wealth were anathema. The rich are rich, Hayek believed, because they are morally and even genetically superior, better adapted to those 'natural forces' of innate human greed and competition.

'My personal preference leans toward a liberal dictatorship

rather than toward a democratic government devoid of liberal-ism,' Hayek once said, commenting on the regime of Augusto Pinochet, who was adored by Thatcher and had led the 1973 coup against Chile's democratically elected left-wing President Salvador Allende.

Throughout the sixties and seventies, Hayek's philosophical worldview had been enthusiastically promoted by an opaque network of think tanks, lobbyists and academics on both sides of the Atlantic, funded by some of the world's richest individuals and businesses. They had found a plausible narrative to justify their wealth – and one that promised to make them even wealth-ier. As long as the narrative held, their wealth could only keep growing, the share of the planet's resources flowing more and more to them.

When Thatcher came to power in Britain and Ronald Reagan in the US, the devotees of Hayek – and those of the Chicago School economist Milton Friedman – watched his ideas enacted: massive tax cuts for the rich, the neutering of trade unions, the sell-off of public housing and state-owned industries, the emasculation of local authorities, outsourcing and competition in public services, deregulation of the financial markets. All of these ideas had been contained in *The Constitution of Liberty*.

So pervasive had neoliberalism become in the 1990s, having captured nearly all of our society's functions, that oppositional voices had been neutered too. Tony Blair told the Labour Party conference in 2005 that we must be 'swift to adapt, slow to com-plain – open, willing and able to change'. Simultaneously in the US, Bill Clinton was trying to win meagre concessions from the new rulers of the world. But the 'Third Way' was never likely to gain any meaningful traction, for it violates everything the neoliberal purists hold dear.

So we've ended up here, with a rampant elite, increasingly

unaccountable to any idea of nation states or their citizens. And in 2008, largely as a result of neoliberal deregulations, we had a financial crisis that meant every man, woman and child in Britain had to pay £19,721 each to bail out the bankers. The economy tanked. The Tories, when they got into power in 2010, blamed Labour for the mess, saying it had thrown good money after bad into public services. It was straight out of the Hayek playbook, blaming state interference for corrupting the pure principles of the market.

Austerity is the necessary corrective, they claim, inflicting terrible punishment on ordinary people and, in the process, ripping up the social contract. The process had been started by Thatcher, but was being finished off by the Tory class of 2010 and 2015. I'd spent twenty-eight days walking through the carnage and despair. Today, the average worker earns less after inflation than they did in 2008. Meanwhile bonuses in the City and executive pay are soaring – in 2016, an average FTSE 100 boss earned £4.5 million.

Their project is almost complete, but things could get much worse. As the social contract is destroyed, and people become more fearful, more precarious, something even darker might emerge.

'The result is first disempowerment then disenfranchisement,' wrote George Monbiot in the *Guardian*. 'If the dominant ideology stops governments from changing social outcomes, they can no longer respond to the needs of the electorate. Politics becomes irrelevant to people's lives . . . The disenfranchised turn instead to a virulent anti-politics in which facts and arguments are replaced by slogans, symbols and sensation.'

I turned away from Parliament and walked along Whitehall, past the Cenotaph, to the gates of Downing Street. On 29 May 1981, a delegation from the People's March for Jobs had walked up to No 10 to hand their petition to Margaret Thatcher. She had refused to meet them. On 29 May 2016, I couldn't walk up to No 10 even if I'd wanted to. For unlike in 1981, when it was still an open road, with an unarmed copper standing outside the door, Downing Street was now one of the most heavily secured residential places on earth, huge fortifications at its end, manned by Robocop police officers with submachine guns and body armour, security cameras everywhere.

I spoke to one of the armed officers, an Asian man who looked in his mid-thirties. He told me, surprisingly openly, about morale in the force, how low it was, about the changes to pensions and to the retirement age. He told me how much his gun weighed and all of the rest of the kit he now has to carry to do his job. How, he asked, was he supposed to still be doing that into his sixties.

He said that his wife wanted the family to move from east London to Southall. He wasn't sure about it. I said that I had just walked from there, that the community seemed amazing, that he would love it.

As we talked, a girl, perhaps twelve or thirteen years old, came up to us and asked, in faltering English, whether we could help. She was on a school trip from Belgium and she and her classmates had a project to complete. She held up a sheet of A4 paper. Could I tell her who this woman was in the photograph? It was Margaret Thatcher.

As I walked along Whitehall, I thought about Thatcher and about the interview she'd given to *Woman's Own* magazine in October 1987. One of her answers would become her enduring legacy:

'I think we've been through a period where too many people have been given to understand that if they have a problem, it's the government's job to cope with it. "I have a problem, I'll get a grant." "I'm homeless, the government must house me." They're casting their problem on society. And, you know, there is no such thing as society. There are individual men and women, and there are families. And no government can do anything except through people, and people must look to themselves first.'

I thought of all the people I had met on my walk and about my own experiences of life. The neoliberal view of what it was to be human simply did not tally. We are essentially social animals and, given the right conditions, remarkably unselfish. Modern psychology, neuroscience and my own lived experience largely bore that out. Was it any wonder that a system of individualism and self-interest made so many of us unhappy? For the behaviour it sanctioned violated the fundamentals of what it was to be human, and swept us all along in its madness and greed.

But having been repeatedly told that there is no alternative, are we all becoming so tired and broken that we've started to believe the narrative? Have we become so alienated from our true natures that we've forgotten who we are? Friedman, Hayek, Thatcher, Reagan, Cameron, Osborne, Farage, Trump – we hear their stories every day.

Our parents tell us who we are; our politicians too. But it's not the truth. Those who get to tell the stories rule the world. Perhaps it is time for some new stories.

I looked ahead of me. I could see Nelson's Column a few hundred yards up the road. I suddenly felt a weariness descend – the terrible weariness and emptiness of endings, of loss, of letting go.

The People's March for Jobs had walked triumphantly into Trafalgar Square on that day thirty-five years before, and a hundred thousand people had greeted them with a spirit of hope – a sense that the tidal wave they'd seen out at sea heading for shore could be stopped.

I walked alone into the square, fairly empty on that day. I might have been thirty-five years late, but I'd finally got there. I undid the straps of my pack, pulled it off my back and laid it on the floor. I leaned against a railing, removed my shoes and socks, and wiggled my toes. Then I closed my eyes and rolled my sore shoulders and then my neck, so that it made little clicking noises.

When I opened my eyes again, I saw a middle-aged woman heading straight towards me.

'You must be Mike,' she said.

She worked with a friend of mine, she said. He'd mentioned my walk. She'd been waiting for a while, and when she saw a middle-aged man with a big backpack walk into the square, she'd guessed it must be me.

'I just wanted to come and say well done,' she said. 'I knew your dad. He'd have been very proud of you.'

ACKNOWLEDGEMENTS

First of all, many thanks to the team at Guardian/Faber: Laura Hassan for wanting to take the book on, Fred Baty for his patience and skilful guidance in editing it, and Paul Baillie-Lane for his role as project editor. Thanks, too, to my agent Lucy Luck. I'd like to thank Katharine Viner and Nigel Willmott at the *Guardian* for giving me the time off to write, and all of my amazing and generous colleagues who covered for me and supported me every step of the way. Clare Brown and Andrew Mayers both read the manuscript and made valuable suggestions. They are both very special people and I'm hugely in their debt. Thanks, too, to Simon Shore and Wendy Swan for being there when needed. Rory Foster is the best copy editor on the planet. Imo endured me and supported me throughout the whole painful process, with love and care. I'm so grateful to her. Fiona Coleman was there for the 'lightbulb' moment. I'd like to thank my brother, Andrew, and his family for putting me up at the start of my journey, and my amazing sister, Sue Tycer, for her continuing faith in the fundamental goodness of people. Thanks to all of the people who walked alongside me or shared a pint with me, and thanks to the People's Marchers, those I met and those I didn't. They did an incredible thing and I'm sorry it took me thirty-five years to join them. Finally, thanks to Pete, for his righteous anger about social injustice and inequality, an anger that never dimmed. I miss him more than I ever imagined possible.